LABOUR-MANAGEMENT RELATIONS UNDER GLOBALISATION

LAW AND POLICY PERSPECTIVES

Labour-Management Relations Under Globalisation

Law and Policy Perspectives

K. Krishna Murty

AKANSHA PUBLISHING HOUSE
NEW DELHI - 110002 (INDIA)

AKANSHA PUBLISHING HOUSE
4649-B,Ansari Road,
Daryaganj, New Dellii-11 0002
Phones:23268193, 9811582579, 09435116718
Email: ektabooks@yahoo.com
visit us: www.akanshapublishinghouse.com

Labour-Management Relations Under Globalisation: Law and Policy Perspectives

First Published 2009

ISBN 978-81-8370-182-2

PRINTED IN INDIA

Published by Akansha Publishing House, New Delhi-110002 and printed at Mehra Offset Press, Delhi.

Dedicated

to

My Parents

Smt. Kayala Seetamma

&

Late Sri Kayala karreyya

CONTENTS

ACKNOWLEDGEMENTS

I wish to record my heartfelt thanks and deep sense of gratitude to my mentor Prof (Dr) D.S. PRAKASA RAO, Professor, Dr. B.R. Ambedkar College of law, Andhra University, Visakhapatnam, for his inspiration, constant guidance, academic encouragement and cooperation, he has given me in getting this work done. Words cannot express my indebtedness to him.

I take this opportunity to express my deep sense of gratitude to Prof. R. Venkata Rao, Dean, Dr. B.R. Ambedkar college of Law, Andhra University, Visakhapatnam, for his constant support, valuable suggestions and the keen interest, he has evinced in the pursuance of my research work.

I take this opportunity to express my deep sense of gratitude to Prof. Y.Satyanarayana, Vice-Chancellor, A.P. Law University, Visakhapatnam, Prof. A. Rajendra Prasad, Principal, A.U. College of Law, Andhra University, Visakhapatnam, Dr. Y. Satyanarayana, Asst. Principal, Dr. B.R. Ambedkar College of Law, Andhra University, Visakhapatnam.

I am also grateful to Prof A. Subramanyam, Chairman, Board of Studies in Law, Andhra University; and all the other faculty members of Dr. B.R. Ambedkar College of Law, Andhra University, Visakhapatnam, for their kind support and encouragement for the completion of this work.

I express my deep sense of gratitude to Prof. M.S. Chakravarthy, Department of Marine Living Resources, Andhra University, Visakhapatnam and Sri R. Rama Krishna, LIC, Visakhapatnam for encouragement and inspiration.

I am thankful to non-teaching staff and library staff of Dr. B.R. Ambedkar College of Law, Andhra University, Visakhapatnam, for their cooperation in completion of my research work. I am also thankful to my relatives and well wishers Mr. G. Kishore, Software Engineer, HCL Technologies, Dr. N. Govinda Raju, Teaching Associate, Dr. B.R. Ambedkar Univeristy, and Mr. S.T. Naidu, advocate, for their encouragement, endearment support in completion of my study.

It is my immense pleasure to express my whole-hearted gratitude to my beloved parents, brothers, life partner and other family members for their affection, constant support and encouragement for completion of the present study.

Finally, I am thankful to Mr. M.P. Misra, Director, Akansha Publishing House, New Delhi for evincing keen interest and bringingout it elegantly in the present shape.

– K. Krishna Murty

Preface

Despite most comprehensive Labour legislation, India has not been able to maintain peaceful employer-employee relations. There has been a spurt in industrial disputes and work stoppages which have hampered faster industrial development of the country. More than 100 labour laws have not succeeded in checking growing militancy in industrial relations, embezzlement of provident fund money and other undesirable trends in industrial relations. Too many labour laws have been enacted due to emphasis on high ideals. But faulty implementation has, instead of protecting labour, deprived them of their due benefits. Too much and defective legislation has made the task of employers and labour administrators and workers too complex. They have started sinking under the ever, increasing workload of labour laws. The mushroom growth of labour legislation in India is the result of the mania of bringing forth new pieces of legislative measures every year without bothering for their implementation and proper execution.It is emphasized that the labour laws should have to be made comprehensively and should solve the problems related to the Labour and Industry amicably and effectively without making any further dispute. It must have a proper economic gain to be made within the new labour laws. A complete overhaul the labour policy is needed for self-reliance and substantial surpluses have to be done. Social justice cannot remain an abstraction of volatile slogans and words but should be severely conditioned by economic logic of affordability. The India should be able to develop a force of efficient and committed employees.Generally, the various labour policies have undoubtedly by resulted in large scale industrial sickness and the number of sick units was more than 3 lakhs, blocking more than Rs.10,000 crores of the most valuable money resources. It is an irony that in the protected environment, India had not gained much either in the area of social justice and equity. The legislation governing the labour had benefited only the organised industrial workers, constituting 10 percent of the total work force and hardly 1 or 2 percent of the total population.Maintenance of Industrial discipline is another area where labour laws have failed. Even for severe indiscipline, termination of workers was not generally up held. Industries are saddled with inefficient and indisciplined workers. In the context of globalisation, India's Labour policies should blend the traditional virtues with the imperative need to achieve quality and productivity. De-regulation of conditions of entry, and attempt to evolve new strategies for "exit" and new policy to facilitate the process of structural adjustment, with a certain degree of deregulation and labour and management relations were needed. The object to promote the welfare of people of India cannot be achieved unless we have socioeconomic laws. Indian constitution and other labour oriented legislations emphasized that there are provisions which enjoin on the state to provide equal opportunity of work and to provide socio-economic justice and this also cannot be achieved unless the condition of the labour class is improved. Employers are now compelled to view industrial relations and human resource management from a strategic perspective; in other words, not only from the traditional viewpoint of negotiating terms and conditions of employment and performing a personnel and welfare function. Industrial relations and human resource management are directly relevant to competitiveness, and how they are managed will impact on enterprise performance e.g. its productivity and quality of goods and services, labour costs, quality of the workforce, motivation, prevention of disputes and not only their settlement, and aligning employee aspirations with enterprise objectives. Most countries (other than those in transition to a market economy) have long-standing dispute settlement procedures at the national level (conciliation, arbitration, industrial or labour courts). Essential as these are, they operate only when a dispute arises. Equally important are dispute prevention through communication, consultation and negotiation procedures and mechanisms which operate largely at the enterprise level. They are not particularly common in many Asian enterprises. Their importance has increased in the current decade when changes in the way organizations are structured and managed have created the potential for workplace conflict. A more positive movement from personnel management to strategic human resource management is called for.

Industrial Relations Legislation fall under three categories: (*i*) Trade Union Legislation, (*ii*) Industrial employment Standing Order Legislation and (*iii*) Industrial Dispute Legislation. The Indian Trade Union Act of 1926 and its amendment govern the trade union movement in our country. The main object of the Act is to give registered trade unions a legal and corporate status and their executives and members immunity from civil and criminal liability in respect of strikes.The Industrial Employment (Standing Orders) Act of 1946 requires employers in industrial establishes to define with sufficient precision the conditions of employment under them and to make the said conditions known to all men employed by them. Legislation for setting labour strikes was introduced by the Trade Disputes Act of 1929. Under the Act, the Government was empowered to appoint a Court of Enquiry or a Board of Conciliation. The Court or Board tried to bring about a settlement, but the decision was not legally binding on the parties concerned. Strikes and lock-outs in public utility service, without proper notice were made illegal. The emergency war-time legislative measures convinced the Government of their utility and led it to incorporate them in the permanent labour code of the country. The Industrial Disputes Act was accordingly passed to replace the Trade Disputes Act of 1929. The Industrial Disputes Act was passed in 1947 with a view to improve the existing industrial relations between employers and the employees and for avoiding strikes and lock-outs specially in public utility services and essential undertakings and for providing machinery for peaceful settlement of industrial disputes and constituting joint works committees for enquiring into and settling individual grievances and day to day difficulties. The Industrial Disputes Act introduced the principles of compulsory arbitration and prohibited strikes without notice in respect of public utility services.

Labour policies seek to be an integral part of the overall economic policy of a nation, just as the industrial policy and the fiscal policy. The Indian Labour policies having been mostly diversed from our economic policy had narrowly focused on the protection of the existing employment in the organised sector, than on the creation of employment. Creation of employment was more important. The present study of Labour Management Relations in the context of Globalization is relevant today to understand the problems involved in the Labour Management Relations in Post Globalization era. The present study focuses on the law relating to labour Management relations in liberalization era. For the purpose of the present study, the legislations dealing industrial relations viz. Industrial Disputes Act 1947, The trade unions Act 1926 and The Industrial employment (Standing orders) Act 1946 were studied in the light of the changing labour management relations in post globalization era. The issues like demand for changing labour management relations to avoid protectionism to the labour in the organised sector by creating special economic zones and address the problems faced by the workers in unorganized sector are also taken up for the present study.

I would be very grateful to the readers if they can send me their suggestions and comments to improve the usefulness of the book.

– Kayala Krishna Murty

LIST OF CASES

1. Excel Wear V. Union of India (1979) 1 SCR 1009 : AIR 1979 SC 25
2. Kalinga Tubes Ltd. V. Their Workers : AIR 1969 SC 90
3. Assam Oil Co. Ltd V. Workmen, AIR 1960 SC . 1264 at 1268
4. Burn and Co. V. Their Employees, AIR 1957 SC 387
5. All India Bank Employees Association. V. National Industrial Tribunal
6. Damayanti, V. Union of India ; AIR 1971 SC 966
7. Bunkingham Carnatic Company, case
8. Kameswar Prasad V. State of Bihar (1962) LLJ 294 (SC)
9. Jay Engineering Works V. State of West Bengal ; AIR 1968 Cal 407
10. T.K. Rangarajan V. Government of Tamil Nadu & Others 2003 (98) IFLR 1009: SC (2003) LLR 863
11. Indian Drugs & Pharmaceuticals Ltd. V. RK Shewarmani (2005)6 SCC 76
12. Glaxo Laboratories V. Labour Court (1984)1 LLJ 16
13. T.K. Rangarajan. V. State of Tamil Nadu (2003) 6 SCC 581
14. Pyare Lal Sharma V. Managing Director and Ors 1989 (3) SCC 448
15. Central Inland Water Transport Corporation Ltd Another Brojonath Gangualy and another; AIR 1986 SC 1571
16. West Bengal State Electricity Board V. Desh Bandhu Ghosh AIR 1985 SC 722 at 723

17. Punjab National Bank V. Ghulam Dastgir; 1 LLJ 1978 SC 321

18. In India Tourism Development Centre v. Presiding Officer, Labour Court), 2000 LLR 262 (Del HC).

19. Purafil Engineers, Pune v. Shaikh Anwar Abdul Rahman, (2000) 84 FLR 144: 2000 LLR 268 (Bom HC)

20. Manager Air Control Engg. Company Ltd. v. Kanaiyalal Ghusabhai Kunvaria, 2000 LLR 592 (Guj HC).

21. Management of Triplicane Urban Co-operative Society Ltd. v. The Presiding Officer, Principal Labour Court, 2000 LLR 1228 (Mad HC).

22. Management of Indian Iron and Steel Company Ltd. v. Prahlad Singh (2001) 1 5CC 424: AIR 2001 SC 69: 2001 LIC 26: 2001 LLR 157 (SC).

23. L.K.P. Merchant Financing Ltd. v. Government of National Capital Territory, Delhi, 2003 LLR 367: 2003-I LLN 1044: 2003 (97) FLR 460 (Del HC).

24. L.K.P. Merchant Financing Ltd. v. Government of National Capital Territory, Delhi, 2003 LLR 367: 2003-I LLN 1044: 2003 (97) FLR 460 (Del HC).

25. N.S. Ravichandran v. Management of Thanthal Periyar Transport Corporation, 2003 LLR 380:2003-I LLJ 729: 2003-I LLN 415 (Mad HC).

26. Creative Garments v. Kunwar Prasad, 2003 LUR 424 (Born HC).

27. United Commercial Bank v. P.C. Kakkar, (2003) 4 5CC 364: AJR 2003 SC 1571: (2003) 2 LU 181: (2003) 2 SUR 445: 2003 LLR 436: 2003-I LLN 825 (SC).

28. Novapan Industries Ltd. v. S.K. Murthy, 2003 LUR 569: 2003 (97) FUR 342 (AP HC).

29. B.C.C.L. v. Presiding Officer, Central Government, 2003 LLR 618: 2003-Il LU 92 (Jhar HC).

30. Bharat Coking Coal Ltd. v. Presiding Officer, Central

Government Industrial Tribunal-II, Dhanbad, 2003 LLR 954: 2003 (98) FUR 718 (Jhar HC).

31. L.S. Sharma v. Presiding Officer (I) Uttar Pradesh Ghaziabad, 2003 LLR 1021: 2003 (98) FUR 922 (All HC).

32. Mahaveer Conductor v. Nand Kishore, 2003 UUR 1167: 2003 (99) FUR 354 (Raj HC).

33. Kattabomman Transport Corporation v. Labour Court, 2004 LLR 246: 2004 (100) FLR 580 (Mad HC).

34. T.C.M. Employees' Union, Kalamassery v. T.C.M. Ltd., 2004 LLR 285: 2004-I LIJ 280 (Ker HC).

35. Vasant C. Hanhad v. Chairman, Oriental Insurance Company Ltd., 2004 LLR 372: 2004-I CLR 791 (Guj HC).

36. Metallurgical Engineering Consultant (I) Ltd., Ranchi v. State of Bihar, 2004-I LU 793 (Jhar HC).

37. Muriadih Collery of Bharat Coking Coal Ltd. v. Bihar Colliery Kamgar Union through Workmen, 2005 LLR 1085 (SC).

38. S. Chandraiah v. The Presiding Officer, Additional Industrial Tribunal, 2005 LLR 1172 (AP HC).

39. Kamla Nehru Memorial Hospital v. The Presiding Officer, Labour Court, Allahabad, 2006 LLR 5 (All HC).

1

INTRODUCTION

The origin and growth of labour law can be traced to the rise of modern factory system. Under the handicraft system, every production unit was small and there was direct personal contact between the employer and the craftsmen. After the industrial revolution, large scale industry came into being. In a modern industrial unit, a large number of workers are employed. As the workers had no bargaining capacity with capitalist employer, they had to work on nominal wages for long hours and under the most unhealthy conditions. Even women and children were employed under conditions which were detrimental to their health, safety and welfare. The workers were unable to protect themselves from exploitation by the industrialists. As a welfare state, the government stepped in to protect the interests of workers. It enacted labour laws to impose statutory obligations on employers to provide reasonably good working conditions and facilities to workers.

On the recommendations of the Factory Commissions appointed in 1880 and 1890, the first Factories Act was passed in 1881 and amended in 1891. The Mines Act was passed in 1951 to ensure safe working conditions in mines. However the labour laws enacted before the World War I were designed mainly to protect the interest of Great Britain. Such protective legislation was of an elementary and haphazard nature.

After the World War I, politicians and trade unions became increasingly aware of the plight of workers. In 1919, India became a member of the ILO. In 1918, the textile workers of Ahmedabad successfully launched a strike under the leadership of Mahatma Gandhi. In 1926, The Trade Union Act was passed. The Act granted immunity to registered trade unions and their members from legal proceeding in Civil Courts. But the Act made no provision for settlement of industrial disputes.

In 1928, there were too many strikes. As a consequence the Trade Disputes Act was passed in 1929. In the same year, the Royal commission on Labour was set up to study the problem of labour. During the 1932-37, two dozen new laws were passed to protect the interests of workers. In 1935, Labour legislation was put on the concurrent list, with the advent of provincial autonomy in 1937, the pace of labour legislation was accelerated. During the World War II, the Defense of India rules were applied to prevent strike and lock-outs.

Rule 81 gave powers to the appropriate government to intervene Labour Management Relations. The Industrial Disputes Act was passed in 1947. Industrial Disputes Act, 1947, continues to govern industrial relations on the legislative side. On the voluntary side, the Code of Discipline in Industry (1958) and the Industrial Truce Resolution (1962) continued to have their impact on industrial relations in the country. The conciliation machinery set up under the ID Act, 1947 continues to play its role in bringing the parties together and exploring ways for promoting amicable settlements.

Labour Law for the Protection of Employer and Workers Interests

The term 'Labour Law' refers to that body of laws which are enacted to protect and promote the interests of the working class in the society. Labour Laws comprise all those laws by which relationships between employers and employees are governed. All Laws which have a bearing on labour are included in the category of Labour Laws. Labour laws deal with the employment, wages, working conditions, Industrial relations, social security, labour welfare etc. Labour Law seeks to establish a harmonious relationship between the employers and the employees and to strike a right balance between capital and labour. The objective of labour laws is to ensure good working and living conditions for workers and to maintain industrial peace and cordial relations between employers and workers[1].

Need for Reform in Labour Legislation

Employers have also criticized labour legislation on the ground that it leads to waste of time, money and energy on their part. The twin objectives of our labour policy; economic growth and social justice, could not be achieved by labour legislation. This, however, does not mean that labour legislation has made no contribution towards improving the lot of working class in India. Labour laws have been very helpful in protecting and promoting the interests of labour. But there have been several undesirable consequences and the desired objectives of labour legislation have not been realized to a satisfactory extent.

Constitutional Framework of Labour Legislation

Employers and workers are partners in industry and in the process of national development. Both individual employers and the community as a whole are under an obligation to protect the well-being of labour. Workers must be given their due share in the gains of economic development. Labour legislation helps to maintain industrial peace which is essential for increasing productivity and prosperity. It is also designed to improve the service conditions of workers by providing for them ordinary amenities of life. It also seeks to ensure the workers, who cannot bargain on equal terms, a fair return for their labour.

Indian Constitution serves as the most important basis for labour laws in our country. Labour legislation in India is designed to fulfill the pledge and ideology enshrined in the Indian Constitution. The Fundamental Rights and the Directive Principles of State Policy enshrined in our Constitution provide guidelines for labour legislation in the country.

Fundamental Rights

The Constitution of India has guaranteed some fundamental rights to all the citizens of the country. Some of these are:

(i) The State shall not deny to any person equality before the law or the equal protection of laws.

(ii) There shall be equality of opportunity to all citizens in matters relating to employment or appointment to any office under the State.

(iii) All citizens will have the right to form associations or unions.

(iv) People will have freedom of speech and freedom of assembly.

(v) All citizens have the freedom to practice any profession.

(vi) No discrimination will be made on grounds of religion, race, caste, sex or place of birth.

(vii) All citizens enjoy protection of life and personal liberty.

(viii) People have the right to be protected against exploitation.

(ix) Article 23 of the Constitution specifically provides that no child below the age of 14 years shall be employed to work in any factory or mine or engaged in any other hazardous employment.

Individuals can enforce the Fundamental Rights in courts. Any law which contravenes a fundamental right can be declared by the appropriate court to be void. Labour is in the concurrent list on which both the Centre as well as the States have the power to make laws. In case of any repugnancy between the Union and the State legislation, naturally the legislation of the Union shall prevail.

Directive Principles of State Policy

The Directive principles lay down the guiding principles which the state ought of follow in framing and enforcing various laws. However, they are not enforceable by any court and provide no legal rights to individuals. Nevertheless, these are a good guide to the State in the governance of the country. They are the sheet anchor of the labour legislation and constitute the substratum of industrial jurisprudence.

The Directive Principles, which are relevant to Labour legislation, are given below:

1. Article 38 lays down that the State shall strive to promote the welfare of the people by securing and protecting as effectively as it may a social order in which there is economic, social and political justice for all.

2. Article 39 lays down the basic philosophy of the ideal of democratic socialism which is enshrined in the Preamble of Indian Constitution and which is the motivating force behind the Directive Principles. It states that the State shall direct its policy towards securing:

   a) That the citizens, men and women, equally, have the right to an adequate means of livelihood;

   b) That the ownership and control of the material resources of the community are so distributed as best to subserve the common good;

   c) That the operation of the economic system does not result in the concentration of wealth and means of production to the common detriment;

   d) That there is equal pay for equal work for both men and women;

   e) That the health and strength of workers, men women, and the tender age of children are not abused and that citizens are not forced by economic necessity to enter vocation unsuited to their age or strength;

   f) That childhood and youth are protected against exploitation and against moral and material abandonment.

3. Article 39 A provides that the State shall secure that the operation of the legal system promotes justice, on a basis of equal opportunity and shall, in particular, provide for legal aid, by suitable legislation or schemes or in any other way, to ensure that opportunities for securing justice are not denied to any citizen by reason of economic or other disabilities.

4. Article 41 lays down that the State shall make effective provision for securing the right to work, to education

and to public assistance in cases of unemployment, old age, sickness and disablement and in other cases of undeserved want.

5. Article 42 lays down what the State shall make provision for securing just and humane conditions of work and for maternity relief.
6. Article 43 provides that the State shall endeavour to secure, by suitable legislation or economic organization or in any other way, to all workers, agricultural, industrial or otherwise, work a living wage conditions of work ensuring decent standard of life and full enjoyment of leisure and social and cultural opportunities and, in particular, the State shall endeavour to promote cottage industries on an individual or cooperative basis in rural areas.
7. Article 43 – A lays down that the State shall take steps, by suitable legislation or in any other way to secure the participation of workers in the management of undertakings, establishments or other organization engaged in any industry.
8. Article 46 mentions that the State shall promote with special care the educational and economic interests of the weaker sections of the people and, in particular, of the scheduled castes and the scheduled tribes and shall protect them from social injustice and all forms of exploitation.
9. Article 47 describes that the State shall raise level of nutrition and the standard of living and improve public health and shall endeavour to bring about prohibition of the consumption (except for medicinal purposes) of intoxicating drinks and of drugs which are injurious to health.
10. Article 48 lays down that the state shall endeavour to organize agriculture and animal husbandry on modern and scientific lines.

Principles of Labour Legislation

The fundamental principles on which labour legislation is based are as follows:

1. Social Justice

Our constitution enshrines the concept of social justice as the basic object of State policy and action. The tune of social justice is most vibrant in industrial jurisprudence. In industry social justice implies an equitable distribution of the benefits of industry among employer and employees. It also means protection of the health, safety and welfare of workers. The Workmen's Compensation Act, 1923, the Minimum Wages Act 1948, the Factories Act, 1948 are attempts at securing social justice to labour.

2. Social Equity

Social justice provides definite standards to be adopted in labour legislation. But as the conditions change there arises need to change the standards and the law. The Government has acquired the power of changing the law. It can make rules regarding certain specified matter to enforce the law. The Government may modify or amend the law to suit the changing circumstances. Such legislation is based on the principle of social equity.

3. National Economy

The general economic situation of the country is another principle on which labour legislation is based. The purpose of the law may be defeated if this is not considered while enacting labour legislation. For example, the quantum of minimum wages, the level of compensation, the standards of safety, etc. are all influenced by the state of the national economy.

4. International Uniformity

The International Labour Organization (ILO) has done commendable work to develop uniform standards of labour legislation among the member countries. It has formulated several conventions and recommendations for the welfare of labour.

Member countries who ratify these conventions are required to implement them through appropriate legislation. The ILO. conventions have served as the guide to most of the labour laws in India.[2]

Despite most comprehensive Labour legislation, India has not been able to maintain peaceful employer-employee relations. There has been a spurt in industrial disputes and work stoppages which have hampered faster industrial development of the country. More than 100 labour laws have not succeeded in checking growing militancy in industrial relations, embezzlement of provident fund money and other undesirable trends in industrial relations. Too many labour laws have been enacted due to emphasis on high ideals. But faulty implementation has, instead of protecting labour, deprived them of their due benefits.

Too much and defective legislation has made the task of employers and labour administrators and workers too complex. They have started sinking under the ever, increasing workload of labour laws. The mushroom growth of labour legislation in India is the result of the mania of bringing forth new pieces of legislative measures every year without bothering for their implementation and proper execution. According to B.K. Tandon, "we have been pursuing a labour policy which has resulted in so much legislation that it was neither warranted nor it could be implemented with any degree of success."[3]

It is emphasized that the labour laws should have to be made comprehensively and should solve the problems related to the Labour and Industry amicably and effectively without making any further dispute. It must have a proper economic gains to be made within the new labour laws. A complete overhaul the labour policy is needed for self-reliance and substantial surpluses have to be done. Social justice cannot remain an abstraction of volatile slogans and worlds but should be severely conditioned by economic logic of affordability. The India should be able to develop a force of efficient and committed employees.[4]

But so long as the private ownership of an industry is recognized and governs overwhelmingly a large proportion of our economic structure, is it possible to say that the principles of socialism and social justice can be pushed to such an extreme so as to ignore completely or to a very large extent the interests of another section of the public namely the private owners of the undertakings. Most of the industries are owned by limited companies in which a number of shares holders : both big and small hold shares. There are creditors and depositors and various other persons connected with or having dealings with the undertakings. Does socialism to the extent of net looking to the interests of such persons? In a state-owned undertaking the government company is the owner. If they are compelled to close down, they can protect the labour better by several other methods at their command and even sometimes at the cost of the public exchequer. It may always be advisable to do so, but that is a different question obviously the two methods involved in running it are not only the same footing. One part of the management and business is done by the owner or their representatives and the other is running the business for return to the owner, not only for the purpose of improving his livelihood or expenses but also for the purposes of the growth of the National economy by formation of more and more capital.

Generally, the various labour policies have undoubtedly resulted in large scale industrial sickness and the number of sick units was more than 3 lakhs, blocking more than Rs.10,000 crores of the most valuable money resources. It is an irony that in the protected environment, India had not gained much either in the area of social justice and equity. The legislation governing the labour had benefited only the organised industrial workers, constituting 10 percent of the total work force and hardly 1 or 2 percent of the total population.

The protected economic environment backed by antiquated labour law and the slow and cumbersome judicial process have also been a major cause of the undesirable substitution of the cheap labour by expensive capital. This explains the present situation where employment in the organised industrial sector has shrunk deposit massive investments over the past decade forcing a number of economic activities in the informal sector where the terms and conditions of employment are not comparable to those in the organised sector.

Maintenance of Industrial discipline is another area where labour laws have failed. Even for severe indiscipline, termination of workers was not generally up held. Industries are saddled with inefficient and indisciplined workers. In the context of globalisation, India's Labour policies should blend the traditional virtues with the imperative need to achieve quality and productivity. De-regulation of conditions of entry, and attempt to evolve new strategies for "exit" and new policy to facilitate the process of structural adjustment, with a certain degree of deregulation and labour and management relations were needed. Deregulation which does not rule out the supervision and evaluation of performance by the state but also requires removal of obstacles and rationalization of rules and procedures of industrial workers is what we want. We need policies which can motivate the labour force. It is necessary to orient such policies towards increased production, through efficient utilisation of resources, relaxation of the provisions and restructuring the closure of sick units, emphasis on national community needs as against the industrial labour's own selfish interests, which permit effective steps to be taken by the management to maintain acceptable standard of labour discipline. Case of individual workmen or groups violating discipline have to be settled on merits and on priority basis within a time bound schedule. The policy should be such that differentiates between labour unrest based on industrial problems and labour agitations generated by politically oriented trade unions. It is necessary to have a trade union legislation in place to prevent minority groups among workers or trade unions to disrupt or destroy agreements or settlements voluntarily made or to interfere where labour relations are satisfactory. It should afford a bigger degree of discretion to the management and should effect re-employment of the displaced persons in the organisation (as for as possible) and voluntary separation of the remaining underemployed or idle workers displaced from the jobs, following introduction of new technologies and rationalization in the systems and methods of work. It is now widely acknowledged that if India is to succeed as a global player, one of its major objectives should be the creation of a low cost economy.

In the ultimate analysis, labour market intervention should focus on improving the employability of the work for through training, rather than reinforcing the protective layers of the legislation.

Change in the law of nature and the law should pay special attention towards the basic objectives of the overall economic policy, namely, encouragement of new units, Industrialisation of backward areas, self initiative of the technically skilled people. It must be ensured that there are no difficulties in the way of all such initiatives contributing to long scale employment creation and to attain the socioeconomic upliftment of our own people. We have dynamic laws, because in the society conditions are changing very fast. We cannot have laws which are static. Depending on the situation, the labour laws and other policies must continue changing.[5]

The object to promote the welfare of people of India cannot be achieved unless we have socioeconomic laws. Indian constitution and other labour oriented legislations emphasized that there are provisions which enjoin on the state to provide equal opportunity of work and to provide socioeconomic justice and this also cannot be achieved unless the condition of the labour class is improved.

As we are aware of that there should be nexus between productivity and the wages. This nexus can be achieved by making the workman as a partner and this can be achieved either by providing production bonus in a substantial amount or to contribute some percent of the profit towards fund, which is managed by the employer and the workmen and they invest the amount in Government securities and the earnings from it are distributed among the workmen. So this can be one of the ways of making the workman as partner in production.

We are living in a competitive world but we will have to cooperate the wages with production, cannot have wages which are not realistic and which cannot provide competition. We are abolishing economic barriers. As in Europe, they have a common market, economic market in a way they are contemplating to abolish the barriers in the movement of manpower and have a common currency India cannot have these objectives achieved unless and until we remove the misunderstandings amongst ourselves. We should try to remove all irritants which are outstanding. Unfortunately in India, though the budget amount is very limited is being spent substantial amount on defence. Then should be a reduction in defence expenditure otherwise, we cannot have that productivity. After the second world war, Germany was more or less destroyed, Japan was also economically hit. But since under the peace treaty they were not allowed to raise sizeable armies, they concentrated on development and now these two countries are the most developed country and they are dominating the world. Unless we reduce and reflix the priorities in our budget, we cannot have that achievement which we desire[6].

The Role of the Law in Labour-Management Relations

Labour Management Relations systems are founded on a framework of labour law, which exerts an influence on the nature of the industrial relations system. However, recourse to the law and its potential to influence the resulting industrial relations system may sometimes be over-emphasized. It is useful, therefore, to examine, from three points of view, the role of the law in influencing an industrial relations system – what it objectives should be and the areas it should cover, as well as what the law cannot achieve.

In any working situation people need to cooperate with each other if there is to be maximum gain to themselves, to management and to society as a whole. Cooperation, however, is not easily obtained as people working together have conflicting interests. Employees are primarily concerned with the security of their jobs and what they can earn, and the employer with what he can produce as cheaply as possible to obtain the maximum profit. When these conflicting interests have taken definite form and shape, the State has often stepped into protect some of these interests through legal control. Labour law has amply demonstrated the sociological theory that Law is social institution which seeks to balance conflicting interests and to satisfy as many claims as possible with the minimum of friction.[7] Since the law must necessarily determine those interests which most urgently require protection over and above other interests, those of labour, where they lack self-reliance, have invariably formed a significant class of interests which the law protects. Hence, especially in some developing countries, the legal rules of an industrial relations system have been judged to some extent by the degree to which they further this end.

The three main functions of the law in an industrial relations system have been described[8] as auxiliary, regulatory and restrictive. First function is the support it gives to the autonomous system of collective bargaining, its operation and observance of agreements. The second function is one of providing a set of rules governing the terms and conditions of employment and supplementing those created by the parties themselves. The greater the coverage by collective bargaining, the less will be the regulatory function of the law. The third function prescribes what is permitted or forbidden in industrial conflict with a view to protecting the parties from each other, and the public from both of them.

One major objective of labour law is to create the legal framework which is necessary for employers, workers and their organizations to function effectively and as autonomous groups in the industrial relations system. Hence the law should protect the freedom of association so that the two parties are accorded the protections and guarantees found in the ILO Convention on the Freedom of Association and Protection of the Right to Organize No. 87 (1948). Since one of the major purposes of such association is to enable workers and employers to protect and further their interests, the law should also provide the legal framework needed to promote collective bargaining. In this connection the ILO Convention on the Right to Organize and Collective Bargaining No. 98 (1949) would provide the necessary basis for such legislation.

A second important function of labour law is to prescribe the minimum terms and conditions of employment which should be observed by employers in the course of conducting business. Therefore, the legal system often contains provisions stipulating the minimum conditions which must be observed in areas such as compensation for industrial accidents, social security, safety and health in enterprises, the minimum age of employment. Some countries may consider it appropriate to prescribe minimum wages. The basic rules to be followed in terminating employment may be another area of the employment relationship which would need to be covered by minimum standards. Methods for settling disputes, both individual and collective, through institutions such as labour courts, arbitration and conciliation systems, have not been an uncommon feature of State intervention through the law.

A third, and more general role for the law in industrial relations is as an instrument of social change. The law does not always merely or solely reflect contemporary thinking in society and does not necessarily lag behind social and other values. It sometimes anticipates them and can, on occasion, be employed to fashion new ideas and to effect changes in behavior. It is not always possible to leave crucial and complex social issues to be solved through purely voluntary action such as collective bargaining. Sometimes, especially in developing countries, the absence of strong and independent trade unions reduces the effectiveness and role of voluntary action, and necessitates greater regulation through legal prescription. In such situations desirable measures such as remedies for unfair dismissal, protection against acts of anti-union discrimination, the minimum conditions of contract of employment should conform to, safety requirements, etc., are prescribed by the law. But intervention on this ground should not lead to the introduction of rigidities in the labour market through overregulation.

Legal prescription should be viewed as merely laying down minimum terms and defining the permissible boundaries of action within which the two parties (employers and workers) must operate. Over regulation through law could have adverse consequences on building a sound industrial relations system through voluntary action, and on the competitiveness of enterprises. This has been perceived to be so in countries such as India and Sri Lanka, where employers have for some time canvassed for greater flexibility and less legislative control over industrial relations. A plethora of laws makes rapid adaptation to change difficult, and avoidance of laws can be a preoccupation of employers in such circumstances. Over regulation is sometimes based on the misconception that sound industrial relations can be achieved through the law. The creation of harmonious industrial relations needs to be achieved by other, non-legal means; the law cannot 'compel' parties to establish good relations. By way of analogy, in a different field of human relations, the law can prescribe the rules to be followed if people wish to marry. But the law cannot create a happy relationship or marriage. Similarly, harmonious industrial relations can be achieved not primarily through the law but through better human relations and human oriented practices at the enterprise level. Some countries, such as those in South Asia, which have a tradition of a plethora of labour laws, have tended to overlook the fact that if the energy expended by the State in enacting and enforcing a mass of labour laws had been spent in finding ways and means of encouraging mechanisms and systems geared to achieving sound labour relations, better results may have been achieved. In such countries parties tend to look to the law for the solution of what are essentially human relations problems, and creativity and innovation in industrial relations are consequently stifled. As a result, attention is focused more on dispute settlement rather than on dispute prevention, when emphasis on the latter is one way of building a sound industrial relations system.

Statute law is one of the specific means used by the State to condition industrial relations outcomes, and represents the most direct means of State intervention. Statutory regulation of minimum terms and conditions such as minimum wages, working conditions, safety and health, social security and protection become terms and conditions in contracts of employment which must conform to them; they cannot be 'bargained' away. Other statutory provisions may be of a more facilitating nature such as ones which establish the conditions and the environment for collective bargaining (e.g. rights of association, unfair labour practices, conciliation services); they are no less fundamental and important. Another - and more indirect - method through which the State influences industrial relations is the system of labour courts, tribunals or arbitration, which are a common feature in many countries. Through these institutions the State seeks to dispense equity in the employment relationship, and they may also protect collective interests as in the case of trade union rights. Such institutions have been considered necessary where the normal system of courts does not have the power or jurisdiction to apply equitable principles and to take into account the realities of the employment relationship, which results in a rather 'legalistic' view of labour relations. The pronouncements of these courts often constitute important limits to the freedom of action of the actors in industrial relations. Still another method of State intervention is through its 'administrative' role, for example, as conciliator or mediator.

Some Current Industrial Relations Issues

Employers are now compelled to view industrial relations and human resource management from a strategic perspective; in other words, not only from the traditional viewpoint of negotiating terms and conditions of employment and performing a personnel and welfare function. Industrial relations and human resource management are directly relevant to competitiveness, and how they are managed will impact on enterprise performance e.g. its productivity and quality of goods and services, labour costs, quality of the workforce, motivation, prevention of disputes and not only their settlement, and aligning employee aspirations with enterprise objectives.

Dispute Prevention

Most countries (other than those in transition to a market economy) have long-standing dispute settlement procedures at the national level (conciliation, arbitration, industrial or labour courts). Essential as these are, they operate only when a dispute arises. Equally important are dispute prevention through communication, consultation and negotiation procedures and mechanisms which operate largely at the enterprise level. They are not particularly common in many Asian enterprises. Their importance has increased in the current decade when changes in the way organizations are structured and managed have created the potential for workplace conflict. A more positive movement from personnel management to strategic human resource management is called for.

Industrial Relations Legislation

Industrial Relations Legislation falls under three categories: (*i*) Trade Union Legislation, (*ii*) Industrial Employment Standing Order Legislation, and (*iii*) Industrial Dispute Legislation.

The Indian Trade Union Act of 1926 and its amendment govern the trade union movement in our country. The main object of the Act is to give registered trade unions a legal and corporate status and their executives and members immunity from civil and criminal liability in respect of strikes.

The Industrial Employment (Standing Orders) Act of 1946 requires employers in industrial establishments to define with sufficient precision the conditions of employment under them and to make the said conditions known to all men employed by them.

Legislation for setting labour strikes was introduced by the Trade Disputes Act of 1929. Under the Act, the Government was empowered to appoint a Court of Enquiry or a Board of Conciliation. The Court or Board tried to bring about a settlement, but the decision was not legally binding on the parties concerned. Strikes and lock-outs in public utility service, without proper notice were made illegal. The emergency war-time legislative measures convinced the Government of their utility and led it to incorporate them in the permanent labour code of the country. The Industrial Disputes Act was accordingly passed to replace the Trade Disputes Act of 1929.

The Industrial Disputes Act was passed in 1947 with a view to improve the existing industrial relations between employers and the employees and for avoiding strikes and lock-outs specially in public utility services and essential undertakings and for providing machinery for peaceful settlement of industrial disputes and constituting joint works committees for enquiring into and settling individual grievances and day to day difficulties. The Industrial Disputes Act introduced the principles of compulsory arbitration and prohibited strikes without notice in respect of public utility services.

Why Need of a Sound Industrial Relations System at the National and Industry Level?

Labour-Management Relations Policy formulation is one of the significant tasks at the national level, and its successful formulation and implementation can influence the labour relations climate at the industry and enterprise levels. Such policy formulation, however, can be formulated not only at the national level through a tripartite process, but also at the industry level on a bipartite basis as between employers' and workers' organizations. Whether bipartite policy formulation becomes a part of national policy depends largely on the respective strengths of employers' and workers' organizations. In some of the industrialized market economies there is a greater likelihood than in developing countries of bipartite policy formulations being reflected in national policies due to the strength of the employers' and workers' organizations. In Sweden, for instance, in the past, the agreements between the union and the employers' organization tended to be translated into national policy instruments. The policies and methods of training of workers, for example, reflected what the two social partners had identified as appropriate for the industry. Or again, in Belgium the State recognizes the two social partners as the main formulators of social policy through collective bargaining; even the social security system is managed by the two social policy through collective bargaining; even the social security system is managed by the two social partners. The pervasive influence of bipartite arrangements is felt only where there is a 'balance of power' between the social partners. There is less likelihood of bipartism impacting on national policy formulation in developing countries due to strong central governments in many cases, and their assumption of the role of identifying the direction of economic and social policies. The relative weakness of employers' and workers' organizations or of one of them, or the inability of such organizations to agree on the fundamentals of what the labour relations policy should be, often prevents bipartism from influencing national policy formulation.

Tripartism and Labour Policy Formulation

Tripartism is the process the process through which the foundation for a sound industrial relations system can be laid at the national level. Ideally, tripartism is the process whereby the government, the most representative workers' and employers' organizations as independent and equal partners, consult with each other on labour market and related issues which are within their spheres of competence, and jointly formulate and implement national policies on such issues. However, this ideal situation is seldom reflected in practice, especially in developing countries or in societies with fairly authoritarian governments which believe that the direction of economic and social development is largely their responsibility. A more realistic model where developing countries are concerned is one in which a government consults the most representative employers' and workers' organizations on labour market and related issues which are within their spheres of competence, and takes account of their views in national policy formulation and its implementation.

Labour Management Relations Policy formulation may take place and be reflected in basic agreements or codes or industrial relations charters in which all three parties in the labour relations system have participated. Some such agreements may be bipartite, and may cover a variety of subjects including principles and procedures of labour relations such as freedom of association, trade union recognition, collective bargaining, labour-management cooperation mechanisms, procedures for the prevention and settlement of disputes, etc. The 1983 Australian national consensus (Accord) and the succeeding Accords on economic questions among the government, trade unions and employers contributed towards increased employment and profits, and a reduction in the days lost on account of strikes[9]. Other examples include the agreements negotiated by the Tripartite Labour Conference in India (in particular the Code of Discipline of 1958), the Code of Practice for Industrial Harmony (Malaysia 1975), the Code of Practice for the Promotion of Labour Relations (Thailand 1981), the Pancasial Labour Relations (Indonesia) and the labour policies resulting form tripartite consultations in Pakistan. Referring to the failure to implement some of these last mentioned arrangements J. Schegle[10] points out:

> "However, failure in practical implementation is not necessarily a valid argument against the concept as such of basic agreements or negotiated industrial relations charters or codes of conduct. The very idea of reaching agreement on these matters between the social partners is in line with a forward-looking tripartite approach to labour relations. The alternative is legislation and increased government intervention, a proposition to which most employers, and also many trade unions, in the region would object as a matter of principle. So the only remedy is to improve the practical application of basic agreements by delegating more power and authority to the central bodies of employers' and workers' organizations."

The contribution which Tripartism can make to the establishment of a sound industrial relations system can hardly be over-emphasized. Tripartism's rationale is to be found in the principle of democracy, the essence of which is a sharing or diffusion of power flowing from the encouragement or recognition of various pressure groups in a society as an effective safeguard against the centralization of power. It has been aptly remarked that "every source of independent power in a democracy is part of its strength, so long as it can be guided to seek its outlet through the democratic political system".[11] Tripartism as a process is a part of a pluralistic outlook on society through which stability is maintained, freedom of association being the sine qua non, because without the right of association the interest groups in a society cannot function effectively. As expressed by H.A. Clegg[12], pluralism's

> "Theme is that men associate together to further their common interest and desires; their associations exert pressure on each other and on the government; the concession which follow help to bind society together; thereafter stability is maintained by the further concession and adjustments as new associations emerge and power shifts from one group to another."

Acceptance of the principle of sharing power entails recognition of the fact that capital and labour represent two important pressure groups in society, if for no other reason than that both of them taken together are the principal providers of goods and services and wealth-creators in a market economy."

Impact of Globalization

Globalization first appeared towards the end of the 20th Century. It is true that in the new millennium, globalization is the central driving force behind the vigorous rapid social, political and economic changes that are reshaping the world order. The developing countries interestingly or uninterestingly have to integrate their national economies in the process of globalization. Internally they have to adjust their economic structural arrangement to face the global challenges. The information revolution has made us one world to think about global interests rather than individual interests. It is globally recognized that "Free trade is not only desirable, but it is the biggest single impetus for global prosperity," Geographical limitations had nothing do with global connections. In this process "labour and their status" is no exception. In the Global market, the priorities are changed. It is felt that "If the workers push their demands too hard, then companies will simply pack up their bags and move elsewhere. If governments implement meaningful reforms, then new investments will simply flow to more profitable parts of the. world."[13] There are many definitions for globalisation. The Human Development Report of South Asia 2001 has defined globalisation as "the free movement of goods, services, people and information across national boundaries. It creates and in turn, is driven by an integrated global economy,' which influences both economic as well as social relations within and across countries. The opening up of the economy increases competition internationally as well as eternally, leads to structural changes in the economy, alters consumer preferences, life styles and demands of citizens." Mr. Kofi Annan, Secretary General of the United Nations at World Economic Forum in 2002, appealed to the rich countries to open their markets to labour intensive products from poor countries and pleaded that developing countries be given a fair chance to export their products.

Significance of the Present Study

Labour policies seek to be an integral part of the overall economic policy of a nation, just as the industrial policy and the fiscal policy. The Indian Labour policies having been mostly diversed from our economic policy had narrowly focused on the protection of the existing employment in the organised sector.

The present study focuses on the law relating to labour management relations in liberalization era. For the purpose of the present study, the legislations dealing industrial relations viz., Industrial Disputes Act 1947, The Trade Unions Act 1926 and The Industrial Employment (Standing Orders) Act 1946 were studied in the light of the changing labour management relations in post-globalization era.

The present study is a modest attempt to study the following objectives.

1. Trace out the evolution of law and policy relating to Labour Management Relations in India.
2. Examine the present Labour Management Relations in the context of Globalization in India.
3. Examine the impact of International Labour Organization (ILO) on the Labour Management Relations in India.
4. Examine the present industrial administration and adjudication in India including the Judicial response to Industrial Disputes.
5. Study of the First and Second Labour Commissions reports relating to Labour Management Relations.
6. Examine the various alternatives for amicable settlement of Industrial Disputes and Maintaining Industrial peace and give suggestions for effective harmonious Labour Management Relations.

As already mentioned, the present work is an attempt to study the law and policy of Labour Management Relations, problems involved in industrial adjudication, Reports of National

Labour Commissions as well as various cases decided by Judiciary regarding industrial disputes. This is based on information gathered from various legislations brought from time to time, the decisional law of the Supreme Court of India and various High Courts, International Conventions and reports of International Labour Organization, constitutional framework relating to labour policy, New Industrial Policy and its impact on Labour Management Relations in Globalization era, First and Second Labour Commissions Reports.

The doctrinaire approach is adopted for the purpose of the study.

The present work is divided into the following seven chapters.

In the First Chapter need for reform in Labour Legislation, Constitutional Framework of Labour Legislation, Fundamental Rights, Directive Principles of State Policy, Principles of Labour Legislation are discussed. The role of the Law in Labour Management Relations, some current industrial relations issues were also discussed. The researcher opined that there is an urgent need of sound industrial relations system at the national level and Industry level. After having identified the objectives of the study, the scope of the study was limited to the Labour Management Relations in organized sector in the context of globalization. Methodology adopted for the present study is doctrinaire approach. Hypotheses and plan of the study are also dealt in this chapter.

In *Chapter II*, Labour Management Relations, Functions and objectives, approaches and theories are discussed. Evolution of Law and Policy relating to Labour Management Relations is provided in this chapter. Workers and Industrial culture is also discussed in this chapter.

Chapter III deals with main functions of I.L.O., various conventions of I.L.O. relating to right to association, freedom from forced labour, the impact of the I.L.O. on the Indian labour scene. It also deals with I.L.O. standards and the adaptation of them into Indian Labour Legislations, Labour Policy under different five year plans. Trade union rights are also discussed in this chapter.

Chapter IV deals with the role of the state in Globalization era, changing face of trade unions in a liberalized economy and impact of Globalization on Labour Management Relations. Need for social security for workers even in Globalization era and challenges of globalization are also discussed in this Chapter.

In *Chapter V*, trade unions and Industrial Relations, workers participation in management, Labour Administration, the province of Industrial Adjudication, Reference, Industrial Relations machinery, Mediation, Conciliation etc., are discussed. The recent Supreme Court judgments in post-globalization era which are deviating from welfare concept and vanishing rights of workmen are also dealt in this chapter.

In *Chapter VI*, the reports of first and second National Labour Commissions regarding Labour Management Relations are discussed. Need to establish Industrial Relation Commission is also discussed in this Chapter.

In the concluding last chapter the problems of both Labour and Management with reference to large number of Legislative enactments are discussed. There is also need to revise the traditional conflict models of Industrial Relations. For having effective and harmonious Labour Management Relations, apart from giving suggestion to implement Second National Labour Commission report immediately, some other suggestions are also made in this chapter.

REFERENCES

1. Tripathi, P.C. Gupta, C.B., *Industrial Relations and Labour Laws*, Sultan Chand & Sons, New Delhi, 1996.

2. See also Tripathi, P.C., Gupta, C.B., *Industrial Relations and Labour Laws*, Sultan Chand and Sons, New Delhi, 1996.

3. Tandon, B.K., *Collective Bargaining and the Indian Scene*, Sultan Chand & Sons 1973, p. 43.

4. Mr. P.R. Kumaramangalam, Member of Parliament, in his Keynote Address in third SAARC Law Conference, New Delhi, Dt. 29-01-1994.

5. Govind Hari Singhania, President, ASSOCHAM, India in his Response address, in third SAARC Law Conference, New Delhi, Dt. 29-01-1994.

6. Ajmial Mian, Co-Chairman, SAARC, in third SAARC Law Conference, New Delhi, 29-01-1994. (Law an Instrument of Economic Change in the SAARC Region"-3rd SAARC Law Conference, New Delhi – 29-01-1994, (Session 1-C) Labour laws and the new economic agenda. Published by SAARCLAW-INDIA CHAPTER, New Delhi.)
7. Roscoe Pound, "A Theory of Social Interests" in Papers and Proceedings of the American Sociological Society, May, 1921.
8. Ottokhan – Freud, "Industrial Relations and the Law – Retrospect and prospect", *BJIR*, Vol. VII, (1969).
9. Oliver Clark and John Niland, "The Dynamics and Dimensions of Change" in *Agenda for Change: An International Analysis of Industrial Relations in Transition, Ibid*, p. 68.
10. The Role of Employers' Organizations in Industrial Relations" in ILO Round Table for Pan-Asian and Pacific Employers Organizations (ILO, 1980, p. 87).
11. Clegg, H.A. *A New Approach to Industrial Democracy*, Blackwell, Oxford 1960s, p. 20.
12. Pluralism in Industrial Relations, *BJIR*, volume 13, 1975.
13. Jeremy Fox, *Chomsky and Globalisation*, Icon Books UK, Totem Books, USA 2002, pp. 23-39.

2

EVOLUTION OF LAW AND POLICY RELATING TO LABOUR MANAGEMENT RELATIONS

The term 'industrial relations' or 'labour management relations or 'employee relations' is difficult to define precisely because it is too complex. This is particularly so in a democratic society which allows freedom of action to the workers and their organisations and to the employers and their organisations and a series of laws are enacted to regulate their relations. In a totalitarian country trade unions were banned, as in Germany under Hitler or Italy under Moussolini. But even such a society has to enact laws to provide an acceptable relationship between the industrial employer and employees. In a Communist country where all persons employed are workers, industrial relations cannot result in any form of industrial action. But changes are taking place even in the so-called Communist countries; the upsurge of industrial workers in Poland and Yugoslavia are cases to point.

Industrial relations as being synonymous with employer and employee relations may be defined as the relations between employers and employees in industry. According to *Encyclopaedia Britannica,* the industrial relations include individual relations and joint consultation between employers and work people at the place of work, collective relations between employers and the organisations and the trade unions and the part played by the State in regulating these relations.

Thus:

(i) Industrial relations include individual relations in an industry;

(ii) The collective relations between employers and labour/trade unions;

(iii) The role of the government in the regulation of these relationships;

(iv) Besides these, there is the international aspects, particularly in terms of the influence exercised by certain international bodies like the ILO in shaping and developing the pattern of industrial relations in several countries.

(v) In order that the term 'industrial relations' covers every sector of the labour force in all parts of the world, the International Institute of Labour Studies has defined it as 'social relations in production'.

Industrial relations is an art, the art of living together for the purposes of production. The emphasis is on the process of accommodation whereby the parties involved develop skills and methods of adjusting to and cooperating with each other.

There is no uniform pattern of industrial relationship even in democratic societies. However, there are standards of industrial relationships which are contained in the Philadelphia Declaration of the ILO (1994) embodied in the series of Conventions and Recommendations evolved in the ILO conferences in which most of the democratic countries of the world participate. If a country ratifies a convention, its national laws have to conform to it. In fact, most of India's labour legislation after Independence has been influenced by such conventions and recommendations.

There is no uniform pattern that can be prescribed for nations. The kind of industrial relations required to ensure harmony and cooperation will depend on a number of factors including the form of ownership of industry that prevails, the state of technology that is utilized, the state of techniques and relations of production in that society, the nature and character of the government, the views of the Government in relations to its own role, the instruments that the society has as its disposal to formulate public opinion, the socially-accepted concept of sanctions in the field of industrial relations and the socially accepted limitations on the use of action in the industrial field— whether it be by the employer or the employee.

Following Robert W. Cox enumeration of the patterns of relationship may be as follows:

(1) The peasant-lord system (in industrial employment it represents master-servant relationship).

(2) The primitive market system.

(3) A small manufacture system (beginning of industrial revolution where workers are getting slowly organised).

(4) The lifetime commitment system as in Japan where there is lifelong employment.

(5) A bipartite system of which collective bargaining is the main function as in USA and other democratic countries.

(6) A tripartite system in which the Government also plays an important role in labour management relations as in India.[1]

Functions

Industrial relations system fulfills at least three major functions. First, it defines the relative rights and responsibilities of workers managers and the state and establishes the power relationships between them. Secondly, it channels and controls the responses of workers and managers to the dislocation, frustrations and insecurities inherent in the industrial process. Thirdly, it establishes the net-work of rules - both substantiative and procedural which govern the workplace and work community. In short, the industrial relations system provides the structure and the machinery for the functional relationship between the managers and the managed in any industrial society.

There are three basic approaches to labour management negotiations - unilateral, bipartite and tripartite. In the unilateral approach, the employer alone decides the terms and conditions of employment for his workers. In bipartite approach, the employer negotiates with his workers. This is collective bargaining. In the tripartite approach, a third party – the Government also participates in the negotiations.[2]

Objectives of Industrial Relations

Basically the objectives of industrial relations are as follows:

- To maintain and develop good employer-employee relations.
- To maintain industrial peace.
- To safeguards the interests of labour and management.
- To avoid as far as possible, industrial conflicts.
- To establish industrial democracy.
- To help the economic development of the country.
- To encourage collective bargaining as a means of self-regulation.
- To help maintain discipline amongst workers.
- To help Government in making laws.
- To help union and management develop constructive attitudes to one another.

Approaches to Industrial Relations

Industrial relations which refer to the formal process of consultation and negotiation are as old as industry and being inherent in industry, will always remain as a feature of industrial life. The participants in it are mainly three– the workers and their organisations, the employers and their associations and the agencies of the government. The participants should build up a stable, workable relationship among themselves and provide for the people a constant flow of consumption goods. The sectional groups in society sacrifice its broader interests to further their own ends and the conflict between the two assume the shape of industrial unrest. The agencies of Government which is the custodian of the interests of the community as a whole, play a significant role in shaping the pattern of relationships in the industrial setting. Industrial relations are collectively conducted between the workers and the employers through collective bargaining.[3]

In the pre-industrial society, productive work was mostly organized on a small scale. Workmen frequently owned the simple instruments which they needed for their work. Hence, they either worked on their own or offered services to others with whom they would have direct and personal relations. With the advent of modern industrialisation, work organisations have undergone a basic transformation in terms of the scale of activity.

Modern industrial work has the following peculiarities:

(i) Industrial work is a group work. It brings together a large number of workers who work for the employer with whom they have scarcely any personal relationship. What is possible between them is a collective relationship. The other significant aspect of this feature is the relations among the workers themselves. Some leaders come up from among the workers and they wield considerable power.

(ii) It involves division of labour. A worker seldom makes a complete product. Work is fragmented and repetitive. The worker spends the best part of his life at the work place but his work does not interest him.

(iii) Industrial work is carried on under the control and direction of the employer. The workers do not own the instruments of production. They have only their services to offer to employers who own the instruments of production. As a result, workers have lost their freedom as independent producers.

(iv) Lastly, industrial work is wage work. Employers buy and workers sell their services. The buyer wants labour to be more productive and the sellers want it to be more rewarding.[4]

Evolution of Industrial Relations

In India when the doctrine of laissez-faire prevailed, workers were at a great disadvantage as they contracted themselves with their employers. They were exploited – they received low wages and worked long hours in miserable physical conditions of work. The relationship between unequals inevitably resulted in the exploitation of the weak by the strong. This exploitation sowed the seeds of dissatisfaction and bred protest. Therefore, workers got together and formed trade unions; they built up their organisations to mobilize their own power. In the sphere of collective relationship trade unions emerged for the protection and furtherance of the workers' interests for the worker individually could not take up his own cause effectively with the employer.

As the industrial units grew large their ownership was increasingly divorced from management and a new managerial group was interposed between the owners / employers and the rank and file of workers.

The other important aspect of industrialization is the formation of employers' associations to safeguard and promote the interest of their members through collective action.

The basic inequalities of the contracting parties in the employment relationship have called forth intervention by a third party, i.e., the Stage, in favour of the weaker section to ensure fair treatment to all concerned. The major instrument with the Government is legislation whereby norms to regulate the relationship between the two parties are specified and enhanced through the apparatus created for the purpose. The Government is prompted to influence the relationship between the employers/ management and the workers and their trade unions, for it has the responsibility of satisfying the economic needs of the community. Therefore, the major influence in the field of industrial relations are the workers, the management and the Government. They play their roles, act and interact and evolve a process to regulate employment relationship.

Upto the late 20's of the 20th century, the employer-employee relationship in India was practically that of master and servant. The British Government followed a policy of laissez-faire and regarded the problem of industrial relations mainly from the point of view of law and order. Policy of the Government was to protect the social system from workers rather than to protect workers from the social system.[5]

Workers were hired and fired as the principle of demand and supply governed industrial relations. The employer was in a commanding position and the conditions of employment and wages were very poor.

In the decades following the World War I, the mounting industrial unrest and political excitement within the country, the Soviet Revolution, the establishment of ILO and the rise of the working class in Britain made the Government conscious of the danger and limitations of the prevailing policy.

After the World War I, the industrial relations concept assumed a new dimension in the sense that the workers now resorted to violence and employers to lockouts. There were numerous strikes and disturbances during 1928-29. As a result, the Government enacted the Trade Disputes Act 1929, to expedite the early settlement of industrial disputes. With the passing of the Trade Disputes Act in 1929, State intervention in the settlement of industrial disputes started. The Act vested the Government with powers which could be used whenever it considered fit to intervene in industrial disputes. It provided for only ad-hoc conciliation boards and courts of enquiry. The Amending Act of 1938 authorized the Central and Provincial Governments to appoint conciliation officers for mediating in or promoting the settlement of disputes. The Act, however, was not used extensively as the Government policy at that time continued to be one of laissez-faire and selecting intervention at the most.

The defects of the Trade Disputes Act 1926, were to a certain extent removed by the Industrial Disputes Legislation passed in Bombay in 1934 and 1938. The Bombay Trade Disputes (Conciliation) Act 1934, introduced for the first time a standing machinery to enable the state to promote industrial peace. A permanent cadre of conciliators were envisaged for settling matters which fell within their jurisdiction. The scope of the

Act was limited to selected industries. The experience of the working of the Act led to the enactment of the Bombay Industrial Disputes Act, 1938.[6] The Act provides for (i) compulsory recognition of unions by the employer, (ii) giving the right to workers to get their case represented either through a representative union or where no representative union in the industry existed, through elected representatives of workers or through the Government Labour Officer; (iii) the setting up of an Industrial Court with original as well as appellate jurisdiction, to which parties could go for arbitration in case conciliation fails and (iv) prohibition of strike/lockout under certain conditions.[7]

During the World War II the Government assumed emergency powers for the settlement of industrial disputes. In 1942, the Defence of India Rules was promulgated to meet the exigencies created by the war. Rule 81 A gave powers to the appropriate Governments to intervene in industrial disputes, appoint industrial tribunals and enforce the award of the tribunals on both sides. Under this Rule compulsory conciliation and adjudication were introduced.[8]

After India attained Independence, the Industrial Disputes Act was passed in 1947 which replaced the Trade Disputes Act of 1929. This Act not only provides for the establishment of permanent machinery for the settlement of industrial disputes but also makes these awards binding and legally enforceable. With subsequent amendments, the ID Act still continues to be the main instrument for Government's intervention in labour disputes.[9]

Another development in the post-independence period was the setting up of the Indian Labour Conference, a tripartite body to look into industrial relations problems. It was setup with the objective of establishing co-operation between the trade of the actual workign of these provisions, the decision of the judiciary and the influence of the bipartite and tripartite agreements and also set up with the objective of establishing cooperation between the trade unions, employers and the Government. It met once a year to discuss problem relating to industrial relations.

The ID Act provides for settlement of industrial disputes through conciliation and adjudication. The Act empowers the appropriate Government to appoint conciliation officers and/or constitute Boards of Conciliation to mediate in and promote settlement of industrial disputes. It also empowers the appropriate Government to refer disputes for adjudication by an industrial tribunal. The Act makes a distinction between disputes arising in public utility services and those in other industries and provides for compulsory conciliation and adjudication to resolve the former. Besides, the appropriate Government could constitute a Court of Enquiry to enquire into matters relating to an industrial disputes. Restrictions are placed on strike/lockout in public utility services and during the pendency of conciliation and adjudication proceedings.

In 1957 the emphasis of Government's attitude towards labour shifted from legal enactments to voluntary arrangements. In fact, the period between 1957 and 1965 can be regarded as an attempt to move away from, legalism to voluntarism which dominated industrial relations in India. As a result, the Code of Discipline was introduced in 1958. It enjoins on parties to refrain from taking unilateral action on industrial matters. But unfortunately, the Code has a limited success. As a result, the Government, has to rely on legislation to regulate labour-management relations.

Plan Policies

The Industrial Disputes Act 1947 has been the main legislative frame-work which has provided the machinery and procedure for the settlement of disputes through mediation, conciliation, arbitration and adjudication. Steps were, also taken in the past to provide a voluntary approach to industrial relations through Codes. A general feeling has developed that the existing arrangements have not proved effective' in presenting disputes and promoting settlements. Since the submission of the report of the National Commission on Labour efforts have been made for evolving a new and comprehensive industrial relations legislation but these have not succeeded on account of the divergence of approaches among the trade union organisations on certain basic issues such as the machinery and procedure for settlement of disputes, the criteria and procedure for recognition of trade unions i.e., whether the representative character of trade unions should be determined through verification of paid membership of contending unions or through secret ballot; right to strike in essential industries including public utilities, role of government. In regulating industrial relations etc. While efforts must continue, to minimize the areas of disagreement among the parties concerned and acceptable improvements in law and machinery effected, some of the changes in the existing laws on trade unions, industrial disputes and standing orders, which are generally considered essential for promoting industrial relations, need not be held over and should be carried out. These changes would, help in streamlining the existing procedures and securing speedy justice to workers. The question of providing security of service to such categories of employees who are at present outside the ambit of labour laws also needs consideration.[10]

Some International Practices

In the USA, the State has confined itself to enacting legislation for ensuring the workers' right to organise and bargain collectively and has constituted an independent authority to administer and interpret legal provisions and decide on complaints regarding unfair labour practices. Intervention of the State in industrial disputes is limited to actual work stoppages which could impair the national economy. But even within this area of State intervention, a wide latitude is given to the parties for settling their differences. The Government does not envisage direct interference in the process of collective bargaining.

Legislation has been introduced in the USA to cover a wide-range of aspects of industrial relations and although it would be an exaggeration to claim that industrial negotiations are solely the province of lawyers, legal profession comes close to dominating the scene. The National Labour Relations or Wagner Act of 1935 govern collective bargaining; the National Labour Relations Board can determine who shall have bargaining rights and issue over which they may bargain. The Labour Management Relations or Taft-Hartley Act of 1947, made collective agreements legally enforceable, introduced the concept of a 'cooling off period' (during which strike action has to be suspended), enabled a district court to issue an 80-day injunction against a strike or lockout which was causing a national emergency, regulated the internal affairs of trade unions and provided protection for workers who refused to join a union. The provisions in the Taft-Hartley Act concerning the internal affairs of trade unions were extended to the Landrum-Griffin Act of 1959.[11]

In the UK, the industrial relations system has been marked by the primacy of free collective bargaining between the parties.

Many writers have argued that prior to the 1960s, UK has a 'voluntary' system of industrial relations. The adjective 'voluntary' means that the State plays no part whatsoever in industrial relations. If voluntary system of industrial relations means the absence of State intervention of any kind, the British system has never been voluntary. The State in Britain has always intervened on certain issues. For example, the State has intervened through the Factory Acts (1961), and associated legislation (such as the Mines Acts and the Offices, Shops and Railways Premises Act). These regulate working conditions by laying down rules for the notification of accidents and industrial diseases, the provision of proper ventilation, sanitation and maximum hours of work.[12]

The assertion that UK had a voluntary system of industrial relations does not imply that the State has not taken an interest in or intervened in industrial relations in UK; rather it implies that the State has played a restricted role and has tried to keep industrial relations and trade unions away from the courts.

The role of the State in British industrial relations changed in the 196Os. First, the State intervened more decisively in the area of wages and salaries, a move crystallised in the notion of 'incomes policy'. Second, Governments attempt to introduce the law more centrally into collective bargaining, conciliation and arbitration. The Industrial Relations Act 1971 marks the high point of this policy.[13]

The Australian system has had a long tradition of State

regulation. The Government intervenes for the settlement of disputes. Collective bargaining in Australia is dominated by the law. Compulsory arbitration is not reserved for exceptional cases as in the USA, rather it is accepted as a normal part of industrial relations. So, collective bargaining, as it is understood in Europe, does not exist in Australia.

In Japan, the right to collective bargaining is guaranteed under the Constitution and the State has enacted legislation to promote collective bargaining. Direct state intervention is permissible in strikes which might jeopardise the national economy and public life. In other industrially advanced democratic systems, direct State intervention in industrial disputes is generally the exception rather than the rule.[14]

In the erstwhile USSR, three important factors regulate the industrial relations system. First, the formation of a socialist society is characterised by the public ownership of the basic means of production. The building up of a workers' state makes the interests of labour and management non-antagonistic. Second, the operation of a centrally planned economy introduces its own constraints on labour and management. However, recently increasing powers are given to local trade unions and individual enterprises to take decisions on matters of employment, wages and productivity. Lastly, the influence of a single political party in running the government and in organising unions makes it necessary for the unions to perform a double role. They have to help in carrying out party policy and look after production interests and at the same time assume the traditional role of unions in furthering the interests of labour.[15]

In the three developing countries in Asia—Myanmar, Malaysia and Philippines, the concern of the State in industrial relations has been more marked. Besides laying down rules and procedures for the settlement of disputes, the State has provided arbitration machinery. In the last resort, Government has reserved to itself the right of making a reference to such machinery in cases where the public interest so demands or where a joint request is made by the parties.[16]

Practice of India

In India labour legislation was undertaken in advance of the emergence of labour organizations. The incentive to labour legislation was furnished not by the humanitarian considerations of enlightened manufacturers but by the discovery of certain Manchester Cotton manufacturers in 1870 that a cotton textile industry was developing in Bombay. At that time industrialists in India could use their labour in any manner they liked as there was no factory laws. The result was the exploitation of labour, especially of children and women labour by employers. Thus industrialists in India had the advantage of cheap labour in comparison with the British industrialists where labour laws existed and the Manchester Cotton manufacturers became jealous of the Indian Cotton mill and wanted to curb its development. The Manchester Chamber of Commerce sent in 1874 a deputation to the Secretary of State for India to apply the same factory laws to the Indian mills as were applicable to the British factories so as to neutralize the unfair advantages which the Indian manufacturers were enjoying due to long hours of work and large scale employment of child and women labour. A Factory Commission was appointed in 1875, to investigate the need of the required legislation. The Commission revealed the fact that the mills worked from sunset to sunrise, there was no fixed weekly holiday and even children of 7 were engaged in the factory. The Bombay Government shelved the Commission's Report as the majority did not favour the idea of regulating working hours in the factories, through legal measures. But the Manchester interests, however, continued to carry on their agitation for factory legislation.

It was in 1875 when some social workers of Bombay under the leadership of Mr. Sorabjee Shaporjee Bengalee started an agitation to draw the attention of the Government to the miserable conditions of the workers and to the need for some factory legislation. As a result of the agitation the first Factories Act was passed in 1881.

In the early days the policy of the Government was to protect the social system from workers rather than to protect workers from the social system. Moreover, whatever labour legislation was undertaken, was also with reference to specific industries and not for the general class of industrial workers.

The defects of labour legislation in India have been due to the lack of proper development of a National labour policy. Prior to World War II, there was practically no social attitude of public opinion on the labour question and no demand was made for an adequate solution of any outstanding labour problem. Most of the measures were, therefore, forced upon Government by extraneous circumstances. Plantation legislation was, for instance, enacted for granting planters a security over their labourers; factory legislation owes its origin to the rivalry of Manchester interests and even in the recent past labour legislation was undertaken for the fulfillment of international obligation, which, however important in itself, cannot take the place of a National Labour Policy.

It has been rightly criticized that many of the labour laws are 'half-baked and hastily devised'. Close at the heels of an Act come amendments and then more amendments to amend the amendments.

Employers complain, not without reason, that government's labour legislation programme is quite unrelated to the needs of the present situation in India. They contend that the obligations imposed on employers under various labour laws contribute to raise the cost of production and weaken India's competitive position in the world market.

India, by 1980 had a spate of labour legislations not to be found in any country at India's level of economic development. The standards laid down by the ILO have been accepted and measures are undertaken to come into closer conformity with the provisions of the International Labour Code. Although satisfactory progress has been achieved in the directions of labour legislation, nevertheless we have yet to travel a long way on the road to social justice.

For industrial relations system to help in both economic development and democracy, the challenge lies in promoting their stability and flexibility, so that the twin goals of both efficiency and equity are met. To achieve these goals individual countries must devise their systems and institutions that are congruent with their national culture, institution history and other macro policies. Widespread acceptance of these goals is the only concrete principle for the industrial relations actors of the present century. The output of industrial relations has so far been measured in terms of network of rules and regulations, strikes and lockouts, grievances and indiscipline, etc. New technologies and changing work place and demographics are bringing transformation in work place governance which will result in greater say and stake for employees, customers as well as for the country. The trade unions have to take into consideration the effects of globalisation and international competition. The highest challenge for them is that the Indian Foreign Trade policies have unleashed a market economy where a large proportion of labour force is made a redundant resource. They find it difficult to accept large- scale workforce reductions or displacement without a credible system of compensation or social safety net.

The content and purpose of labour policy and labour law should focus on facilitation rather than regulation, proaction than reaction and on harmonious relations conducive to social and economic development rather than dispute resolution. When the private sector becomes the engine of growth, the State needs to play a much stronger role in ensuring a balance between the rights of both labour and management. The policy should focus on the entire labour force. There is a need for a thorough review of the Centre-State relations in the sphere of labour with respect to legislation, labour administration and labour judiciary. The key issue is, how much uniformity and how much diversity can states have in labour matters. The crucial issue is the law and procedure relating to the protection of retrenched/dismissed workers. The ILO conventions and recommendations have played a significant role in India as regards the legal framework on wages, working conditions, welfare, social security, protection of the vulnerable sections of society, human resource development, equity and non-discrimination, etc. It has also ratified three of the eight conventions that constitute the fundamental principles. However, India has opposed proposals to link labour standards and trade through "social labeling". The purpose of law should be to achieve a delicate balance between conflicting and competing claims. It should be pro-people and pro-humanity.

Thus, the labour law regime in India is a conglomeration of a large number of legislative enactments. It is a large mosaic of laws in which no discernible pattern emerges. These parts of the mosaic are all disparate entities.

Yet this large quantity is only superficial. For, underneath a large number of these laws are not applicable to a vast majority of the workforce. Furthermore, though the number of laws is large, many important issues such as compulsory recognition of a trade union, protection to white-collar workers etcetera don't find any mention in the laws. Another important aspect of the volume of laws is that a bulk of the provisions are merely procedural in nature. The substantive aspects of the employment relationship comprise only a small part of legislations. Thus, while the employers are concerned merely with filing returns and maintaining registers, the worker gains nothing substantial. What happens is just the increased control of business by the Government. While control is necessary, it should not partake of the character of throttling business. What is needed is just regulation, pure and simple. Legislative despotism in the form of excessive legislation and legislative anarchy in the form of total absence are two extremes. The need of the hour is a golden mean between these two extremes. For, legislative monitoring through legislations is essential. It is the protector of the unprotected. This function cannot be abdicated; for, if gold rusts what will iron do? Law should merely regulate in conjunction with other social forces.

State intervention in India has assumed a more direct form. The State has enacted procedural and also substantive laws to regulate industrial relations. In the distant past, State intervention in labour matters was for protecting the commercial interests of the British Rulers. Later, pressures from the public to guard the interests of workers in the face of difficulties created by the operation of the economic system prevailed. Since independence, State intervention in labour matters has been necessitated by larger need for the regulation of the economy with the focus on rapid overall growth. Apart from planned development, the requirements of the Welfare State envisaged in our constitution have been another important reason for State intervention.[17]

Apart from the different roles played by the State, there are others which have a special significance in our context. The first is that of the State as an employer which has two aspects—direct employment of labour by the State and employment in industrial corporations constituted by the State. Handling of industrial relations in the case of its own employees, to whom all legislation framed from industry is applicable, falls in this category. This function of the State as an employer has been there over a very long period. To this was added another when, as a matter of policy, it was decided to operate a mixed economy wherein industries were to be run by both private entrepreneurs and the State. The policy statements show that as an employer the State binds itself to the rules which it frames for private employers. Where standards of good employment are disparate, the State seeks to set standards with a view to influencing the employers in the private sector. While this is the policy, in practice, it so happens that there is a fair amount of interaction between what the employers do for their employees in the two sectors. And this interaction is influenced by the new consciousness among the workers and ease of communication within the working class.

The second role which the State has to play in our context is the outcome of its Federal Constitution, and the fact that labour is a subject in the Concurrent list for the purpose of legislation. It has been a tradition in the country for long that the Central Government assumes the responsibility of enacting legislation on many aspects affecting labour, whereas the State Governments look after implementation, though they can legislate on their own also. In either case, a considerable measure of consultation has been the rule.

It is obvious, therefore, that the State cannot be a silent

spectator in the development of healthy labour practices. It has to play a role which the parties to a dispute find acceptable.

Industrial relations in India have been shaped largely by principles and policies evolved through tripartite consultative machinery at the industry and national levels.

Tripartite bodies like the Indian Labour Conference/Standing Labour Committee/Industrial Committees were set up for setting union norms to guide industrial relations. Tripartite meetings provide a useful forum of communication between the parties represented on them. They help in narrowing down differences among the three groups in reaching consensus over matter of common interest, in providing a forum for communication among the parties and in sharing the responsibility of Government in maintaining industrial harmony.[18]

Industrial Relations Practice at the Plant-level in India

There are five types of the prevailing patterns of industrial relations in India at the plant-level. These are:

- Regulative (Standing Orders)
- Consultative (Voluntary Jt. Consultation)
- Preventive (Works Committee/Joint Committee)
- Cooperative (Collective Bargaining Codes)
- Conflictive (ID Act)
- Participative (JMC).

By and large, the regulative and conflictive patterns in industrial relations seem to predominate at the plant-level in India. The positive patterns begin in consultation and culminate in participation via cooperation.

The regulative pattern marks the beginnings of industrial relations. It is characterised by the application and administration of the Industrial Employment (Standing Orders) Act and the enforcement of Standing Orders.

The consultative pattern will begin only if both management and employees believe in voluntary joint consultation and bilaterally practice it within the framework of their terms of jurisdiction.

There is a provision for the preventive pattern of industrial relations illustrated by statutory bodies such as Works Committee and Joint Committee as machinery for the avoidance of problems of industrial relations. These are intended to prevent any industrial unrest and conflict and pave the way for the positive philosophy of cooperation in industrial relations reflected in collective bargaining.

Alternatively, the conflictive pattern is reflected in the working of the industrial disputes legislation as applicable to different industries in the country.[19]

There is a long way to go from the regulative pattern to the participative pattern of industrial relations but this movement is essential for the progress of the country.

Theories of Industrial Relations

1. Unitary Theory

The essence of the unitary theory of industrial relations, held by Halford Reddish and others, is that every work organization is an integrated and harmonious whole existing for a common purpose. They assume that each employee identifies with the aims of the enterprise and with its methods of operating. By this view, there is no conflict of interest between those supplying financial capital to the enterprise and their managerial representatives, and those contributing their labour and job skills. By definition the owners of capital and labour are joint partners to the common aims of efficient production, high profits and good pay in which everyone in the organization has a stake. It follows that there cannot be 'two sides' in industry. Indeed managers and managed alike are merely parts of the same 'team'. This team, however, is expected to be provided with strong leadership from the top to keep it working and to ensure commitment to the tasks to be done and to its managerial office holders.

One implication of unitarism is that factionalism within the enterprise, is seen as a pathological social condition. Subordinate employees are not expected to challenge managerial decisions or the right to manage, while trade unionism is viewed as an illegitimate intrusion into the unified and cooperative structure of the workplace. More than this, trade unionism competes almost malevolently with management for the loyalty and commitment of employees to their employer. In other words, unitary theory in its traditional or classical form denies the validity of conflict at work whether between management and employees, between management and unions, or even between the organization and its customers. The concepts of common purpose and harmony of interests further imply that apparent conflict is either (a) merely frictional, e.g. due to incompatible personalities or 'things going wrong', or (b) caused by faulty communication', e.g. misunderstanding' about aims or methods, or (c) the result of stupidity in the form of failure to grasp the communality of interest, or (d) the work of agitators inciting the supine majority who would otherwise be content.[20]

Collective bargaining and trade unions are therefore perceived as being anti-social, anti-managerial mechanisms, since acceptance of two opposed and competing interest groups within the enterprise, in the persons of management and union representatives, only precipitates and crystallizes unnecessary and destructive industrial conflict between what are viewed as two non-competing, cooperative parties.

A variant of unitary theory, 'neo-unitary' theory, appears to have emerged in some organizations since the 1980s. It builds on existing unitary concepts but is more sophisticated in the ways it is articulated and applied within enterprises. Its main aim seems to be to integrate employees, as individuals, into the companies in which they work. Its orientation is distinctly market-centered, managerialist and individualist. By gaining employee commitment to quality production, customer needs and job flexibility, employers embracing this frame of reference have expectations of employee loyalty, customer satisfaction and product security in increasingly competitive market conditions. Companies adopting a neo-unitary approach to managing people share a number of ways in which they do this; they try to create a sense of common purpose and shared corporate culture; they emphasize to all employees the primacy of customer service; they set explicit work target for employees; they invest heavily in training and management development; and they sometimes provide employment security for their workers.[21]

2. *Conflict Theory*

Conflict theory is based on two interrelated views of society and of industrial relations between employers and employees. The *first* is that although Western industrialized societies are still class based, they are essentially 'post-capitalist' in the sense that political and industrial conflict or increasingly institutionally separated within them and that industrial conflict has been less violent because its existence has been accepted and its manifestations have been socially regulated through agreed constitutional arrangements. The *second* view is that work organizations are microcosms of society. Since society comprises a variety of individuals and of social groups, each having their own social values and each pursuing their own self-interests and objectives, those controlling and managing work enterprises similarly have to accommodate the differing values and competing interests within them. It is only by doing this that private or public enterprises can function effectively. Industrial relations between employers and unions and between managers and trade unionists, are an expression of the conflict and the power relations between organized groups in society generally. As such, industrial conflict between managers and their subordinates has to be recognized as an endemic feature of work relationship and managed accordingly.

A major element in post-capitalist theories of contemporary society and industrial relations is the proposition that the nature of class conflict has substantially changed from that suggested by Marx in his nineteenth-century analysis. In Marxist theory class conflict is perceived as being synonymous with industrial conflict and political conflict. Under market capitalism, Marxists argue, the capitalists or the owners of the means of production are identical with the ruling class in industry and politics, while wage-earners, owning only their labour-resources, are relatively powerless in industrial relations and in politics. Capitalists are the social elite and the proletariat are the socially weak.

First, we now live in a more open and socially mobile society compared with the class-based social divisions associated with nineteenth-century and early twentieth-century capitalism. The widening of educational opportunity, the democratization of politics, and the growth of public sector industry have opened up recruitment to a whole range of sought-after roles in society, including those within industry, politics, education, the professions, arts and so on, which would have been inconceivable a hundred years ago. Moreover, the creation of the welfare state, mitigated the worst effects of social deprivation, economic inequality and abject poverty.

Second, the distribution of authority, property and social status in society is more widely diffused than in the past. The positions which individuals occupy in the authority structure of industry, do not necessarily correlate with their positions in the political structure or with their social standing in the community. The village postal worker can become the local councilor, the school teacher a Member of Parliament and the trade unionist a Justice of the Peace. Similarly, the union convener within the workplace might have potentially more industrial power than the senior management with which he negotiates. In other works, post-capitalists take the view that dominant and subordinate classes within industry need no longer necessarily correspond with the political or social divisions of society generally.

Thus, the emergence of trade unionism, employer's organizations and collective bargaining, together with union representation at enterprise and workplace level, now effectively regulate the inevitable social conflicts arising between management and subordinates at work. Even where these conflicts seem irresolvable, third party intervention, usually through state agencies providing conciliation and arbitration services, is now available to provide workable remedies. By this analysis, extending worker participation in managerial decision making, as happens in board level worker representation in countries like Denmark, the Netherlands and Germany, is seen as a logical progression in institutionalizing the power relations between managers and subordinates at wok. Post-capitalist society is viewed as an open society in which political, economic and social power is increasingly dispersed and in which the regulation of industrial and political conflict are of necessity dissociated.[22]

A second theoretical concept closely related to that of post-capitalism, and of central importance in the conflict theory of industrial relations, is 'pluralism'. According to Clegg one of its major propounders:

> "Pluralism emerged as a criticism of the political doctrine of sovereignty - that somewhere in an independent political system there must be a final authority whose decisions are definitive. Not so, said the pluralist. Within any political system there are groups with their own interests and beliefs, and the government itself depends on their consent; and co-operation. There are no definitive decisions by finial authorities: only continuous compromises.
>
> A plural society, is a relatively stable one but not static. It has to accommodate to different and divergent pressure groups to enable social and political changes to take place constitutionally. This is achieved through negotiation, concession and compromise between pressure groups, and between many of them and government.
>
> It is from this analysis of political pluralism that industrial relations pluralism is derived. Just as society is perceived as comprising a number of interest groups held together in some sort of loose balance by the agency of the state, so work organizations are viewed as being held in balance by the agency of management. The pluralist concepts of political sovereignty and of managerial prerogative have much in common. Trade unions are viewed as the legitimate representatives of employee interests at work with the right to challenge the right to manage. There are also similarities between the processes of political concession and compromise, one the one hand, and of collective bargaining on the other. Above all, the pluralist argues, 'greater stability and adaptability is given to industrial relations by collective bargaining than

by shackling and outlawing trade unions'. According to pluralist theory, the central features of industrial relations is the potential conflict existing between employer and employed and between management and managed within work enterprises. Unlike in unitary theory, however, trade unionism is accepted by pluralists as having both a representative function and an important part in regulating this conflict, rather than in causing it. Similarly, collective bargaining is recognized as being the institutional means by which conflict between employers and employees over the wage- work bargain, and its adaptation, is regularized and resolved. Industrial conflict, therefore, is accepted by pluralists not only as being inevitable but also as requiring containment within the social mechanisms of collective bargaining, conciliation and arbitration.[23]

There is little doubt that the pluralist and post-capitalist analysis of industrial relations, with their emphasis on the twin virtues of collective bargaining and parliamentary democracy as separate but conflict-resolving and rule-making processes were the predominant academic orthodoxy in Britain during the 1960s and 1970s. Initially they were strongly associated with the thinking of a small group of University of Oxford academics. Their individual and collective views, had an important impact on the deliberations and findings of the Royal Commission, chaired by Lord Donovan between 1965 and 1968, and on its final report. The so-called 'Oxford' approach to industrial relations influenced not only public policy and a generation of scholars in the field but also industrial relations practitioners. During the 1980s and 1990s, however, neo-unitary theory enjoyed a partial renaissance amongst some managers and students of industrial relations, as shifts to the right in British politics, to market economics and the weakening of union bargaining power in segments of the labour market occurred.

3. Social Action Theory

Social action theory in industrial relations emphasizes the individual responses of the social actors, such as managers, employees and union representatives, to given situations. It contrasts with systems theory which suggests that behaviour in an industrial relations system is explicable in terms of its structural features. Social action theory is preeminently associated with the studies of Max Weber. According to Weber, action is social 'by virtue of the subjective meaning attached to it by the acting individual... it takes account of the behaviour of others and is thereby oriented in its course'. He insists that in order for social actions to be explained theory must be interpreted in terms of their subjectively intended meanings, not their objectively valid ones. If only observable behaviour is examined, the significance and value which individual actors place upon their behaviour are likely to be misinterpreted.

Social action theory also has its critics. Marxists argues, that those supporting the action frame of reference neglect the 'structural influences of which the actors themselves may be unconscious.' Whilst the consciousness of individual actors in the industrial relations system towards its politico-economic structures can be to some extent autonomous, it is limited in practice. This is because 'Definitions of reality are themselves socially generated and sustained, and the ability of men to achieve their goals is constrained by the objective characteristics of their situation'. Perhaps the most useful features of social action theory in industrial relations is the 'way in which is stresses that the individual retains at least some freedom of action and ability to influence events'. Although the structures of the industrial relations system may influence the action of its actors, these in turn also influence the system as a whole including its outputs.[24]

4. System Theory

System theory was first articulated by John Dunlop. Its purpose was to present a general theory of industrial relations and to provide tools of analysis to interpret and to gain understanding of the widest possible industrial relations facts and practice.

The system theory views the industrial relations system as a sub-system of the wider society or the total social system. The wider society is seen as providing certain external influences and constraints but not as completely dominating industrial relations. An industrial relations system at any particular time is regarded as comprised of certain actors, certain context and ideology which binds the industrial relations system together and body of rules created to govern the actors at the place of work and work community. The creation of rules is the central aim of the industrial relations system and Dunlop isolates three groups of actors–workers, management and the government–who take part in the rule making process.

In every country, workers, government and the management all interact to build up the country's industrial relations system. Each of these three actors has a role to play in the industrial relations drama. Generally in any economy there is also an ideology which is shared in common by the government, businessmen and workers. Such ideology may be defined in terms of democratic capitalism as in the USA, democratic socialism as in the UK, state capitalism as in Spain or state socialism as in the former USSR. In India, we have another economic system known as mixed economy. Mixed economy philosophy believes in the co-existence of both public and private sectors and there should be no conflicts of interest between the private and public sectors.[25]

Democratic capitalism encourage collective bargaining supported by legislation and government intervention where necessary; democratic socialism also encourages collective bargaining but mainly as a voluntary process, the intervention by the government being rather rare. State capitalism does not allow full freedom in collective bargaining; trade unions are tolerated but not encouraged. State socialism assigns well defined roles to the trade unions, which work within the parameters of the overall political system. In a mixed economy, we have a mixture of all these approaches and there is a good deal of ambivalence.[26]

5. *Marxist Theory*

Marxist interpretations of industrial relations are not strictly theories of industrial relations *per se*. Marxism is rather a general theory of society and of social change with implication for the analysis of industrial relations within capitalist societies. In other words, Marxist analysis is essentially a method of social enquiry into the power relationships of society and a way of interpreting social reality. To understand the relevance of Marxist theory to industrial relations it is necessary to separate out those main features of general Marxist analysis which contribute to its special character as a means of interpreting relations between the capitalist and wage earning classes. Moreover, Marx himself wrote comparatively little about trade unionsim and collective bargaining because neither of these institutions was firmly established in Britain when he was studying 19th century capitalize development. Thus, the application of Marxian theory as it relates to industrial relations derives indirectly from later Marxist scholars rather than directly from the works of Marx himself.

The starting point for the Marxian analysis of society is class conflict. Class conflict is synonymous with industrial conflict since the capitalist structure of industry and of wage-labour is closely connected with the pattern of class division in society. Thus, the conflict taking place in industrial relations between those who buy labour and those who sell it is seen as a permanent feature of capitalism, merely reflecting the power base of the bourgeoisie and the class relations of capitalist society generally.

Marxist model exemplifies the structuralist (technological, economic and political forces) explanation of industrial relations. Industrial relations occur within a dynamic conflict situation which is permanent and unalterable so long as the structure of society remains unchanged. The conflict situation is viewed as a product of the labour market in which on the one hand there are workers who have to sell labour power in order to subsist, while on the other hand there are buyers of labour who own the means of production and purchase labour power.

These two interests are irreconcilable. They are engaged in a perpetual conflict over the distribution of revenue. The two interests have a common purpose in increasing total revenue and so they have. But the conflict over distribution is in no sense lessened by this for the actual distribution of additional increments of revenue is determined by the power situation. Workers with no power may get nothing. There is no automatic distribution based on a sense of equity. Shares have to be fought for sometimes bitterly.

The concept of alienation also played a crucial role in Marxian model on industrial conflict. Alienation arises from the fact that in the capitalist system labour is sold, it is bought by the capitalist and used to satisfy his need rather than those of the workers. Thus, the worker is estranged from the things he creates and thus, in turn violates the essential nature of man.

Alienation is most vividly seen in modern industrial labour. Two aspects are particularly crucial. The *first* is the division of labour which is seen by Marx as a means of promoting wealth for the capitalist but restricting even more closely the freedom of the worker. The *second* is the factory system of production which is looked upon as the most complete method of domination of the worker by the capitalist for he can control every activity of labour. However, it is crucial to appreciate that neither the division on labour nor the factory system were seen by Marx as important in their own right; they were only important because they represented the most developed form of treating workers as a commodity.[27]

Alienation will not be overcome simply by increasing wages, while from some points of view this might be desirable, it will not result in freedom, but merely make the worker 'a better paid slave'. Similarly social reforms will not help to overcome alienation. Alienation will only be overcome with the overthrow of the capitalist system where labour stops being treated as a commodity.

Workers and Industrial Culture

Democracy and democratic values are not merely some techniques of a political system, these are certain basic attitudes to the life process. The Indian interpretation of democratic values has made an impact on *laissez-faire* as understood in the nineteenth and early twentieth century. In India, political democracy adopts and approach of 'co-operative' life process which can be called a 'social' approach that has added a new dimension to the political idea of democratic living, though the experiment was started elsewhere. The possibility of 'public effort' co-existing with 'private effort' with 'determined priority' areas and also with monopoly authority, has now been established beyond question. Therefore, in a democracy the 'state sector' or the 'public sector' can co-exist with equal and more power without jeopardizing the basis democratic values. There is no apparent contradiction between the emphasis on 'public enterprises' in our industrial culture and our democratic pattern of living. In this understanding of democracy perhaps society has an active role in bringing equality in all aspects of life-economic, social and cultural. Equality among unequals only perpetuates inequality and thus it is ultimately an antithesis to democratic values. Democratic values do not, therefore, have a unidimensional or restricted and ascertainable definite formula irrespective of time, social structure or other considerations. In other words, the Indian experiment has established that such democratic values and norms are to be determined in consonance with the type and nature of the society, its basic need, its historical and anthropological cultural values etc. The Indian experiment of industrial culture is bound to fertilize that of the other South Asian countries, in particulaı. The Indian experiment in the democratic process reform may be said to be involved in synthesizing two opposite pulls viz., the intrinsic multicultural conflict that is inherent in the working of the Indian society and the attempt at establishing a cooperative living process between multicultural societal structures through mutual understanding and adjustment. We find these causative phenomena in all walks of Indian democracy, in its political, social and economic milieu.

In that context the standard of norms, norms building *and execution* process in our industrial culture. An industrial culture is possible on account of the contribution of:

(i) Those who *supply the capital* which can be compared with blood circulation of an industrial society;

(ii) Those who supply the labour which can be compared with masculation; and

(iii) Those who add the technology, the technologists and professional managers who can be compared with the brain-action.

Now, a democratic norm is made possible only when there is a demonstration of faith in equality, and importance and equi-existence of each section. Democratic functionality is possible only in an atmosphere of trust and good faith.

The attitude to workers is not merely an attitude of subordination but also of mistrust. Workers are taken as anti-production, incapable of understanding far reaching consequences and, perhaps, dishonest too. Thus there is a belief that if they are given a fair deal they will be high-handed; if one keeps faith in them, they will practice lethargy in production and if they are given a hearing, they will press for an unreasonable deal. Though human beings have a tendency of forming groups, workers are mistrusted when they try to unionize and save themselves from exploitation. This unionization was prevented earlier on the ground of its being (a) anti-production (b) restraining others from exercising freedom of trade (c) a conspiracy against the employer and (d) destroying the financial stability of the country and thus antinational. This industrial psychology of the investors is based on the eagerness to exploit the situational of dependence of the working force. This very attitude is responsible for most of the bitterness in the relationship between investors and workers. A careful study of the history industrial relation in an open society would show that investing managements are often more 'ant production' than the workers. They have been known to restrict supply in the market for unreasonable gains, to resort to all manner of production-cum-trade practices to subvert production in times of necessity, to exercise their capacity to foment conspiracies. On the other hand, workers have stood for the cause of the nation. It is mistaken presumption that when workers unit they become anti-national or become a thereat to industrial peace. It is the investors' scramble for unreasonable gain that alienates the workers from production.

Indian Intellectuals and Indian Labour

The brief of the financiers/employers/private enterprises/ company management, is held by leading intellectuals and advocates who, while they views for the people's vote represent the inters of a few capitalists. One has even advocated that all public sector projects be auctioned to private capitalists[28] where another laments that there are thousands of cases where big industrial undertakings continue to be carried on primarily for keeping the employees and workers engaged and to pay wages, salaries etc, and to pay to the government huge taxes in crores while the employer continues to incur huge losses year after year[29]. While one champions the cause of private enterprises and capitalists holding them out to be panacea of all the economic evils in the country, the other agues that these private enterprises are so Philanthropic that they carry on business incurring huge losses only for the workers' interest! Expect individual judges, the judiciary, as whole, too has demonstrated an eagerness to protect the interests of one section of society. In Excel Wear v. Union of India[30] the Supreme Court argued at length to protect the interest of the employer and investors. It was held: "not to permit the employer to close down is essentially an interference with his fundamental right to carry on business." Similarly, "financial difficulties or accumulation of indisposed stocks may justify the view that the closure is due to unavoidable circumstances beyond the control of the employer", it said in Kalinga Tubes Ltd. V. Their Workers.[31]

The role of the workers in the industrial culture is greatly regulated by their organized strength. As such, the normative structure of the regulations in the context of its industrial culture, is to a large extent determined by the role that labour leaders play in the national scene of politics. In fact, the share that labour has seized so far of industrial culture has been the result of great battles. Their right of partnership is not matter of grace or concession. Workers in the twenty-first century are expected to be innovative and participatory. It is therefore well to remember that rights have been earned so far through persistent struggle, and shall have to be earned as such in future too. It is in this concern that one has to understand the role of Indian Trade Union movement since independence.

Issues Related to Trade Unions

Trade unions are responsible for maintaining a better industrial relations climate in the organisation. A number of studies have been conducted to explore various issues related to trade unionism.

These studies can be broadly classified into three categories: (1) Macro-level studies on trade unionism; (2) Studies on trade union growth, structure and activities; and (3) Behavioural studies.

(1) *Macro-level Studies*: Macro-level studies have focused on economic, social, technical and legal issues and their effect on union functions as well as union-management relationships. Early studies on unions pleaded for legal protection, and the promotion of professional trade unionism through the provision for union recognition, for better interaction between the state and unions.[32] Some studies have discussed the role of unions in economic development, their problems, the attitudes of the government, the emerging trends in trade unionism, and causes for union-management conflict.[33] Monappa (1985) studied the formation of white-collar unions, blue-collar unions, crafts unions, and several other types of unions working in various sectors. Tulpule (1990) emphasized that unions, should pay attention to broader issues like respect for human rights, civil liberties and public policy. Studies also report that unions are organizationally, financially and numerically weak as the industrial working class is docile and economically poor.[34] Recent studies have reported that industrial restructing led to retrenchment, employment loss, casualisation of employment and contract employment. This has resulted in a decline of the union membership and weakening of the union power.[35]

Historical Background of Trade Unions

Labour movement in India is about 150 year old, since it may be traced from 1860s. Early years of movement were led by philanthropists, and social reformers who organised workers and protected them against inhuman working conditions. The first known strike in India was organised by 'Dinabandhu Gupta' a dramatist and social reformer of Bengal to protest against the hardship of the cultivators and the plantation workers. The Government thereupon appointed an 'Indigo' Commission in 1875. It is a Robji Shapuri in Bombay made a protest against the poor working conditions of workers at that time.

In India the period between 1918-1924 can perhaps be best described as the era of formation of modern trade unionism, when the deteriorating economic condition of workers resulted in strike. The wages of workers were increased but it could not keep pace with the soaring prices of commodities. Leaders like Mahatma Gandhi also took interest in improving the deplorable condition of workers. Later on all political parties developed their own trade union wings.[36]

Change is Needed

There is no doubt that trade unions fought valiant battles made great sacrifices to secure economic justice for poor, ill treated workers. They succeeded in making the organised workers prosperous. Now the world has changed beyond recognition. Recently an article published in a Business daily has compared the Trade Unions with that of the Henry Ford's model T car for years, the model T was the best selling car in the US. After some years customers became more prosperous, and wanted something better. Though the market changed, Henry Ford would not and drove his company almost to the verge of the bankruptcy by not allowing a model change for almost 20 years. Though late, the Hindustan Motors have to come with a new version of Ambassador car which remained most favourite choice for bureaucrats and ministers in India for over 5 decades likewise, although capitalists have changed, trade unions have not. Trade Union leader cling to same philosophy obvious of the fact that the involvement of the workers in the trade unions is dwindling with every passing year, Trade Unions still cling to the same philosophy and strategy that they first devised to challenge primitive capitalists.

Present day Trade Unions can be faulted on three grounds:

1. They have forgotten their roots to serve the poor.
2. They have not been adaptable.
3. They often demand something for nothing in return.

Meanwhile, capitalism has modernised so well that free markets have become the latest fashion. Thus, Trade Union have lost three ways.

1. The loss of the moral high ground to social activists due to the neglect of the poor.
2. The loss of the political high ground due to shrinkage in membership.
3. The loss of the intellectual high ground against capitalists due to the outdated strategies.

In fact, Trade Unions need an 'enemy' to survive. Traditionally capitalists have been the enemy. Now it is difficult to cast a modern firm, which pays handsome wages, offers job security and excellent career opportunities too, in the role of villain. Trade unions are mainly responsible for not creating enough jobs because to day five percent wages can be earned by only five percent of the labour force. If the objective is to raise employment in the organised sector to 20 percent of the total wages or have to be brought down from the top five percent level to the top 20 percent, this is not possible without trade unions. By demanding excessive wages, trade unions have not only shrunk job growth but have also reduced the members they can organise. In the normal course, trade union membership will shrink where wages rise faster than the growth rate of the economy.

Remarkably, 50 years ago, socialism and trade unions were at the zenith of their power and prestige. However, the heady success of socialism did not last within [30] years, the Berlin Wall collapsed, and the Soviet Union broke into pieces. The miners strike in the U.K, and the textile strike in India were put down without difficulty for want of public support. The APSRTC strike, L.I.C. strikes were withdrawn due to lack of public support. The life-style of the trade union leaders has become more lavish during the last 50 years. Trade unionism has led to sloth, lethargy, unproductivity and indiscipline. Locking up the horns with the managements on even flimsy grounds has given the trade unions the respectability of militancy. But overall, the movements of the trade unions have so far not been able to create conducive environment for the general economic health of the country.[37]

REFERENCES

1. Dr. Biswanadh Ghosh, *Industrial Relations of Developing Economy (With particular reference to India),* Himalaya Publishing House, Mumbai, 2001.
2. *Ibid.*
3. Srivastava, S.C., *Industrial Disputes and Labour Management Relations in India,* 391, 1984.
4. *Ibid.*
5. Harish Chander, *Contract of Employment and Management Prerogatives,* Vijaya Publications, New Delhi, 1993.
6. Myers, Charles, A., *Labour Problems in the Industrialization of India,* 1958.
7. Malhotra, O.P. and Malhotra K.R., *The Law of Industrial Disputes,* Vol I, 3rd Edition, 1981.
8. *Ibid.*
9. *Ibid.*
10. See *Roport of the National Commission on Labour* 1969.
11. Williams, *Labour Relations and the Law,* (3rd Edition), 1965.
12. Another example of Government intervention in industrial relations in UK prior the 1960s can be seen in the field of wage regulation. The Trade Boards Act of 1909 set up trade boards for some trades where wages were so low and conditions of employment so poor that they had attracted universal condemnation. The boards were empowered to fix statutory minimum wage rates which were backed by an official inspectorate and the threat of legal penalties. Today the functions of trade boards are carried out by wage councils set up in 1945.

13. Supra, note 11
14. Prof. Madhavan Pillai. K., *A Textbook on Labour and Industrial Laws*, Allahabad Law agency, Allahabad, 1994.
15. *Ibid.*
16. Malik P.L. *The Industrial Law*, Eastern Book Company, Lucknow 1974.
17. Bhagoliwal, T.N., *Economics of Labour and Industrial Relations*, 1987.
18. Agarwal. S.I., *Labour Relations in India*, Macmilan Company of India Ltd, New Delhi, 1978.
19. Chaturvedi, S.M., *Labour and Industrial Law*, Central Law Agency, Allahabad, 1995.
20. Supra, note 1.
21. Supra, note 1.
22. Mishra. S.N and Mishra. S.K., *An Introduction to Labour and Industrial Laws*, Central Law Publications, Allahabad, 1997.
23. *Ibid.*
24. *Ibid.*
25. *Ibid.*
26. *Ibid.*
27. Giriappa, S., *Issues in Labour Problems*, Ajanta Publications, Delhi 1990, pp. 13-24.
28. Ram Jethmalani, " The 71 Point Front," *Indian Express* (1 September 1988): "except key defence industries it requires to be demolished or auctioned away...".
29. R. Santhanam, "Closure of Industrial Undertaking" *Indian Judicial Reports Issue 33*, 29, 79, (16 August 1988).
30. (1979) 1 SCR 1009; AIR. 1979 SC 25
31. AIR 1969 SC 90.
32. Ghosh, 1960; Johri, 1967.
33. Padmanabhan, 1980; Nigam, 1984.

34. Ramaswamy & Ramaswamy, 1981; Masilamani and Haribabu, 1986; Sheth, 1993.

35. Mahalingam, 1992; Mathur, 1992; Neogi, 1992; Venkataratnam, 1992; Sheth, 1993.

36. Dr. Biswanath Ghosh, *Industrial Relations of Developing Economy (with particular reference to India)*, Himalaya Publishing House, Mumbai, 2001.

37. H.L. Kumar, Par reaching effect SC verdict; unions must look before leap, *IFLR*; Vol. 99, October 1, part 1 2003.

3

IMPACT OF THE I.L.O. ON THE LABOUR MANAGEMENT RELATIONS

The work of the international organisations has not been without influence on this trend, especially in the developing countries, through their practical activities of international technical cooperation and dissemination of ideals embodied in their constitutions and the various international declarations, charters and other texts adopted over years. To be more precise these ideals have found their loftiest expression in the Universal Declaration of Human Rights, 1948 and the two International Covenants of 1966 drawn up by the United Nations, one on economic, social and cultural rights and the other on civil and political rights. At the national level as well, there has been a natural trend towards greater emphasis on human rights under the influence of such factors as the new prospects opened up by the technical progress, higher standards of education, the growth of mass media, the shrinkage of distance due to improved communications, the spread of the ideals of social progress and human betterment. There are other no less powerful influences which have made the question of human rights a topical issue throughout the world—among them a new awareness of the serious consequences of ignoring or openly infringing these rights, or simply of failing to take resolute action to promote them.

In this regard the declaration said that "poverty anywhere constitutes a danger to prosperity everywhere", and affirmed that labour is not a commodity; that freedom of expression and of association are essential to sustained progress, and that common welfare and universal prosperity are the objectives to be achieved.

To achieve the above objectives, the main functions of the I.L.O. are:

(1) to establish international labour standards;

(2) to collect and distribute information on labour and industrial conditions; and

(3) to provide technical assistance.

However, as compared to other functions, the I.L.O. has primarily relied on standard-setting, which has been its "core activity". The international labour standards take the form of conventions and recommendations. A convention is a treaty which, when ratified, creates binding international obligations for the country concerned while a recommendation creates no such obligation but is essentially a guide to national action. At present, the International Labour Code comprises of 149 conventions and 156 recommendations[1]. which cover mainly basic human rights (including freedom of association, freedom from forced labour and freedom from discrimination), the development of human resources (including employment policy, employment services and vocational guidance, training and rehabilitation), general conditions of employment (including employment security, wages hours of work and leisure, industrial relations, the employment of children, young persons, and women), industrial health, safety, welfare, social security, migration and labour administration and statistics; and some particularly deal with industry, mining, transport, agriculture, shipping and the special problems of developing countries.

However, the International Labour Code is not, of course, a code in the sense of being a logically arranged restatement of law binding in its entirety by virtue of statutory enactment throughtout the jurisdiction to which it applies. Nor is it consistent with its nature that it should at any point attain finality, it is rather, as Lord Chancellor Sankey once said of international law, 'a living and expanding code', in Re Piracy Jure Gentium[2].

The activities of the I.L.O. in the field of human rights is guided both by the Universal Declaration and the two covenants on human rights, and by its own past work and experience in the discharge of its responsibilities. The adoption of the Universal Declaration and the covenants constitutes a recognition of the general trend towards inclusion among human rights of all forms of protection that can free man from fear and want-not only civil and political freedoms but economic social and cultural rights as well.

David A. Morse has rightly said that:

> "This has brought the human rights aspect of all the ILO's activities into particularly sharp relief. The clear recognition in the Universal Declaration that economic and social rights are the corollary of civil freedom is largely due to the existence of the Constitution of the I.L.O. which preceded it by nearly 30 years and of the Declaration of Philadelphia, which did so by nearly five years."[3]

The significance of the matter was thrown into sharp relief in connection with the celebration of tenth anniversary of the adoption by the General Assembly of the United Nations, of the Universal Declaration. In commemoration of this anniversary, the International Labour Conference adopted on 20 June, 1958, a resolution pledging the continued cooperation of the I.L.O. with the United Nations in the promotion of universal respect for and observance of human rights and fundamental freedoms on the basis of the dignity and worth of the human person.[4]

In the resolution that it adopted on the subject at its 50th session (1966), the International Labour Conference provided support in a number of ways. In first place, it emphasized that the protection and advancement of the human rights proclaimed in the Universal Declaration were of fundamental importance for the fulfillment of the objectives of the I.L.O.; which should pursue its standard-setting activities in conformity with the articles of the declaration. It also pointed out the urgent need for concerted and increased efforts at international and national levels, including increased allocations for technical cooperation projects as well as staff and financial resources. Moreover, the conference gave an undertaking to continue cooperation between the I.L.O. and the United Nations in the field of human rights and appealed the member-states to ratify and fully implement the international labor conventions relating to human rights. The year 1968 was celebrated as International year of Human Rights, during which the worker's and employers' organizations were called upon to defend and promote human rights. Finally, the conference invited the governing body of the International Labour Office to take the following action with respect to human rights questions falling within the competence of the I.L.O.; for example, to promote the observance of the fundamental human rights in all member states; to review and assess the role, objectives and activities of the I.L.O. in the field of human rights, including the possibilities of extending standard-setting activities in this field ; to encourage technical cooperation projects and advisory missions designed to promote human rights objectives everywhere; and to consider the possibility of coordinating research, publicity, technical cooperation projects, advisory missions and standard-setting activities into a significant, concerted programme and of allocating adequate financial resources and staff to carry it out.

Economic and social rights, cannot be achieved without promoting fundamental rights and freedoms. The essential justification for freedom of association is thus the defence of the economic and social rights of those concerned. The aim of freedom of labour is to enable workers to choose employment providing them with satisfactory conditions and economic security, while at the same time affording them real opportunities of improving their living standards. The promotion of equality is if fully effective only if it creates opportunities compatible with the requirements of human dignity in everyday life.

The promotion of human rights is indeed of basic importance for the fulfillment of the objectives of the I.L.O. ; unless its activities are pursued with respect for human personality they will not provide a sound foundation for social and economic progress[5].

However, it has been rightly said that the promotion of human rights cannot be left to itself and is not brought about automatically by development or economic growth. There must be a conscious and well-thought-out policy, which, while giving due weight to the absolute need to raise standards of material wealth all round, will ensure that this wealth is devoted to ends that serve the freedom and dignity of man. Constant alertness of human rights is all the more important because full scale programmes of economic and, above all, social policy will increasingly be needed to secure these rights. And further, it is already difficult to enforce legal safeguards of rights and freedoms. Thus in best calculated society, effective legal system and sincere implementation of various essential programmes are the main factors responsible for protection and promotion of human rights. In this sphere the I.L.O.'s work covers principally the safeguarding of freedom of association, the abolition of forced labour, the elimination of discrimination in employment and the promotion of the principle of equal pay for equal work. But it should not be over looked that other aspects of the work of the I.L.O., such as the free choice of employment, fair remunerarion and working conditions, protection of the right to social security and protection against unemployment also fall within the broad framework of the human rights.

In all, nine conventions have been adopted in the field of human right, five conventions deal with the freedom of association, two relate to the forced labour and one each deals with the equal pay for equal work and discrimination in employment. Of these, one relates to non-metropolitan countries.

India has ratified five conventions. Of the conventions not ratified by India, one relates to freedom of association, one relates to the abolition of forced labour and the other to the right to organise and collective bargaining.

Suppose one asks, "Does the non-ratification of these conventions mean that in India "Freedom of association" and the "right to organise" are absent ? Or, "forced labour" is prevalent and "discrimination" is practiced ? In legal sense the answer is 'no'. The fundamental rights have been guaranteed and the guidelines for legislature and state action in the form of directive principles have been laid down in the Constitution.

Right to Association

Workers' organisations cannot exist if workers are not free to join them, to work for them and to remain in them. This is fundamental human right, a civil liberty, which as such appears in the catalogues of fundamental rights in a number of constitutions,[6] including that of India. Article 19 (1) (c) of the Indian Constitution provides that "All citizens shall have the right to form associations or unions." This right has also been secured by the Trade Unions Act, 1926. Freedom of association is a recognised legal right on the part of all persons to combine for the promotion of purposes in which they are interested.[7] Freedom of association is not only essential for the material well-being of the workers through wage-agreements, etc., but for spiritual advancement too in the process of collective bargaining. This freedom is recognised by the Universal Declaration of Human Right, 1948.[8] Among the basic human rights and freedoms of concern to the I.L.O., freedom of association is unique, which is an essential condition for steady progress towards the goal of social justice. It enables the workers to give expression to their aspirations and also strengthens their position in collective bargaining by re-establishing a balance in the strength of the parties.

The International Labour Organisation adopted five conventions in this regard, out of which one is concerned with non-metropolitan countries and the rest four are-Right of Association (Agriculture) Convention, 1921 (No. 11), Freedom of Association and Protection of the Right to Organise Convention, 1948 (No. 87), Right to Organise and Collective Bargaining Convention, 1949 (No. 98) and Rural Workers' Organisation Convention, 1975 (No. 141). Out of that India has adopted only two conventions i.e., No. 11 of 1921 and 141 of 1975.

In India, the government in public interest can ban an association or trade union and detain or arrest a trade union leader under the Essential Services Act, 1967, the Preventive Detention Act, 1950, or any other preventive detention laws; Likewise, the code of discipline in industry, although non-legal and non-statutory one, regulates the organisation of workers and employers in accordance with the set norms and standards. The Constitution of India itself, while guaranteeing freedom of association or unions, empowers the state to regulate, restrict this freedom in public interest and public good. These laws and practices on trade unions do not conform to the requirements of the convention. However, the provisions of the Industrial Disputes Act, 1947, the Bombay Industrial Relations Act, 1946, the M.P. Industrial Relations Act, 1960 protect workers against dismissal as a measure of anti-union discrimination, and sections 33 (3) and 36 of the Industrial Disputes Act, 1947 provide for the right of representation to the workers. The Trade Unions Act, 1926 protects the right of association by providing immunities to the registered trade union from civil, criminal and tortious liabilities.[9]

Here it is deemed proper to be clear about some specific aspects of the right to association like union security, right to strike and collective bargaining. So far as union security arrangements are concerned due to illiteracy and lack of proper understanding and organisation in Indian working-class, it is not prudent to introduce a 'closed shop' or a 'union shop' system and to require the employer concerned to encourage it. Even the Trade Unions Act, 1926 also does not provide for such practices. In *Assam Oil Co. Ltd. v. Workmen,*[10] and *Burn and Co. v. Their Employees,*[11] the Supreme Court of India has held that it is not open to an employer to dismiss his employee solely or principally for the reason that he has joined a trade union. Moreover, man's right to work has been advanced against the 'closed shop'.

In India under article 19(1)(c) of the Constitution a citizen has freedom to form associations. It has been held that the right to form association includes the right to refuse to be a member of the association, the right not to be compelled to join an association, the right not to be compelled to withdraw from an association.[12]

As regards right to strike, which is a necessary weapon to protect the right of association, has although been recognised by the Indian law but not yet guaranteed, towards fulfilling the object of collective bargaining.[13] As back as in 1942 Lord Wright observed in a leading case: "The right of workmen to strike is an essential element in the principle of collective bargaining,"[14] However, after the First World War due to frequent strikes, the Indian Trade Unions Act, 1926 for the first time indirectly recognized the right to strike by legalising certain activities of registered trade unions in furtherance of trade disputes,[15] otherwise those would have been a breach of law and contract and thus actionable, as happened in the case of *Bunckingham Carnatic Company, Madras, in 1920*. Further, government has been authorised to determine its legal and illegal character.[16]

Furthermore, right to strike does not legalise picketing and other incidental acts of omission and commission during strike.[17]

This is the position regarding industrial workers. The position of civil-servants is till worst. For example, section 4-A of the Civil Service (Conduct) Rules, 1955 bans strike by the government servants. In this connection the Supreme Court of India affirming its decision in *Kameswar Prasad v. State of Bihar*[18] held in another case[19] also that right to form an association guaranteed by article 19 (1) (c) of the Constitution does not involve or imply the right to resort to strike, and held section 4-A to be valid.

Besides, it is worthwhile to discuss the legal position of 'gherao', a new form of labour agitation resorted to by the working-class to press upon the employer or the management for acceding to their demands. Legally speaking 'gherao' is the physical blackade of a target either by encirclement or forcible occupation. The 'target' may be a place or a person or persons, usually the managerial or supervisory staff of an industrial establishment. The blackade may be complete or partial.[20]

'Gherao' differs from 'strike' and peaceful picketing in as much as strikes are resorted to put economic and not physical pressure upon the management. Gherao, as an concomitant of freedom of association has been viewed differently by the different political parties. The United Front government of West Bengal which came into power in 1967 characterised gherao as legitimate trade union activity. But many of the political parties like

Congress, Swatantra and labour leaders and legal luminary like P.B. Gajendragadkar condemned it.

However, the judgment in *Jay Engineering Works v. State of West Bengal*[21] settled at rest the legitimacy and the legality of the gherao in which gherao has been held to be illegal and a punishable offence. In various other cases and writ petitions the Calcutta as well as other High Courts have declared gherao illegal, and violative of fundamental rights guaranteed by the Constitution.

Thus, it can be safely concluded that right to strike has got legal sanction in India, as a necessary concomitant of the freedom of association but not gherao.

If we look to the statistics of industrial relations including strikes, lock-outs, and mandays lost, we can say that the present law is misused by the trade unions as well as employers. Necessary checks must be imposed on their indiscriminate and frequent adherence to such practices because that ultimately effects production and national economy adversely. Although to protect human rights it is worthwhile to safeguard the individual rights, yet some safety-valves shall have to be used to check their misuse and their adverse effects on the human rights at large. In this context, it can be said that although right to strike is essential weapon to protect the freedom of association of the trade unions, yet having regard to the other socio-economic rights, that should not be absolute. Thus, the existing law on the point is sufficient to protect the freedom of association of the trade unions, provided that is used honestly and sincerely and not for the sake of unfair labour practices. A developing country like India cannot afford to provide absolute right to strike. The recent Supreme Court Judgement also affirmed this view.

In *T.K. Rangarajan vs Government of Tamilnadu & others*[22], the Supreme court of India interpreted the right to strike in post liberlization developments

In related to above case, the recent strike of nearly twelve lakh employees in Tamilnadu bears ample testimony to the fact that the trade unions are still living in fossilized era of the so called militancy which has caused more harm to the society than any other factor by calling upon strikes even on very flimsy grounds.

Although the supreme court has prevailed upon the state government of Tamilnadu to gracefully re-instate those employees who have been dismissed on a condition that they will submit an apology and an undertaking that they would not strike or indulge in similar activities in future.

Answering the question of right to strike - whether fundamental, statutory or Equitable Moral Right, the Supreme Court held that no such right exists with the Government employees.

There is no fundamental right to go on strike:

Law on this subject is well settled and it has been repeatedly held by this court that the employees have no fundamental right to resort to strike. In *Kameshwar Prasad and other v. State of Bihar and another*[23] this court (C.B) held that the rule insofar as it prohibited strikes was valid since there is no fundamental right to resort to strike. In *Radhey Shyam Sharma v. The Post Master General, Central Circle, Nagpur*[24] the employees of Post and Telegraph Department of the Government went on strike from the midnight of July 11, 1960 throughout India and petitioner was on duty on that day. As he went on strike, in the departmental enquiry. Penalty was imposed upon him. That was challenged before this court. In that context. It was contended that sections 3. 4 and 5 of the Essential Services Maintenance ordinance No. 1 of 1960 were violative of fundamental right guaranteed by clauses (a) and (b) of Article 19(1) of the Constitution. The Court (C.B) considered the ordinance and held that Sections 3, 4 and 5 of the said ordinance did not violate the fundamental rights enshrined in Article 19(1) (a) and (b) of the Constitution. The court further held that a perusal of Article 19(1) (a) shows that there is no fundamental right to strike and all that the ordinance provided was the respect to any illegal strike. For this purpose. The court relied upon the earlier decision in *All India Bank Employees Association v. National Industrial Tribunal and others*[25] wherein court [C.B) specifically held that even very liberal interpretation of sub-clause (C) of clause (1) of Article 19 cannot lead to the conclusion that trade unions have a guaranteed right to an effective collective bar gaining or to strike either as part of collective bargaining or otherwise. In *Ex-Capt Harish Uppal v. Union of India and another*[26] the court (C.B) held that lawyers have no right to goon strike or give a call for boycott and even they cannot go on a token strike. The court has specifically observed that for just or unjust cause, strike cannot be justified in the present-day situation. Taken strike in any field. T can be easily realized that the weapon does more harm than any justice. Sufferer is the society - public at large. In *Communist Party of India (M) v. Bharat Kumar and others*[27], a three-Judge Bench of this Court approved the Full Bench Decision of the Kerala High Court by Holding thus:- there cannot be any doubt that the fundamental rights of the people as a whole cannot be subservient to the claim of fundamental right of an people section of the people. It is on the basis of this distinction that the High Court has rightly concluded that there cannot be any right to call or enforce be any right to call or enforce a "Bandh" which interferes with the exercise o the fundamental freedoms of other citizens, in addition to causing national loss in many ways. We may also add that the reasoning given by the High Court particularly those in paragraphs 12, 13 and 17 for the ultimate conclusion and directions in paragraph 18 is correct with which we are in agreement.

The court further held in the prevailing situation, apart from being conscious of rights, we have to be fully aware of our duties. Responsibilities and effective methods for discharging the same. For redressing their grievances, instead of going on strike, if employees do some more work honestly, diligently and efficiently such gesture would not only be appreciated by the authority but also by people at large. The reason being, in a democracy even are part and parcel of governing body and owe duty to the society. Misconduct by the Government employees is required to be considering the gravity of the situation and the fact the on occasion. Even if the employees are not prepared to agree with what is contended by some leaders who encourage the strike, they are forced to go on strikes for reasons beyond their control. Therefore, even though the provisions of the Act and the Rules are to be enforced. They are to be enforced after are to be situation and the capacity of the employees to resist. On occasion there is tendency or compulsion to blindly follow the others.

This Judgment would have for reaching effect on Industrial Relations particularly in the case of government and public sector units employees.

Freedom from Forced Labour and Bonded Labour as Human Rights

In some industries, there is a possibility of forced labour and bonded labour. The I.L.O provided various guidelines to abolish bonded labour and Forced labour. Forced Labour or slavery is as old as history. It was widespread in many parts of the world in the ancient times. Aristotle justified slavery as a divine and beneficent human institution, not only sanctioned by nature but justified by the circumstances of social existence. However, in the middle ages slavery was not a significant element in the economic structure and as such the institution of slavery gradually fell into disuse. Then came serfdom. Slaves were treated as commodities, capable of being purchased and sold but not serfs. But the use of slave manpower again reappeared with the discovery of the new world i.e. America. India was not exception but here slavery or forced labour did not assume the classical form as in the west Asiatic and Mediterranean countries.

In India, forced labour as one of the forms of slavery is a relic of colonial and feudal system. Its origin can, therefore, be traced to our land problems, which is the axis of Indian economy. An official report stated:

Tenants are compelled to do some type of agricultural labour in their (landlord's) fields for a number of days in a season either without wages or for some very meagre wages; some times his family members are also made to work for the landlard. Such service may be free in lieu of grant of land, or payment of very meagre wages. The tenants cannot refuse to work or bargain for wages, because there is a danger of being ousted from the land or house-sites. These are common characteristics of bonded or forced labour exacted by landlords in many rural parts of India where landlordism exists.[28]

Further, forced labour is not only the outcome of land relationship, but also of 'debt-bondage' which means the debtor had to do manual labour for his creditor in lieu of the advance or debt or interest thereon till repayment. The debt is, in fact, seldom cleared off. Not only this but even government machinery or functionaries like sarpanchas, tehsil panchayats, gram sevaks, forest guards, primary teachers and socio-political workers were subjecting the tribals to this slavery like practice.[29] The remnants of bonded labour system was also found in 'contract labour', who were nothing but contractor's slaves. Moreover, the condition of forest labour was also not better than the bonded labour. However, to regulate the employment of contract labour in certain establishments and to provide for the abolition in certain circumstances and for matter connected therewith the Contract Labour (Regulation and Abolition) Act, 1970 was enacted, but nothing substantial has been done toward, ameliorating the condition of forest labour.

Thus, freedom from slavery, servitude or bonded labour must hold a central place in any conception of human rights. Exaction of forced labour is a crime against humanity itself, wherever and in whatever form it may be, which is banned by the Universal Declaration of Human Rights, 1948. The International Labour Organisation has adopted two conventions on forced labour, one convention concerning forced or compulsory labour, 1930 and another concerning the abolition of forced labour, 1957, out of which the earlier was ratified by India in 1954, after long deliberations and second still remains unratified because of certain practical difficulties of implementation. Jenks has rightly observed that the Abolition of Forced Labour Convention, although in a sense supplementary to, is entirely independent from the forced labour convention, 1930 and the exemptions from scope provided for in the earlier convention have no application to it.[30]

The Constitution of India also prohibits forced labour and makes it a punishable offence. Article 23 (1) provides that "Traffic in human being and beggar and other similar forms of forced labour are prohibited and any contravention of this provision shall be an offence punishable in accordance with law." But it has been permitted, in certain circumstances, that the state can impose compulsory service, as provided in article 23 (2) which states: "Nothing in this article shall prevent the State from imposing compulsory service for public proposes, and in imposing such service the State shall not make any discrimination on grounds only of religion, race, castes, or class or any of them." Here, it is for the government to decide as to when compulsory service be imposed for public purposes.

However, the most unique and exemplary incident in this connection is that when there was national emergency in India in 1976, the compulsory service could be imposed or made permissible, the Government of India passed the Bonded Labour System (Abolition) Act, which was a milestone towards curbing beggar or forced or bonded labour and rehabilitation of bonded labourers. Articles 39 and 46 are also very relevant in this regard, which provide for adequate means of livelihood and protection from social, economic injustice and from all forms of exploitation. Thus, we see that one of the most humane gains of the emergency has been the emancipation of bonded-labour, who for centuries had survived under grueling lashes and sadistic whims of medievalism. According to this Act every bonded labourer stands "freed and discharged from any obligation to render any bonded labour". However, it is painful to note that in spite of all above constitutional and legal measures, about 21.7 lakhs of bonded labourers are still existing according to a preliminary report of the national survey on the incidence of bonded labour conducted by the National Labour Institute, New Delhi, in collaboration with the Gandhi Peace Foundation.

The report stated:

Deprived of basic human rights (freedom of movement and freedom of seeking employment), subjected totally to the mercy of landlord, bereft of bargaining power, devoid of any property and themselves being the property of their masters, they seek opportunities to survive for which they are forced to go into bondage for the pettiest amount of debts. They subordinate themselves with increasing intensity to the systems of exploitation of cheap labour controlled by the moneylender-farmer. Social customs, or unproductive purposes like festive occasions, no longer constitute the main reasons for the indebtedness of the poorest of our rural society. According to our findings the poor peasants and agricultural labourers take loans for immediate consumption. Their economic situation is characterised by total absence of any assets. Most of them belong to the scheduled castes and scheduled tribes.[31]

Thus, it is true that till this pernicious system of bondage is eradicated. India's commitment to democracy and human rights will be a matter of serious controversy, which is not possible by mere legislation but by its effective implementation, removal of poverty, eradication of illiteracy and spiritual teaching of equality, fraternity and brotherhood.

So far as judicial attitude in this regard is concerned, no direct case is reported to have reached the Supreme Court on the forced or bonded labour. Although various labour legislations prohibit exploitation of child labour, like Factories Act, 1948, Mines Act, 1952, Plantation Labour Act, 1951 and Motor Transport Worker's Act, 1961, yet such exploitative practices is common in industrial as well as agricultural sectors. The child labour of the country is exploited at the hands of the employers due to the rampant poverty, increasing population, and other factors which compel children to accept any job at any wage including starving wages and at any service and working conditions imposed by the employer. Thus, practically their protection from moral and material abandonment is negligible.

The problem of forced or bonded labour is a matter of human rights, which should be tackled quickly and properly. For this, the government is doing something in its own way but social workers and philanthropists should also come forward. Moreover, legal aid programme can also be useful in emancipation of bonded labour. At last, not the least, poverty should be stricken and suitable and adequate amendments in laws, particularly in land laws, be introduced to make these landless bonded labourers landholder-farmers to enable them to lead their life as human being with dignity and share their efforts in development of the country as free citizen.

Generally bonded labour is the result of poverty which nourishes feudalism. Thus, labour legislation prohibiting bonded labour and mere provision for their rehabilitation will not help much unless viable measures are taken to remove poverty, to provide employment and minimum income for livelihood.

Right to Equality

"Men are born and remain free and equal in respect of rights", says the French Declaration of the Right of men of the Citizens, 1979. So proclaimed the founding fathers in the Declaration of Independence of the United States, 1776 which stated ; - "All men are created equal". The principle of equality and non discrimination has been internationally recognized as back as 1919 when the preamble of the International labour Organisation provided for principle of "equal remuneration for work of equal value", for the first time. The Philadelphia Declaration of 1944 proclaimed that:

All human beings, irrespective of race, creed or sex, have the right to pursue both their material well-being and their spiritual development in conditions of freedom, dignity, of economic security and equal opportunity.

So far as equality of opportunity is concerned it includes not only equality of opportunity in employment and occupation, but also equality of opportunity in educational and vocational guidance programmes. In this connection David A. Morse, the then Director - General of I.L.O. has observed that the two major concerns of the I.L.O. in this sphere are the elimination of inequality of treatment and the promotion of equal opportunity, which are obviously inter-related. Indeed the body of interlocking measures called for a connection with these two problems should provide for the protection of individuals and groups against arbitrary actions by prejudice or hostility, the removal of defacto inequality in the case of certain sections o0f the community and the creation and maintenance of conditions which will enable all groups of society to enjoy increasing equality of opportunity and prospects of self-fulfilment and of improving their social and economic status.

Before coming to the international as well as national labour standards on equality of opportunity, it is essential to study the relevant provisions of the Universal declaration of Human Rights. Alike French Declaration article 1 of this Declaration says that "All human beings are born free and equal in dignity and rights", and article 2 says that:

Everyone is entitled to all the rights and freedoms set forth in this Declaration, without distinction of any kind, such as race, colour, sex, or language, religion, political and other opinion, national or social origin, property, birth or other status.

Article 7 further says:

All are equal before the law and are entitled without any discrimination to equal protection of the law. All are entitled to equal protection against any discrimination in violation of this Declaration and against any incitement to such discrimination.

In the same spirit, the constitution of India is not lacking in any way in this regard. Article 14 states: "The State shall not deny to any person equality before the law within the territory of India". And the main anti-discrimination provision is found in article 15(1) which says that "the State shall not discriminate against any citizen and grounds only of region, race, caste, sex, place of birth or any of them", but clause (3) provides that "Nothing in this article or in clause (2) of Article 29 shall prevent the State from making any special provision for the advancement of any socially and educationally backward classes of citizens or for the Scheduled Castes and Scheduled Tribes."[32]

Impact of the ILO on the Indian Labour Scene

The impact of the activities of the ILO on the Indian labour scene is two fold. Firstly, the ILO was the principal source for labour legislation in India through the ratification of the ILO standards. The principles of these standards are incorporated into the existing labour laws. Secondly, the effect of Article 3 of the Constitution of the ILO which provides for the nomination of nongovernment delegates and advisors to the International Labour Conference which is held every year is in furthering the process of organization among employers and workers in India.

The ILO Standards and Indian Labour Legislation

One of the main functions of the International Labour Conference (ILC), the legislative wing of the ILO is to formulate international labour standards. The ILC provides a forum for discussion and deliberation of international labour problems and then formulates the standards in the form of conventions and recommendations. These conventions and recommendations are collectively known as the International Labour Code.

A convention is a treaty, which when ratified by a member state, creates binding international obligations on that state whereas a recommendation creates no such obligations, but is essentially a guide to national action.

LABOUR POLICY AND THE FIVE-YEAR PLANS

Soon after India attained Independence in 1947, the Central Government convened a conference which was attended by the representatives of state governments, employers and workers with a view to developing means to increase industrial production. At this conference they adopted a resolution called the Industrial Truce Resolution, the object of which was to evolve measure to improve relations between employers and labour and ensure conditions that would not interrupt production. After this resolution was adopted, the Government of India setup two tripartite committees, namely, the Committee on Fair Wages and the Committee on profit sharing. The recommendations of these committees later formed the basis for the planned and orderly progress of industrialization.

The Planning Commission was set up later in March 1950. The basis for formulating the five-year plans was an initial in-depth analysis by experts as to the priorities and the manner of utilizing the scarce resources available in a developing country.

The strategies for growth, the mix between industry and agriculture, generation of employment and improving the standards of living were to be chalked out and given as guidelines to the Central Government and then to the state for implementation. This would ensure a phased and balanced growth of the various sectors of the economy.

This study is, however, mainly concerned with the labour policy enunciated in the 5 Five-Years Plans which we shall discuss at length in the following pages.

For the Planning Commission's approach to labour, the first consideration is related to the well-being of the working class and, secondly the plan's contribution to the economic stability and progress of the country.

First Five Year Plan (1951-1956)

The recommendations of the Planning Commission with regard to labour policy, when accepted, from the basis of the labour policies of the Central and State Governments which it revises from time to time according to the specific needs of industry and the requirements of a planned economy. Labour policy was first formulated by the Commission in 1951.

The First Five-Year Plan concentrated on five aspects of labour policy:

(i) Industrial relations; (ii) wages; (iii) working conditions; (iv) employment and training; and (v) productivity.

1. *Industrial Relations*

The Planning Commission in consultation with the Ministries of Labour and Commerce and industry had worked out certain proposals to govern industrial relations. According to these proposals the industrial development committee composed of representatives of employers and workers agreed upon certain conclusions in respect of an industrial relations policy. The main features of this agreement are that the workers had a right to strike, to resort to direct action for the defence of their rights. At the same time the disruptive effects of a strike had to be considered and therefore curtailed as far as possible.

Since India, soon after independence, was moving in the direction of planned productions and distribution, realization of social justice and welfare of the workers was of utmost importance. The plan thus recommended that the states arm themselves with legal powers to refer disputes for settlement when there was a deadlock between the two parties in a dispute, by arbitration if other peaceful methods failed.

The stress was to be on avoidance of disputes and as far as possible on internal settlement of disputes. For this, the plan recommended that terms and conditions of employment and responsibilities of the employers and workers should be clearly defined, that a grievance procedure should be developed and standing orders laid down.

In order that there be harmonious labour-management relations there was to be close collaboration between employers and workers through consultative committees.

Works committees were to be set up for on-the-spot settlement of differences between the workers and management and the evolution of tea spirit and a sense of belonging to the enterprise and its viability was to be fostered. The process of collective bargaining was to be encouraged for which there would be a single bargaining agent over as large an area of industry as possible. In other words, industry-wide agreements were to be encouraged.

Another point of agreement was the determination of norms to govern the relations between employers and workers. The machinery for this was to be tripartite in nature. When agreement was not possible the government was to decide unilaterally. These decisions were to be incorporated in legislation.

2. ***Wages***

The recommendations in this regard were that there should be some control on wage increases, in fact some kind of regulation and monitoring. The planning commission felt that "advances to a living wage can be achieved through a fall in prices, an increase in the productivity of labour, or an improvement in the capacity of industries to pay, brought about by nationalization of industry or modernization of the plant etc."[33]

The tripartite machinery for wages was to develop norms to guide wage boards in setling questions relating to wages. A suitable and proper basis had to be worked out by this machinery for awarding periodic bonus by the industrial tribunals and courts wage boards has to be established in the industrial tribunals and courts wage boards has to be established in each state and the centre in order to deal with the questions relating to wages. A statutory provident Fund for industrial workers was to be instituted to provide for old age.

3. *Working Conditions*

The plan emphasises that administrative measure are to be developed for the implementation of such pieces of legislation as the Factories Act, 1948, the Mines Act, etc. Which regulate conditions of work. As suggested by the plan, the action should take the following course. The Factory Inspectorate was to be strengthened for achieving standards of enforcement of these laws. In cases where lower standards prevailed those areas were to be given greater attention. An inspection code for each industry regarding its working conditions was to be prepared and the provisions of this code were to be followed strictly; the employers were also to be concerned with workers education, health, and other social needs. Finally, to promote the effective implementation of the provisions of the Factories Act, a national industrial health museum was suggested, to create awareness in the minds of the public at large.

4. *Employment and Training*

The recruiting arrangements of the individual concerns were to be improved so that the exploitation of the workers was avoided (collection of money for giving a job). An enquiry was recommended to examine the working of the employment exchanges.

There was to be coordination in the provision and facilities for technical and industrial training between the ministry of labour and apprenticeship training scheme in industrial undertakings. It was suggested that as assessment be made of the requirements, short-term as well as long-term, of the different types of skilled manpower.

The process of rationalization (installation of new machinery in industry) was to be facilitated, based on safeguard like fixing work loads, standardization of working conditions, stopping fresh recruitment, offering work to surplus workers in other departments without causing a break in the continuity of service and offering of gratuity to induce voluntary retirement etc.

The Planning Commission pointed out that in fulfilling these recommendations there would be a progressive rise in the productivity of industry.

5. ***Productivity***

Productivity studies were suggested to find out the productivity per worker. Method were to be evolved to conduct these studies with a view to understanding the factors responsible for high or low levels of productivity in different industries.

Thus the First Plan was drawn up with awareness of one aspect, i.e. the importance of industrial labour in the national economy. Social security measures were implemented in the form of ESIS Act, 1948, Employees Provident Fund (EPF) Act, 1952, etc. A Central Labour Institute was planned to study the problems of production in relation to the health and safety of workers and state Governments opened welfare centres for industrial workers.

ILO and Freedom of Association and Collective Bargaining

A survey report of the International Labour Organization (ILO) holds:

As an essential condition for the defense of workers and forming, as it does, a part of basic human rights, freedom of association assumes special structure. Owing its existence largely to the will and efforts of the trade union organizations, the ILO could not fail to recognize in its Constitution of 1919 the principle of freedom of association as one of the objectives of the programmes of action. The preamble to part XIII of the Treaty of Versailles mentioned 'recognition of the principles of freedom of association' among the objects to be promoted by the Organization, and the general principles set forth in Article 427contained a provision concerning 'the right of association for all lawful purposes by the employed as well as by the employers.'[34]

ILO Administration on Freedom of Association

The ILO survery report suggests that ILO standards on trade union matters should be supplemented and developed by the principles enunciated by a number of bodies, in particular the governing body committee on freedom of association and the fact finding and conciliation commission on freedom of association set up to promote and supervise the application of these standards. These principles are properly regarded as constituting a body of accepted cases laws in the field of freedom of association and are also applied to member nations.

Trade Union Rights

It is already pointed out that freedom of association i.e., the trade union right has been declared as an important component of the human rights and civil liberties in view of prescription of article 19 of the Universal Declaration of Human Rights. This declaration which was adopted and proclaimed by the general assembly on 10 December, 1948, sets the standard of international morality, the declaration being not legally binding on nations. It sets up the tune and tenure of imitational legal standard that soon started developing. While article 8 of the Covenant on Economic, Social and Cultural Rights emphatically provided the general legal standard of international law regarding fundamental nature of trade union rights as a human right and article 22 of the Covenant of Civil and Political Rights, providing the same right of freedom of association including right to form and join any trade union, ILO's proclamation in the international labour conference in 1944 sets the particular legal standard regarding trade union rights. The conference which proclaimed the Declaration of Philadelphia as a part of ILO Constitution, thus declared that freedom of association and expression were essential to sustain progress and referred to the fundamental rights which were an inseparable part of human dignity. ILO then started adopting conventions in particularising the international legal standards in the affair and also recommendations in formalising and acatualising these standards. In 1970, the International Labour Conference adopted a resolution concerning trade union rights and their relation to civil liberties[35] which stipulated that there exist firmly established universally recognised principles defining common standard of achievement for all peoples and all nations, and, that the rights conferred upon workers' and employers' organisations must be based in respect to those civil liberties which I have been enunciated in particular, in the Universal Declaration of Human Rights and in the International Covenant on Civil and Political Rights, and that the absence of those civil liberties removes all meaning from the concept of trade union rights. The conference explicitly listed the fundamental rights essential for the exercise of the freedom of association and in particular:

(i) the right to freedom and security of person and freedom from arbitrary arrest and detention;

(ii) freedom of opinion and expression and in par1icular, freedom to hold opinions without interference and to seek, receive and impart information and ideas through any media and regardless of frontiers;

(iii) freedom of assembly;

(iv) the right to a fair trial by an independent and impartial tribunal; and

(v) the right to protection of the property of trade union organisations.

Freedom of Movement

The restriction of a person's movements to limited area, accompanied by prohibition of entry into the area in which trade union operates and in which he normally carries on his trade union functions, is inconsistent with the normal enjoyment of the right of association and with the exercise of the right to carry on trade union activities and functions. This was the observation in *United Kingdom/Southern Rhodesia,*[36] *Republic of*

South Africa[37] and many other cases. Similarly, in *Bolivia*[38] and Chili[39] the committee held that the imposition of sanctions, such as house arrest or banishment for trade union reasons constitutes a violation of the principle of freedom of association. The committee has considered it unacceptable that sanction of this nature should be imposed by administrative action. It considered particularly in *Chili,*[40] that the exile of trade union it is in violation of human rights and is particularly grave.

Today the world has become so complex that everywhere we find competitions, in which man is used as an instrument to achieve materialistic objects. Exploitation of man by man is the main characteristic of the present competitive materialistic world. Spiritual values have almost vanished. The era of laissez faire, which restricted any sort of interference on the freedom of trade and commerce by the state, was nothing but a blessing to capitalist-employers, who became exploiters of mankind. Rich became richer and poor became poorer. The concept of laissez faire, gave birth to labour exploitation and victimization at the hands of resourceful employers, because labour being weaker class. In fact, laissez-faire gave birth to two classes of opposite interests-one exploiters and the other exploited. However, with the passage of time and with the advent of the concept of welfare state the whole situation has undergone a tremendous change. With the democratic setup of welfare states, industrial democracy emerged which ultimately resulted in participative management. For providing all these healthy standards, ILO's role is commendable.

The Second Five-Year Plan (1956-1961) - on Labour Policy

The Second Five-Year Plan was framed in the light of the socialist pattern of society which was built not only on monetary incentives but on ideas of service to society.

Thus the labour policy of the Second Five-Years Plan set as its objective better discipline, increased production and improved productivity. Towards this objective the planning commission constituted a panel of labour that concluded certain agreements from which the recommendations in the second Five-Years Plan have emerged.

These recommendations were as follows:

The second Five-Year plan continued the policy laid down in the first plan with certain changes.[41] In the matter of Industrial Relations the Plan stressed mutual negotiations, conciliation and voluntary arbitration. Where the cases were intractable there was to be recourse to government intervention to remedy this situation. Since inadequate implementation of awards and agreements led to friction between labour and management, as appropriate tribunal was to be constituted to enforce compliance with the directions of the awards. Penalties for violation, it was suggested, should be deterrent in nature. This plan recommended the setting up of standing joint consultative machinery at the center, in the states and in individual units for bringing about cooperation between labour and management and setting up of a council of management to discuss matters relating to an enterprise and to recommend steps for harmonious working.

Wages

The Second Plan identified the factors which could solve difficulties in the implementation of the principle of fair wages, namely, improvement of the working of marginal units. One way was to combine such units into larger ones consistent with the requirements of a decentralized economy. Surveys had to be made to determine which units fell in this category. The other recommendations for improvement of wages were:

(i) improvement of working conditions; and

(ii) introduction of payment by results. The plan also recommended the setting up of a wage commission to lay down the principle of an acceptable wage policy.

The Wage Commission was to examine the relevant data and formulate the principles for defining the relationship between wages, prices and profits, keeping in view the social objectives of the community. In order to have an adequate data base the plan recommended "the wage census before formulating the principles". Not only was the wage census to be taken into account but the causes of wage disputes were also to be considered.

This plan recommended that a tripartite wage board, consisting of an equal number of representatives of employers and workers and an independent Chairman should be instituted for settlement of wage disputes since the industrial tribunals could not resolve issues satisfactorily.

The third aspect of labour policy emphasized by the second Five-Year Plan was its recommendation for extension of social security measure like the EPF scheme. The EPF scheme was implemented on a statutory basis during the First Plan. The Second Plan recommended that the EPF be extended to cover industries and commercial establishment having 10,000 workers or more in the country as a whole.

The enhancement of the rate of contribution from 61/4 % to 8.33% and extending to provisions of medical benefit to worker's families under the ESIS scheme was suggested. Another recommendation was to combine different social measures into an overall social security scheme, to reduce overhead costs and to provide more benefits form the savings so effected.

The Second Five-Year Plan also recommended measure for certain groups of workers who needed separate treatment because of their unique problems. A few such groups were contract labour, agricultural labour and women workers. The suggested measures were regulation of working conditions of contract labour, ensuring their continuous employment, region-wise determination of the level of minimum wages for agriculture labour and its effective enforcement, and effective implementation of various statutes for protection to women workers.

The Second Five-Year Plan aimed at provision of development programmes for the training of craftsmen (to provide 19,700 seats in addition to 10,300 seats available) to increase the period of training. The training schemes were to be implemented by the state Government in collaboration with the Ministry of Labour, Government of India and a National Council for Vocational Training. The introduction of an apprenticeship scheme for training skilled craftsmen, to increase the number of employment exchanges and expand the scope of their activities, expansion of the Central Labour Institute, setting up of a film unit for a

Workers Education Programmes, and housing programmes for industrial workers, etc, were a few of the improvements suggested by the plan.

One of the points worth mentioning in this plan was the development of the concept of workers' participation in management. Joint management councils were established in 23 units (Third Plan) on an experimental basis. These council were given the responsibility for matters such as workers' welfare, training and other related matters, to act as a link between the employers and workers in maintaining relations between them. In a seminar in March 1960, the work of the councils, was reviewed and it was found satisfactory.

The plan period witnessed significant advances in the area of workers' education. It was found that such programmes have helped to "raise the confidence of the workers" and "increased their ability to take advantage of labour laws." Most of the suggestions given in the Second Five Year Plan were incorporated in various labour laws.

The Third Five-Year Plan (1961-1966) – on Labour Policy

This plan aimed at consolidating, stabilizing and expanding the measures taken during the second plan. In the matter of industrial relations, the Third Plan emphasized the implementation of the Code of Discipline. This plan maintained that the principle of voluntary arbitration was to be followed for settlement of disputes in preference to adjudication. In this connection, it was suggested that the government should take the initiative in drawing up panels of arbitrators on a regional and industry-wise basis. The plan strongly recommended that in order to improve their work efficiency the functions of the works committees be demarcated so that they were distinct from trade union activity. It also made recommendations for progressive extension of the scheme of joint management councils, and consequent to this step, undertaking of an intensive programmes of workers education in the establishments where such councils were set up to improve the rate of literacy among workers. Finally, the plan recommended the need to recognize trade unions as a step towards recognizing their role in the industrial and economic administration of the country.[42]

Wages

The recommendation of the second plan to set up wage boards for the settlement of wage disputes was extended to many industries in the Third Plan, as in the iron and steel industry. On the question of payment of bonus it was decided to appoint a commission to study the problems connected with bonus claims and to evolve guidelines with principles and norms for the payment of bonus.[43]

Social Security and Labour Welfare

The coverage of workers under the ESI scheme was 17 lakhs industrial workers at the end of the second plan and during the Third Plan period the scheme aimed at a total coverage of 30 lakhs. A scheme was also proposed to add 6000 hospital beds by building additional hospitals (Third Plan). The coverage of the EPF scheme was also to be extended. The EPF scheme which coverage 58 specified industries/establishments was to be extended. The employment level for coverage was to be lowered from 150 to 20 persons.

To ensure the safety of mine workers, a National Mines Safety Council was proposed to be set up to familiarize those in the mining industry with safety rules and measures. The question of separate safety legislation for building and construction workers was also examined by this plan. As recommended by the plan, special welfare funds were constituted for welfare measures for coal and mica mining workers. In some industrial centres workers' cooperative housing societies exist.

Employment and Training Scheme

By the Third Plan period it was intended to increase the number of industrial training centres, with adequate in-plant training facilities for training educated youth in the methods of business managements. The capacity of the three central training institutes for craft instructors was to be raised. The apprenticeship training scheme which was carried out on a voluntary basis in the Second Plan was sought to be made compulsory. It was also intended to increase employment exchange, especially rural employment exchanges.

Another aspect which was covered in this plan was the need to develop a scheme to provide relief to retrenched workers on a contributory basis, with the assistance of government, the relief was to be in the form of loans.

Productivity

The Third Plan also laid stress on raising the level of productivity for which the employer, the workers and the rest of the community were to work together.

Research

During this period one aspect which was given equal importance with the other routine aspects of planning was labour research in the areas of working conditions, family budgets, absenteeism, etc. It was decided to constitute a central committee, tripartite in character, for coordinating labour research.

The Fourth Five-Year Plan (1969-1974)[44] - on Labour Policy

In the matter of Industrial Relations, continued emphasis was laid on measure recommended in the earlier plans. As a result many acts were enacted, e.g. the Payment of Bonus Act, 1965, the Shops and Commercial Establishment Act and the Labour Welfare Fund Act in the states. The National Safely Council was set up in 1966 as per the recommendations of the Third Plan. All the wage boards of the 19 major industries had submitted their reports. Under the Minimum Wages Act, 1948, the minimum wages were fixed for agricultural and other trades. The Government of India set up the National Commission on Labour to study and make recommendations on various aspects of labour relations.

The coverage of social security measures as in the case of ESIS and EPF was extended.

The Fourth plan laid great emphasis on employment and this idea was given wide coverage. Thus, in 1968, a committee of experts was set up by the Planning Commission to enquire into estimates of unemployment worked out by other plans, the census and the National Sample Survey to advise the Planning Commission on these issues. The committee submitted its report which recommended the collection of employment data in India.

The strategy developed by the Fourth plan was unique in the sense that it emphasized labour intensive programmes through the development of agriculture and the rural infrastructure like electrification, water management, and so on. This plan laid stress on schemes such as roads, minor irrigation, housing and urban development.

Thus, many of the programmes launched during the Fourth Plan period were with the goal of increasing employment opportunities and providing unemployment relief in the rural areas.

During this plan period the Maharashtra and Gujarat governments formulated employment scheme. Other schemes formulated for employment growth were in the mining and manufacturing industries, the transport sector, the construction industries etc.

The Fifth Five-Year Plan (1974-1979)[45] - on Labour Policy

The Fifth Plan document had a chapter on employment, manpower and labour welfare. The thrust was on a few themes, which are discussed below:

The need to generate more employment opportunities and help to reduce underemployment, either in the wage employment category or in the self employed category for which labour intensive projects were suggested. The need to examine more closely, in view of the changed economic environment, the linkage between current education systems and population growth was also highlighted. It was felt that given the populations explosion, besides family planning to control this phenomenon, there was a need to reorient education towards practical skill formation.

There was an extensive review of the demand and supply for the various types of specialist manpower, such as, engineers, doctors, teachers, scientists, managers, agriculture specialists and craftsmen. It was suggested that craftsmen should be given training to improve and diversify their skills to meet the needs of the current environment.

The need for greater mobility of labour was also stressed, especially from labour surplus to labour starved areas. It was felt that geographic barriers would result in artificial shortages and excesses.

The government provides an employment service through employment exchanges. These services were to be expanded to cover a comprehensive package, consisting of career counseling and vocational guidance.

It was suggested that there was a need to improve labour welfare amenities already existing by integrating them into more comprehensive social security package and expand the coverage of the employees state insurance scheme and the family pension scheme.

Finally, a national labour institute was to be set up, to function as a coordinating agency for research in labour matters.

The plan allocation was Rs. 57 crores for craftsmen training, employment service and labour welfare programmes.

The Sixth Five-Year Plan (1980-1985)[46] - on Labour Policy

The Sixth Plan had a chapter on labour and labour welfare. After a brief overview of the labour situation in the country, which highlighted the wage and bonus issue, in terms of wage differentials, national minimum wage and the need for productivity-linked bonus, the document highlighted a few thematic concerns. They are:

- The need to strengthen and revitalize scheme of workers' participation, according to the Sixth Plan.
- It should be make a vehicle of transforming the attitudes of both employees and workers for establishing a cooperative culture which may help in building a strong, self – confidence and self-reliant country with a stable industrial base.

- A 21 Member Committee comprising the representatives of employers, trade unions, government and academicians has studied the matter in depth and recommended, among others, a legislative scheme of workers' participation providing three-tier participative forums at shop floor, plan level and corporate/board levels. An enlarged area of participation to cover matters relating to operational economic and financial, personal, welfare and environment areas has also been recommended.
- An effective agency for monitoring and evaluation would greatly help in making participative management a success.[47]

Next, the role of trade unions, particularly in the organized sector, was examined. A reorientation of the role of trade unions was suggested. It was estimated that the extent of unionization in the organized sector as a whole was around 30% several factors like the proliferation of unions, inter-union rivalry and the role of outside leaders have combined to "undermine the effectiveness of collective bargaining and led to industrial unrest". (Sixth Plan, p. 405). The trade union's role and orientation of attitude needs to be changed, given the nation's priorities of growth the development. There needs to be a better identification of the worker's goal with that of the enterprise's viability. At the same time the trade unions have major role to play in improving the quality of life of workers, through education, health and family planning, recreational and cultural activities.

Expansion of two major social security measures was suggested: first that the Employees' Provident Fund scheme should be extended to employees in smaller establishments and those in rural areas. The second was the need to extend the Employees State Insurance scheme to newer areas. In both the schemes, the coverage of employees was somewhat limited and these two important benefits could help ease the privations of many wage earners.

Concern was also expressed about safety and working conditions. A broader framework was suggested to include the effect of occupational diseases, the environment in which workers live and work. It was felt that these two factors had a direct bearing on increased production.

The document examined in detail, the problems of the rural and other special deprived categories of labour. It suggested the need for the proper organization of rural labour, in order to protect their interests, either through existing trade unions or through their own efforts. The need to periodically revise the minimum wages of agricultural labour was highlighted. Special problems of bonded labour, child labour, women labour, contract labour, construction labour and inter-state migrant labour were identified and steps that ought to be taken to mitigate their problems and the special care and attention that groups deserved was highlighted.

An outlay of Rs. 161.9 crores was proposed for labour and labour welfare the programme for the plan period.[48] Thus in different plan periods, the government adopted various labour friendly policies to strength Labour-Management Relations.

REFERENCES

1. I.L.O., *International Labour Standards* (1978).
2. [1934] A.C. 586, 589 – Quoted by C. W. Jenks, *Social Justice in the Law of Nations – The I.L.O. Impact After Fifty Years,* (1970).
3. David A Morse, *The I.L.O. and Human Rights* (1968).
4. C.W. Jenks, *Human Rights and International Labour Standards* 5-6 (1960).
5. G.A. Johnston, *The I.L.O. Its Work for Social and Economic Progress,* 150 (1970).
6. O. Kahn-Freund, *Labour & the Law* (1977).
7. Laski, Freedom of Association, V-VI, *Encyclopidia of Social Sciences* 447 (1957).
8. Arts. 29 (1) and 23 (4).
9. Sec. 17 to 19.
10. A.I.R. 1960 S.C. 1264 at 1268.
11. A.I.R. 1957 S.C. 38.
12. Sec. *All India Bank Employees Association v. National Industrial*

Tribunal, A.I.R. 1962 S.C. 171 : and *Damayanti v. Union of India*, A.I.R. 1971 S.C. 966.

13. A.P.S.R.T.C. *Employees Union v. Andhra Pradesh State Road Transport Co.*, 3 Lab. I.C. 1225 (1970).

14. *Croffer Harris Tweed v. Veitch*, (1942) A.C. 435 at 463.

15. See Ss. 17 and 18 of the Indian Trade Unions Act.

16. See ss. 22 to 25, 13 (3) (4A) and 10 A of the Industrial Disputes Act, 1947.

17. *All India Bank Employees Association v. National Industrial Tribunal*, Supra note 13.

18. (1962) 1 L.L.J. 294 (S.C.)

19. Supra note 13.

20. Jay Engineering Works v. State of West Bengal A.I.R. 1968 Cal. 407 at 417 (per Sinha, C.J.)

21. *Ibid.*

22. 2003 (98) IFLR 1009 ; SC = 2003 LLR 863.

23. (1962) suppl 3 SCR 396]

24. [(1964) 7 SCR 403],

25. [(1962) 3 SCR 269]

26. [(2003 2 SCC 45]

27. [(1998) 1 SCC 201

28. Government of India, Ministry of Labour, *The India Year Book*, 1948-49, p. 268.

29. *Indian Express*, dated 10 September, 1978, p. 6.

30. Supra note 4 at 39.

31. Report of National Survey, 4 (1978).

32. O.P. Parmar, I.L.O. and India in pursuit of Human Rights through labour standards, *JILI*, 1981.

33. Government of India, First Five-Year Plan, New Delhi, Planning Commission, 1951, pp. 181-192.

34. (ILO, Freedom Association and Collective Bargaining, General Survey by the Committee of Experts, International Labour Conference, 69th session 1-2 (1983))

35. (ILO, *Record of Proceedings*, ILC 54th session 733 (1970))

36. Id.,58th Report, case No. 251 para 596

37. id., 85th Report, cases Nos. 300, 311, 321, para 110

38. id., 205th Report, case No. 983, para 37.

39. id., 217th Report, case No. 1096,para 298.

40. id., 165th Report, case No. 823,para 62

41. Government of India, *Second five-Year Plan*, New Delhi, Planning commission, 1956, pp. 571-584.

42. Government of India, *Third Five-Year Plan*, New Delhi, Planning Commission 1961, pp. 250-263.

43. Sonarikasr, S., *Implementation of Labour Enactments*, Bombay, Popular Prakashan, 1976, p. 33.

44. Government of India, *Fourth Five-Year Plan*, New Delhi, Planning Commission, 1969, pp. 424-432.

45. Government of India, *Fifth Five-Year Plan*, New Delhi, Planning Commission, 1974, pp. 83-84.

46. Government of India, *Draft Fifth Five-Year Plan, 1974-79*, New Delhi, Planning Commission, pp. 267-273.

47. Government of India, *Sixth Five-Year Plant 1980-85*, New Delhi, Planning Commission, pp. 402-412.

48 Tripathi. P.C., Gupta C.B., *Industrial Relations and Labour Laws*, Sultan Chand and Sons, New Delhi.

4

LABOUR MANAGEMENT RELATIONS IN THE CONTEXT OF GLOBALISATION

Globalisation has become a dominant feature of the world economy over the last decade; as more and more nations are becoming integrated into the global economy through trade and capital flows.

During these days capital, trade and labour were all free to move from one country to another. Many have observed that in the globalisation that we see today only capital is free. Labour or human resources are not.

Alam Rugman (2000), understands globalisation as the worldwide production and marketing of goods and services by multinational enterprises. According to Anthony Giddens and John Tomlinson (1999), Globalisation is multidimensional. The Human Development Report of South Asia explains Globalisation as the free movement of goods, services, people and information across national boundaries.

In Favour of Globalisation

Globalisation promotes economic growth and prosperity to all nations. It promotes technology, creates more quality jobs for the community, the free foreign investment supplements domestic savings and encourages more investment in the community.

The entire theory of globalisation is based on the following aspects:

(i) Sustained economic growth, as measured by gross national product is the path to human progress.

(ii) Privatisation, which moves functions and assets from government to the private sector, improves efficiency.

(iii) The primary responsibility of the government is to provide the infrastructure necessary to advance commerce and enforce rule of law with respect to property rights and contracts.

(iv) Free markets, without intervention from the Government generally result in the most efficient and socially optimal allocation of resources.

(v) Economic globalization, achieved by removing barriers to the free flow of goods and money anywhere in the world, spins competition increases economic efficiency, creates jobs, lower consume prices increases consumers' choice, increases economic growth and is generally beneficial to every one.

Critics of Globalization

While many Indian Economists feel that the process of globalization is irreversible and inescapable, many economists, scholars and thinkers in the western world do not feel so.

Alan Rugman (2000), feels that there is no globalization that it is a trial based production in the US, Japan and Europe. According to him business is not global. Michel Chossudovsky (1997), feels that globalization, IMF and World Bank policies have ruined many countries and have only brought about the globalization of poverty. According to Jerry Mander and Edward Goldsmith (1996) The process of globalization must be brought to a halt as soon as possible, and reversed. They described free trade as a great destroyer. They feel that globalization will destroy employment and local communities.

In a brilliant review of the international economic relations in the 20th century. Ian Clark (1997) argues how fragmentation of communities and countries are interlinked with globalization. Nobel laureate Mr. Joseph Stiglitz has described the present globalization in the following words "Needy Nations are subject to

1) Privatization
2) Free flow of capital
3) Market based price.
4) Free trade before extending financial loans by the World Bank.

The U.S. economy is fast collapsing; the entire world economic order is heading towards total bankruptcy the world needs a complete review of economic order in terms of continental co-operation while preserving sovereignty of state nations.

The Human Development Report on South Asia 2001 comes to the conclusion that "During the globalization phase about half a billion people in south Asia have experienced decline in their incomes. The benefits of globalization have remained limited a small minority of educated urban population, and also the report concludes that South Asia, which is the home of the largest number of poor people in the world (515 million) did not make much progress towards poverty reduction as a result of globalization and also the report comes to the conclusion that the number of people in poverty have increased. The poor are being marginalized. The resource allocations to the poverty alleviation programmes are declining; reducing their effectiveness.

The report also comments on the growth rates of countries in South Asia and says that in most countries growth rates are declining. All these make one wonder whether globalization has promoted growth and brought prosperity.

Dani Rodrik of the Harvard University has argued that import liberalization is not really essential for growth. W.T.O. is anti-democratic and that the world-trading regime has to shift from a market-access to a development perspective and he suggests that globalisation is an outcome, not a pre-requisite of a successful growth strategy as evidenced from the experience of East Africa and China.

Mr. Kofi Annan, Secretary General of united Nations is one of the critics of globalisation. Recently after the meeting of the world economic forum in January-2002, he appealed to the rich countries to open their markets to labour intensive products from poor countries. Developing countries be given a fair chance to report their products.

At present in the name of green box and blue box subsidies, agricultural products of developed countries are highly subsidized and such products enter the market of developing countries and compete with them.

There are a number of instances where the developing countries are not given equitable treatment. W.T.O. follows a policy of green room consultancy, where by only rich nations come together and take decisions. Developing countries have no options but only to follow these decisions.

If a product from a developing country is competitive in the market anti-dumping duties are levied or non-tariff barriers used and access is denied to products of developing nations in the markets of developed countries.

Diminishing State – A 21st Century Challenge

An activist state is one which takes interest in all forms of the activities of their subject some times leading to undue interference. Presently most of the countries are very conscious of the crises of ingovernability. To adopt to the new structure of the societies governments have chosen to de-legalise and deregulc1tc and often transfer most of the status dominant sphere to the private. The old sovereign states shrink largely in the process of regionalisation as well globalization. These in total give a picture of diminishing state. What should learn from this emancipated paradigm shift at the beginning of millenium, especially developing countries endeavouring to achieve better levels of economic and political living without repeating the whole dialectic process?

India is bringing about fundamental changes in the economic field aiming at globalisation through liberalised economic policies. Free market has been accepted as the model in India. Foreign capital and multinationals are not only welcome but are being positively induced to participated in a big way in the economic resurgence of India. These contemplated changes in India's economic system will be fall reaching importance with regard to the question of reach of fundamental rights.

The liberalised policy of the recent times in India or else where is the best example for this. For example, without changing the socialistic pattern envisaged in Preamble and Part III dealing Fundamental Rights and Part IV dealing Directive Principles of State Policy of the Constitution of India, economic relations are radically changed in India.

The solution for this is only that the thesis of more market, less state and the antithesis of the constitutional call for social solidarity and welfare must merge into a synthesis immediately to achieve social justice because without social justice, no social stability will last longer otherwise the system is going to be collapsed. In this back drop the Labour Management Relations in the context of Globalization are to be understood.

The period following liberalization witnessed the arm of state shifting in favour of the employers as against the employees in the earlier period. Consequently, the workers were on the defensive and this led to a sharp decline in mandays lost due to strikes by 36.9 percent during 1992-97 as against 1986-91. Since workers remained subdued in the liberalization period, the employers did not need to declare lockouts either as a retaliatory measure or as a normal weapon to subdue workers. This is corroborated by the fact that mandays lost due to lockouts declined by a relatively smaller percentage i.e., 25.7 per cent in the post-liberalization period as against the pre-liberalisation period.

In the wake of the so called New Industrial Policy (NIP) there was widespread expectation in certain quarters that the time had come for labour policies to be dovetailed with industrial policies so that both moved in a unified direction than in opposite directions. There was much talk about the so called 'exit policy'. In October 1999, the Government constituted the Second National Commission on Labour on the recommendations of the Indian Labour Conference.

The social and labour effects of the new policies have been a major source of concern. New investments are taking place not where job losses are the most but where job losses are, relatively the least. As a result, job creation, if at all, is not occurring where it is needed most. Productive employment creation and maintaining the social order being the responsibility of the state, state governments would have to strive hard to preserve the employments and create a conductive environment for further job creation. It then becomes imperative for them to review their industrial and labour policies to woo investment and facilitate the growth of industry and business for further job creation. Whether and how state governments can make a difference in adopting and practicing competitive labour policies is, then, a moot question.

The Government of India would articulate and implement social and labour issues till the 1960s when the same party used to rule at the Centre and in most states. But since 1969, non-Congress and regional parties came to power in the states and four times at the center. State Governments began to ask for greater provincial autonomy including in maters relating to labour, which has been on the 'concurrent list' since the British days. Both trade unions and employers' organizations submitted memoranda reflecting their views on labour issues to the Sarkaria Commission set up in the 1980s to review Center-State relations. The problem is compounded by the definition of "appropriate government" particularly in the case of Central Government undertakings with plants or operations extending to more than one State. While the administrative machinery in the Central Government is responsible for the overall performance of the enterprise, labour-management relations in plants came, in several cases, under the jurisdiction of the Government of the State where the enterprise was located. Political differences among parties in power caused problems for individual enterprises. Also when major policy issues were discussed at labour ministers 'conference, Government representatives would take a stand on the line of ideology of the ruling party at the Centre and or the States. Given the diversity of the context, the seriousness of the political ferment and pendulum-like swinging of

Government policies over the years, one wonders whether India will ever have a unified labour policy.

State Governments are business too. According to a report of the Comptroller and Auditor General of India, the number of State Government companies increased significantly from 168 in 1969-70 to 840 in 1986-87 and to over 1,000 in 1990s, more than 3000 in 2006. In every State, the state electricity boards and state road transport corporations were the biggest with a total investment of over Rs.137 crore in 1986-87. The electricity boards had a negative return of 13 percent on average. The cumulative losses of 514 State Government enterprises were over Rs.20 billion.

Some State Governments are endeavouring to make adjustments and improve their image so that they can attract investment and save/create jobs. While the Central Government did not resort to even a single privatization overtly till the end of 1999, many states were ahead with privatization openly. Raipuria refers to the privatization and restructuring of electricity boards (Meghalaya, Orissa, Andhra, Haryana and U.P.), profit-sharing with employees (Rajasthan Roadways), a renewal fund on the lines of the National Renewal Fund (Rajasthan) for employees of sick units which were closed, issue of project-specific bonds (Gujarat and Rajasthan) and promotion of tourism through the private sector (Sikkim). Andhra Pradesh, Orissa, Karnataka and many other states also resorted to open privatization. Several State Government have a variety of welfare programmes as well. Some political parties continue to oppose privatization of central public sector undertaking in their own states, regardless whether they are in opposition or a part of the ruling coalition at the Centre even though in their own states as a ruling party, they pursue privatization, often vigorously.

The industrial relations scenario in different states in India present glaring contradictions. In West Bengal, politically affiliated trade unions, particularly those subscribing to the leftist ideology, are widespread. In Maharashtra – which is the hub of economic activity and widely acclaimed as the commercial capital of the country-enterprise-level unions, which are independent and unaffiliated to any Central federation or political party, have a major presence. In Karnataka, particularly Bangalore, which has been christened the Silicon Valley of India, many firms in the new, non-traditional, high-technology industries are 'union-free'.

In some parts of Gujarat, "footpath unionism" is growing. Some briefless lawyers, among others, mobilize signatures of several disgruntled employees, register a union and pursue their individual grievances on the lines of contingent litigation; the leaders of such unions will have a sizeable share in the compensation that such workers might get. In Maharashtra, the growing sickness in textile mills and opportunities to reap a bonanza through real estate business in sick and closed mills, opened new vistas for a formidable link between the real estate underworld mafia and trade unions. In some of the industrially and socially backward areas of Andhra Pradesh and Bihar, for instance, radical social movements in some cases assumed the role of trade unions also and began to pursue the cause of workers through militant means, undermining the role of traditional trade unions and making a mockery of the authority of the employer, the district administration and the local police.

Unions may be declining in some parts of the country but not in Orissa, where union leadership is focusing on organizing in small and medium-scale industries.

Changing Face of Trade Unions in a Liberalised Economy

Trade Unionism in India is passing through a critical phase and facing unprecedented challengers in a liberalized, privastised global economy. Labour is being pushed form the organized sector to the unorganized sector leading to an increase in causal and contract Labour. Downsizing, organizational restructuring, labour laws, political instability, the apathetic attitude of Government and gap in knowledge and skill base are the major factors responsible for this state of affairs. Thus, trade unions have to rethink their position and adopt such strategies which would help them to act as responsible partners in the organisation.

C.S Venkata Ratnam rightly opined that trade unions are losing their members grip and their influence is declining as labour has shifted to the unorganized sector. These workers are not protected by unions and no sincere efforts have been made to organize them. Plant-based independent unions have increased without affiliating themselves to any central-level federations and have concentrated on plant-level issues such as productivity-based wage settlements. This has weakened the power of unions. Many sick public sector units, unable to compete in an open market system, have compelled trade unions to adopt "concession bargaining" for their existence and survival. The lack of mature leadership and inter-union rivalry continue to be the pertinent issues. Employers are bypassing unions as they find them obstructing the production process. They have started sub-contracting, outsourcing and signing individual contracts. The government has not been able to provide a method for union recognition and choosing the sole bargaining agent. The law has so far been able to take the unorganized sector in its stride. At this crucial juncture, trade unions' role and functions need to be reviewed and redefined so that they can cope with the restructuring process.[1]

Impact of Globalisation on Labour-Management Relations

It is very necessary to improve competitiveness of our industry and economic activities:

(i) to ensure a regime of harmonious industrial relations

(ii) to ensure increasing opportunities of employment

(iii) to ensure at least a minimum level of protection and welfare for workers in all sectors of the economy organized as well as unorganized.

A regime of harmonious Industrial relations is very important to improve competitiveness of our industry and economic activities of our nation:

(i) To ensure a regime of harmonious industrial relations

(ii) To ensure increasing opportunities of employment

(iii) To ensure atleast a minimum level of protection and welfare for workers in all sectors of the economy – organized as well as unorganized.

The above components are essential to improve competitiveness of our industry and economic activities:

Employment, skills and training are necessary for acquiring and retaining employability and employment; healthy industrial relations and laws that can promote a harmonious industrial relations machinery for the speedy and just solution of disputes.

Economic Reforms in India: A Backdrop

During 1980's India had a fairly good economic performance. But towards the last years of the decade, and particularly in 1990-91, Indian economy entered an unprecedented liquidity crises. This was due to the combined effect of many factors.

The economy of the Soviet Union and that of most of the East European countries collapsed towards the end of the eighties. Some of them were India's major trading partners.

The Gulf War in January 1991, resulted in rising oil prices and there was a virtual stoppage of remittances from Indian workers in the Gulf. As a result of these factors, India's credit rating in International market fall considerably. In these markets, there was erosion of confidence in the strength of the Indian Economy. As a result, India found it difficult to raise funds in the international markets.

In the year 2001, we completed a decade of a policy of liberalization and now the government seriously considering introducing a second generation of reforms.

Salient Features of Economic Reforms

1. The government opened major sectors of the economy to the private sector, which were so far reserved for the public sector.
2. Foreign investment was invested in all sectors except agriculture and plantations. The ceiling on foreign equity investment in corporate bodies at 40% was removed. Foreign equity investment upto 51% to 75% in some cases even 100% Foreign Equity Investment was allowed.
3. All restrictions on the entry of the private sector into the

field of infrastructure and strategic industries were removed.

4. Banks can also approach capital markets for raising funds.
5. In order to provide adequate infrastructure, private capital, and foreign investment have been allowed in such areas as construction of roads, ports, airports etc.
6. The government wants to reduce its investment in the public sector enterprises therefore being made for disinvestment in this sector. There is a separate Ministry of disinvestments in the union cabinet. Infact, from April, 2001, all quantity restriction on imports have been removed, and the rates of customs, tariffs have been reduced. India signed the W.T.O. agreement in 1994 and has accepted the commitment to liberalize its trade regime.
7. Subsidies are being cut, tax rates are being reduced and the entire fiscal system is being streamlined.
8. The office of the controller of capital issues stands abolished.

Globalisation and Labour-Management Relations: Dynamics of Change

At the time of Independence in 1947, India opted for a socialist republic and embarked on a planned mixed economy. During late sixties and early seventies, India pursued the policies of self reliance based on import substitution industrialization policy several countries in Asia pursued an export oriented industrialization policy. During 1980s, Indian economy faced the crisis because of macro-economic imbalances resulting in mounting internal and external liabilities, crisis of balance of payment, growing inflation, low growth rate, pledging of gold, devolution of rupee and seeking loans from IMF on constraining conditions. New economic measures were initiated with an object of bringing fiscal economic corrections so as to provide an inherent macro-economic competitive strength through structural adjustment in industries and modification of public sector policies.

The new reforms call for reorganisation of public sector, doing away with over protection and budgetary support to losing enterprises. The government decided to disinvest a part of the equity of selected public enterprise units to expose them to free market conditions and also to usher a new work culture. The disinvestments of public sector enterprises enabled the government to reduce fiscal deficit, but it did not help to improve the performance of the enterprises. Recently, the government disinvested by reducing its equity in Videash Sanchar Nigam Ltd., Indo Burma Petroleum, Paradeep Phosphates Ltd. and some hotels. There is a suggestion that government should take steps in identifying and reviewing the sick units both in public and private sectors.

In the wake of New Industrial Policy (1991), industrial licensing was abolished in all but 18 industries related to security and social environment concerns of the country. Private sector competition was introduced selectively in areas earlier reserved for the public sector. Majority foreign holding is now allowed in almost all industries except those which are of strategic importance. The system of capital issue control was abolished, the import- export procedure was simplified and rupee convertibility introduced on trade account. Even reservation to small sector was withdrawn in most cases. The liberalisation provided a free choice in setting up and management of industries. Steps were taken to facilitate the direct inflow of foreign investment in the form of non-debt inflow to help the introduction of new technology and market expertise. New companies enjoyed automatic approval of foreign equity participation upto 51 percent and more.

On the state of economy, the Economic Survey (2001-2002) points out that the overall growth rate of 5.4 percent this year is supported by a growth rate of 5.7 per cent in agriculture, 3.3 percent in industry and 6.5 per cent in services. There has been a sharp slow down in industry. The government finances are in a mess. There is a big shortfall in revenue collections and despite measures to reduce expenditure, the Centre will exceed the 5.5 per cent target of fiscal deficit as a proportion of GDP. The restoration of high economic growth would be difficult without a significant and sustained reduction in fiscal deficit. The government needs to raise more by way of taxes and reduce subsidies and other revenue expenditure while not shying away from making capital investments even through public borrowings if the returns justify it[2]. In the budget speech (2002-2003), Finance Minister Yashwant Sinha pointed out that the aim in the current year is to consolidate and implement the policies at all levels through a strategy of reform-linked public funding which will continue the emphasis on agriculture and food economy reforms; enhance public and private investment in infrastructure; strengthen the financial sector and capital markets; deepen the structural reforms and regenerate industrial growth; provide social security to poor; and consolidate tax reforms and continue fiscal adjustment at both central and state levels. Economic growth is expected to be about 5.4 per cent, and a fiscal deficit of 5.3 per cent of GDP[3]. A McKinsey study published in 2001. pointed out that India could grow at 10 per cent a year if it could do three key things - reform land markets, privatise state assets and dismantle barriers to Product markets[4]. There is a need for expansion in economic activities, promoting foreign and domestic investments, exploring employment potential in agriculture, rural and small sector and creating export markets and thereby generating employment opportunities.

T.A Kochan (1987) proposed a three tier strategic choice model of industrial relations. For the top tier of strategic decision making, a superstructure of tripartite consultation was built and in the quarter century (1947-72) Since Independence, such tripartite institutions as the Indian Labour Conference (ILC) and Standing Labour Committee (SLC) served a useful role and provided a major thrust towards voluntarism in the face of preference to adjudication over collective bargaining. However, since the early 1970s, tripartite consultation and voluntarism have suffered a set back because the principal actors lost their representative character. Hence indecision, politicised polarization and pendulum tactics often tripartite consultations. Generally tripartitisam is restricted to consultations among the government and the organisations of workers. There is a need to extend the scope to other sections of society including the unemployed, unoraganised and even the consumers. The middle tier refers to such factors as the employment relationship and personnel policy formulation, collective bargaining, labour legislation and labour administration at the enterprise level. Here too, the scenario is equally infirm. At the third level that is, the shop floor level, the strategic choices relate to the organisation of work and the workplace environment. The last two decades have shown considerable innovation and experimentation at this level; yet much of it has not been sustained in organisations where it has been tried. The principal thrust of management is to gain greater flexibility in organisational work and the allocation and utilisation of human resources. Changes in the industrialisation strategies call for changes in labor management policies, to obtain the requisite balance between a social system and technical system in our organisations in order that organisations fulfill the purpose for which they were created.

Globalisation is certainly not good for the country. It is bad for the Indian economy, increases unemployment and hits the poor most. Public sector companies are thrown out of existence. Globalisation is against a just and equitable society. It thrives on inequities in income and opportunities.

A large number of employees are artisans and craftsmen. Their products are threatened by cheap imports from abroad. The Chinese silk or imported carpets and leather products tend to throw silk weavers in Karnataka or leather goods makers in Uttar Pradesh and carpet makers in Kashmir out of job. Also, the Foreign Direct Investment (FDI) facilitated by globalization, helps to boost mechanism and automation, which edge human labour out and drastically cut jobs.[5]

Globalisaiton and Privatisation

Social and Labour Issues in Privatisation: An Overview

Privatisation is one of the major elements of an adjustment process going on in most parts of the world, with a view among others, to making enterprises and economies productive and competitive. In almost all the economies in transition, in Central and Eastern Europe, privatization is under way. Privatisation in Eastern Europe, however, is different from that in other countries in as much as it involves essentially a fundamental change in the concept of property relations in the larger society itself. There is wide gap between rhetoric and reality in terms of avowed and actual privatisations. This paper deals with social and labour matters rather than the technical complexities and dynamics involved in the process of privatization.

With this focus, the concept of privatization and its impact on the social and labour issues involved including employment and job security, trade unions and collective bargaining, employee ownership, industrial relations and tripartite consultation.

What, Why and How of Privatisation

Privatisation has been defined and understood in many ways. Essentially it refers to a process through which the direct involvement of the state or the public sector is reduced through transferring the ownership, control and/or managerial responsibility for government enterprises, functions and activities, fully or partially, to the private sector corporations, individuals or groups of individuals such as employees, customers and citizens, domestic or foreign.

The motives for privatization could be several, embodying a variety of socio-economic and political objectives and may include one or more of the following:

- Fundamental changes in socioeconomic and political systems (as in Central and Eastern Europe)
- Reduce direct involvement of the state in industry, commerce and services and consequential financial and administrative burden.
- Desire to increase efficiency and competition in the economy.
- Achieve better balance between public and private sectors.
- Attract foreign capital.

Privatisation can be accomplished in several ways which include the following: complete or partial divestiture of equity or assets; liquidation, abandonment or return of the assets of nationalised corporations; leasing, contracting out or franchising production, distribution, supplies or services with freedom to manage without government interference; establishment of joint ventures; policy reforms such as liberalisation and deregulation, etc. It may be added that liberalisation, which refers to opening up of any industry to competitive pressures, is a form of privatization and yet it is possible to liberalise without privatization too.

In Eastern Europe, due to peculiar conditions of property relations, paucity of capital and pressure to mobilize the public support, several countries including Hungary and Poland have resorted to what is known as voucher privatization. It means giving the citizens investment coupons worth a certain amount with which they can buy shares in companies being privatized. The shares are either distributed freely or will be vested in the concerned individuals as and when they pay the money. According to some schemes the money need not be paid, but can be adjusted, over time, against dividends payable on the shares held by the individuals as and when the companies make profits.

The major problem in most countries with regard to privatization concern the valuation of assets and the terms on which the sale is effected. There is need for greater degree of transparency in the process of privatization. Additionally there are problems in some countries, which, for political or other reasons wish to discourage foreign investment, at the same time they do not want to divest it locally for fear that it may accentuate the exising ethnic inequalities in property ownership patterns. Often allegations of favouritism and corruption and electoral considerations make the governments shy away from the process itself instead of making it more transparent. There is need to priatie the process of privatisation itself, if at all privatization is carried out effectively. This will reduce further scope for "socialising the losses and privatising the gains."

What to Privatise?

The emotive arguments on the subject grounded in ideology range from one to the other end of the continuum: nothing to everything. Even in 1990s if they can have it their way some governments still envisage an increased role for government in managing the economy, including industry, trade and commerce.

The privatistion decision is difficult particularly because government projected parastatals as symbols of equity and justice. The dilemma in Central and Eastern Europe concerns the fear about the "nomenclature" stealing the show in the new setting also through what is popularly referred to as a "golden parachute" strategy using their clout and collections in the former setup to manoeuvre ownership and control in the new privatized establishments. As the Deputy Finance Minister and Director of Privatisation in the Czeck and Slovak Republic, Mr. Dusan Triska (1991) put it boldly, "We will have to make do with the managers we have now, most of whom are former nomenclatura from Communist Party. The most bitter pill that our nation will have to swallow is to see who will be the winners and who will be the losers in the process of transformation and privatization. The winners certainly will be the old winners and the losers will be those who were losers under the previous regime."[6]

While these and other issues arise in different forms and magnitude in various countries, there can be no particular formula or solution to deal with them and decisions have to be made in the proper text and context as per the specific objectives, both short term and long term, that are sought to be accomplished. Some, like Kornai (1990, p.82), argued that the state "is obliged to handle the wealth it was entrusted with carefully until a new owner appears who can guarantee a safer and more efficient guardianship. The point is not to hand out the property, but rather to place it in the hands of a better owner." Kornai was particularly concerned with the "spontaneous privatization" taking place in Eastern Europe (which may not often be privatization in the real sense) and the consequent emphasis on free distribution of shares through issue of "vouchers" or "investments coupons." There are others (e.g. David Lipton and Jeffrey Sachs, 1992) who argue about the need for rapid privatization through free distribution combined with the advantages of case-by-case approach. The latter viewpoint is guided by concern to pre-empt the accumulation of road blocks to privatisation.[7]

Privatisation and Performance Improvement

Let us agree, for the sake of argument, that private sector failure is one of the causes for nationalisation and public sector failure is one of the causes for privatization. If we have to learn any lesson from this basic fact of history, we would admit that mere change of ownership does not guarantee increased competition, efficiency and other advantages of free play of market forces. The central issue here is, as Bishop and Kay (1988), Vickers and Yarrow (1988) and several others have raised in the context of privatization programme in the U.K., the tension between the failure of markets and the failure of regulation, and the need to find structures which minimize the extent of either and/or both. It is proposed here that the current wave of arguments concerning deregulation are directed at reforming regulation which rendered market forces dysfunctional and contributed to the stifling or non-performance of market forces. The case for privatization could be advanced from the view point that encouraging it could bolster the performance of even the public sector as it happened in the U.K. As Bishop and Kay (1988) observe, "the most significant aspect of the (privatisation) performance has been the change in the culture of the public sector and privatized companies. New management has challenged the previous culture. Privatisation symbolized the government's determination to take seriously the need to instill commercial spirit in the public sector. In contrast to the actions, if not intentions, they would neither interfere in managerial decisions, nor intervene to prevent bankruptcy. Most radically, if the new commercial spirit could best be achieved outside of public ownership, the government was prepared to transfer its business to the private sector. This created an expectation of change (often ahead of any changes actually taking place) which has made effective management at all levels considerably easier." Similar change of heart is seen in most parts of the world. The current debate on privatization made most governments and unions, among others, focus attention on strategies to improve the performance of public sector itself.[8]

Social and Labour Issues

Privatisation and the logical corollary steps to remove the road blocks to free economy involve complex social and labour issues. The heart of the dilemma is that it is difficult for the affected employees to agree to a logic that dictates the necessity to undergo the change process and even make sacrifices, if needed in the overall interests of the survival of an organisation countries actually cut employment either through the Bank programmes or on their own. The situation is not different in industrialized countries. In the U.K., three public enterprises – British Coal, British Steel and British Rail – themselves accounted for a decline of nearly 350,000 jobs during 1979-80.[9]

The relation between job loss and privatization is often incidental and not imperative. Job loss is nil or negligible when an efficient enterprise is privatized such as in Singapore or Malaysia. Job loss is more when a firm needed drastic restructuring. Delayed restructuring may lead to greater job loss than non-restructuring per se. Where privatization brought back to life units in limbo (or non-working units) such as in Bangladesh, for example, it meant retrieving lost jobs, some though not all. In the U.K. within a few years since privatization, several of the privatized firms reported a sizeable increase in employment than the levels reported on the eve of privatisation.

Even where job security is relatively greater in parastatals, job losses may result there too due to accumulated inefficiencies and a host of factors outside the control of the firm or state. Lack of modernization and lack of competition may eventually contribute to job losses. The long-term effects of privatization on employment depends on whether the enabling environment exists for them to operate efficiently and, even if its exists, how efficiently those firms operate. It is easy to provide safeguards in profitable and expanding organisations but difficult in sick and unviable units. While it is extremely important and highly desirable to provide for employment security, the actual practice would be dictated by pragmatism, whatever the intentions with which they have long been associated. Ideally change process should find acceptance at all levels and by all constituents in the organisation. But, often this is more easily said than is the real case. In what follows, aspects relating to employment and job security, trade unions, collective bargaining, industrial relations and tripartite concertation are briefly discussed.

Employment and Job Security

One of the major fears about privatisation concerns the potential loss of present and future employment. The relative decline of employment in private sector and the growth of public service employment in the 70s and 80s may have further strengthened the notion that jobs in public sector are more secure. Public sector employment accounts for half and one-third respectively of formal sector employment in Africa and Asia and there is evidence of growth in public employment (public sector and public services included) in Asia (Edgren, 1988), Africa and Latin America (Ghai, *et al.*, 1989). Though in both Africa and Latin America formal sector employment grew at 1% and 1.8% respectively, it was at the expense of a substantial decline in real wages of the order of 20% in Africa and 7% in Latin America during 1981-86. However, the developments in 1980s indicate that even governments have limits and limitations tc bear the burden of employment through budgetary support beyond a point, particularly when it is unproductive and/or became redundant due to the imperatives of new technologies and competitive pressures. As a result, between July 1981 and February 1987, public employment and pay issues in central governments figured prominently in the World Bank lending operations in 24 Third World countries in different regions. Four countries froze employment and 10 countries actually cut employment either through the Bank programmes or on their own (Nunberg, 1989). The situation is not different in industrialized countries. In the U.K., three public enterprises – British Coal, British Steel and British Rail – themselves accounted for a decline of nearly 350,000 jobs during 1979-80 (Bishop and Kay, 1988).

The relation between job loss and privatization is often incidental and not imperative. Job loss is nil or negligible when an efficient enterprise is privatized such as in Singapore or Malaysia. Job loss is more when a firm needed drastic restructuring.

Delayed restructuring may lead to greater job loss than non-restructuring per se. Where privatization brought back to life units in limbo (or non-working units) such as in Bangladesh, for example, it meant retrieving lost jobs, some though not all. In the U.K within a few years since privatization, several of the privatized firms reported a sizeable increase in employment than the levels reported on the eve of privatisation.

Even where job security is relatively greater in parastatals, job losses may result there too due to accumulated inefficiencies and a host of factors outside the control of the firm or state. Lack of modernization and lack of competition may eventually contribute to job losses. The long-term effects of privatization on employment depends on whether the enabling environment exists for them to operate efficiently and, even if its exists, how efficiently those firms operate. It is easy to provide safeguards in profitable and expanding organisations but difficult in sick and unviable units. While it is extremely important and highly desirable to provide for employment security, the actual practice would be dictated by pragmatism, whatever the intentions be. As the typology of employment safeguards in case of macro-economic pressures and privatization in 10 countries in Asia, Africa and Europe indicate, those countries (Singapore and Malaysia) which are on a sound footing and where unemployment and inflation are not major problems could afford greater degree of protection that others. Even the ILO Convention No. 158 and Recommendation No. 166 adopted by the International Labour Conference in 1982 does not rule out job losses due to economic, technological, structural or similar reasons even as these instruments provided safeguards in Part III to the effect that employer who contemplates such termination must: (a) provide the workers, representative concerned in good time with relevant information including the reasons for the terminations contemplated, the number of categories of workers likely to be affected and the period over which the terminations are intended to be carried out; (b) give, in accordance with national law and practice, the workers, representative concerned, as early as possible, an opportunity for consultation and measures to be taken to avert or minimize the terminations and measures to mitigate the adverse effects of any terminations on the workers concerned such as finding alternative employment; and, (c) notify the competent authority of such terminations as early possible, giving relevant information. Privatisation of Japan National Railways affords one of the best examples where all but 4,000 jobs lost could be retrieved within a few years due to a well-conceived plan of redeployment and retraining which included giving priority in hiring of the affected workers not only in public sector and the privatized railways, but also the firms which have backward and forward linkages with railways and other private sector firms. The question which arises in such cases, however, is whether such preferences would work against the interests of young, future entrants into the labour market. Such trade off is hypothetical where there is no unemployment, but real where unemployment is a significant issue.

The need for developing social security net through setting up National Renewal Fund, as has been done in India, and exploring additional contributions to the fund through sale of surplus land, contributions to the tune of 1 to 2 per cent of the wages and wage bill respectively by employees and employers as insurance against future contingencies and compensation for flexibility could be thought of to provide for additional benefits to the surplus labour over and above normal terminal benefits and/or support for active labour market interventions through retraining for possible redeployment or resettlement in self or special employment/livelihood programmes.

Trade Unions

Trade unions generally oppose and resist privatization on grounds such as the following: (a) The rationale of public sector and public services and the need to preserve them in the larger and long-term well being of the nation (Clements, 1988); and, (b) the concern about security of employment, employment conditions, union security (membership strength and recognition), collective bargaining and industrial relations implications (for detailed statements of each of the tripartite actors in ASEAN countries.[10]

To begin with, however, the free trade union movement must have initially found it difficult to oppose privatization on ideological grounds. As Clements (1988) argues, "A challenge to the principle of privatisation is portrayed as a challenge to the free enterprise system. "Indeed, the AFL-CIO in the U.S.A. was apparently reluctant to oppose privatization, until its Public Employees Department put pressure and published its first major document on the subject. The West European trade union movement raised fundamental issues about the relevance of public sector and public services and articulated the need for toning up the services by making the public managements more responsible than merely transferring the ownership. Generally their opposition to privatization was somewhat mild. The left-led union movement was somewhat in disarray due to sweeping changes in Central and Eastern Europe since mid-1980s. Among the industrialized countries, thus the burden of opposing privatization fell on the Trade Union Congress (TUC) in the U.K., which also happened to be the center stage for privatization programmes in the 1980s. Even in the U.K. a 1983 survey of trade union attitude to privatization covering gas and electricity, freight, construction, telecommunications, health and local government services revealed that as yet there was no pattern to trade union responses and pointed to the need for a new kind of social auditing that demonstrates the real costs and benefits of privatization (*Social and Labour Bulletin*, 1983). Trade Unions invariably focused on strategies to defend the concept, quality and effectiveness of public services and highlighted the negative consequences of privatization not only to employees but also to the customers and the public. When the TUC began to reflect on the future of public ownership, as the discussions in its annual congresses throughout the decade reveal, its leadership was distraught with the growing erosion of confidence in public services among the public and its own members. Therefore it had to enlarge the scope of its campaign against privatization so that it will be seen more as a positive reaffirmation in public ownership manifesting a genuine concern of "Industries for People", than as an agitation by trade unions to merely safeguard the interests of their members.

The unions in developing countries, irrespective of the colour of their political and union affiliations, nationally and internationally, have generally been opposed to privatisation. This is partly because of ideological considerations and largely out of concern for the security of their members jobs and of the unions themselves. For instance, privatization of a scooters plant became still-born and that of a cement plant reversed in India due to opposition from unions.

Admittedly, it is difficult to define conclusively the distinction among concepts such as public sector, public services and public utilities. Keeping this constraing in view, it may be noted that in several developing countries the right to organise, right to collective bargaining and right to strike have been restricted or denied not only in public services but also in public utilities and parastatals like railways, gas, electricity, airlines, banks, etc. Quite a few countries provide for consultation than collective bargaining and government exercises ultimate discretion to influence final decisions on matters concerning pay and working conditions even in public utilities and parastatals.

Several governments and formerly centrally planned economies, with Hungary and Yugoslavia being the notable exceptions, in a certain sense, virtually imposed, at least till recently, single trade union structures aligned with the military regime or ruling party and effectively curbed or limited the trade union rights. In all countries belonging to the above categories that have put in motion a process of privatistion, the workers have gained these rights once their economies began the transition to a free market economy. The most striking examples relate to Indonesia and the former U.S.S.R. The government in Indonesia declared that workers in state-owned enterprises can have rights to organise, bargain and strike once they become private. In the former U.S.S.R. the draft legislation published in 1989 grants workers the right to choose their representatives. The right to strike has already been granted to workers in the Commonwealth of Independent States (i.e., former U.S.S.R.), with certain restrictions. In Japan the right to strike was denied to the workers of the Japanese National Railways (JNR) in spite of a mild condemnation and moral persuasion by the ILO in late 1960s (ILO, 1966). But the right to strike was conceded to the railway workers in Japan after JNR was privatised.

The rights of workers and employers should be recognized and respected irrespective of the nature of ownership of the enterprise. Yet, evidently, workers and unions seem to gain their rights in the wake of privatization! Trade Unions maintain, however, that such improvement in workers rights notwithstanding, in practice they find it more difficult to exercise them in private sector than in public sector, particularly in developing countries. In Central and Eastern Europe both workers and employers organisations are yet to be organised/ reorganised.

There have been quite a few instances in some countries where it can be concluded that the unions ability to impede privatization in general and adjustment and restructuring in particular, seem to be inversely related to the political will of the government to meaningfully carry out the process involved (Waterbury, 1988).

Collective Bargaining

Privatisation usually entails restructuring. This affects bargaining structures, union membership base, and consequently the representative character of the union(s). The case of Cebu Plaza Hotel in Manila, Phillippines is perhaps the only one of its kind that the ILO Committee on Freedom of Association has dealt with so far and concerns directly the side-effects of privatization, among others. This case concerns the successor rights of workers in the event of transfer of ownership from one employer to another and also examines whether negotiated protection can be annulled by special legislations/proclamations concerning privatisation. The Committee held that proprietorial change shall not remove the right to collective bargaining from employees; such change shall not also directly or indirectly threaten unionized workers and their organisations.

The case of privatization of Japanese National Railway also exemplified the trade union dynamics (Suwa, 1989) impinging upon changes in inter and intra-union relations, union-management relations, management approaches to collective bargaining and how unfair labour practices may creep in, deliberately or otherwise, in the course of privatisation.

A trade unionist's analysis of labour conflicts of privatization in the context of Hungary (Neumann, 1991) points out that "the legal frameworks for privatization secure consultation possibilities for the organisations, representing employees interests. The trade unions demands aim at mitigation of unfavourable consequences on employment and social benefits and at the acquisition by employees of the largest possible property share at the best possible terms." Neumann notes that the "State Property Agency takes employees' decisions and evades negotiations on employment and social problems - tolerating even violations by the buyer."

In the case of Poland, legislative changes warranted by the transformation process in the economy may have diminished or altered the powerful role that works councils used to enjoy, at least on paper, at the enterprise level.

Focus on the survival and competitiveness of enterprises before the demands of employees and union will be a characteristic of all firms, both private and public, which are serious about bringing about the adjustment process. Indeed in the case of British Steel, its Chief Executive, Ian McGregor, told the union: Company survival comes first. "Nothing for nothing. Something for Something." Thus marked change in collective bargaining scene can not be ruled out. Indeed it seems more common than an exception to have decentralized bargaining in privatised firms.

Employee Ownership

Trade unions in most countries have generally opposed worker ownership and worker cooperatives due to ideological reservations about "workers capitalism" and also because individual shareholders and unions may not have greater say. However, grant of shares through free distribution (in several Central and East European countries), or on concessional terms, establishment of Employee Stock Ownership Plans (ESOPs), management / employee buyouts are becoming a common element in the privatization strategies. According to a World Bank study11 about 5% of the completed privatizations (20 out of 392) during 1980-87 were through worker / management buyout. 12 of these were in the U.K. and 5 in Cote d' Ivory. Chile, Denmark and Gambia also reported one case each. In Phillippines, the tripartite industrial peace accord (May 1990) provided, among others, that "Workers and Employers agree to recommend to the Asset Privatisation Trusts that in case of sale or privatization of government owned or controlled corporations, the workers affected should be given the right of first refusal to purchase the company of shares/interest there of. Alexandria Tyre Company in Egypt followed an ESOP programme. In Hungary and Poland 20% of the shares have been earmarked for employees through legislation. In Pakistan 26 per cent of the shares in Allied Bank were allotted for purchase by employees on the eve of privatization with promise about allocation of another 25% shares in the same bank a year hence.

It is too early to assess whether this trend will be irreversible. Much depends on the industrial and economic progress and prosperity as also the preferences of employees for ready cash vis-à-vis long term capital appreciation. The effects of such employee financial participation on corporate governance and performance are still to be seen and the available experience and evidence on the subject have been mixed.

Industrial Relations

The major change in industrial relations will most likely be in terms of decentralized bargaining with local unions and with much reduced effective influenced and intervention from national federations of trade unions as well as government. The specific developments will, of course, broadly conform to the trends and practices in private sector bargaining in the respective countries. Increased emphasis on direct communication with employees, a variety of employee involvement programmes and a shift in emphasis from collective to individual agreements in regard to managerial cadres is already evident. There is evidence of significant increases in top management pay in privatized firms in the U.K.[12] This could be so in developing countries too where top management remuneration in public sector is less than their counterparts in private sector. This needed will be the attraction for senior and middle managers to agree to individual contracts. It has, therefore, implications for management trade unionism.

There will be a possible shift in emphasis in the skill composition of the workforce in privatized firms with skilled persons gradually replacing unskilled ones though not in the same proportion. This was evident in the privatised jute mills in Bangladesh. Like managerial employees, skilled employees also will improve their pay, more so when such skills as are in demand and in short supply. This was noticed for instance in the privatization of Bolivian Central Bank. In the case of privatisation of Port of Kelang in Malaysia too the employees pay and benefits improved after privatization, though job security guarantee itself was reduced to five years from the date of privatisation.

A major challenge also awaits the human resource function to effect the changes with a human face and human concern limiting the negative effects on employment, employment conditions and industrial relations without violating the regulatory- moral, legal and contractual- framework defining mutual rights and obligations of unions and of employees. The transfer of ownership clarifies managerial objectives and fosters new patterns of industrial relations. Also, as Colling's (1991) analysis suggests, change in the external environment will be mediated by the needs and perceptions of actors within the process and may expose managers to a range of contradictory pressures.[13]

Tripartite Consultation

Tripartite consultation may be increasingly found useful to achieve consensus on a controversial subject like privatization. Thailand and Phillippines have had tripartite declarations on the subject. In India, tripartite dialogue is supplemented by setting up of industrial committees to consider the future of sick and unviable public sector companies. In Central and Eastern

Europe, however, it is the unions which are consulted by the government in deciding the broad strategy. Genuine tripartite consultation should aim at going beyond privatization and be directed at collective endeavours to create a congenial environment and infrastructure to realize the full potential of individual initiative and free market economy.

The privatisation is one of the major elements of structural adjustment process going on in most part of the world. It involves complex social and labour issues. Fears about privatization concern potential loss of present and future jobs. There is not enough evidence to suggest that privatization per se destroys jobs. However, the focus on efficiency improvement in units with surplus manning usually leads to short-term reduction in jobs, even if there is not privatisation. In countries with significant levels of unemployment and small proportion of labour force engaged in organised sector, this can create a major social problem. Hence the emphasis on job security measures and creation of a social security net. However, a country's ability to provide such security effectively depends mainly on its economic health including low rates of inflation and unemployment, high growth of gross National Product and low debt and deficit.

The trade unions are concerned about privatization due to fears about job loss and potential adverse effects on the dynamics of trade unions and their rights. Trade unions ability to impede privatization in general and adjustments and restructuring in particular, seem to be inversely related to the political will of the government to meaningfully carry out the process involved. To begin with, the free trade union movement had the ideological dilemma that opposition to privatisation is opposition to free enterprise itself. The unions were also handicapped by the growing dissatisfaction of the public with the unsatisfactory performance of public services. In several countries after privatization, the trade unions have raised gains. This is particularly so in case of Indonesia and former USSR where the right to organise collective bargaining and right to strike have been restricted or denied not only in public services but also in public utilities and parastatals. But, with privatization, the restrictions have been generally removed. Trade unions, however, maintain that such improvement in workers rights notwithstanding, in practice they find it more difficult to exercise them in private sector than in public sector, particularly, in developing countries.

The negative effect of privatization on collective bargaining and trade union dynamics was experienced in some countries like Phillippines and Japan. Also, in countries like Poland, the transformation of the economy diminished or altered the powerful role that work councils used to enjoy at the enterprise level. Though the employee ownership has occasionally raised suspicion about the effects of workers; capitalism, financial participation of employees in corporate turn-arounds and privatisation is on the increase in several countries.

The major changes in industrial relations are seen in terms of decentralistion and bargaining with local unions with much reduced effective influence and intervention from national federations to trade unions and government. The new industrial relations practices seem to focus, in some cases, on individualised contracts replacing collective bargaining, skill development and direct two-way communications with employees.

Tripartite consultation is also being considered useful to create a congenial environment and infrastructure to realize the full potential of the structural changes taking place the world over.

Observations of Second National Commission of Labour

The role of labor as human capital can not be determined for economic growth of a nation especially in the era of globalization. The Second National Commission observed "The main principles on which the entire theory of globalization is based:-

- Sustained economic growth, as measured by gross national product is the path to human progress.
- Free markets, without intervention form the government, generally result in the most efficient and socially optimal allocation of resources.

- Economic globalisation, achieved by removing barriers to the free flow of goods and money anywhere in the world, spins competition, increases economic efficiency, creates jobs, lowers consumer prices, increases consumers choice, increase economic growth and is generally beneficial to every one.
- Privatization, which moves functions and assets from government to the private sector, improves efficiency.

The primary responsibility of the Government is to provide the infrastructure essential to advance commerce and enforce rule of law with respect to property right and contracts.

While many Indian economists feel that the process of globalization is irreversible and inescapable, many economists, scholars and thinkers in the western world do not feel so. They are highly critical of the process of globalization and the inequalities that it is likely to promote between the poor and developed nations of the world" It is said that "monetary stability, macro-economic discipline, sound financial systems, and efficiently working market mechanisms are essential for all countries that embrace globalisatioll. But they are not sufficient for any. To fight the fears that globalisation sometimes inspires, countries need policies that promote not just economic efficiency, financial stability, and growth but also equity and high-quality growth. In too many counrrles, the quality of growth suffers from widening distributional inequalities related partly to high unemployment but also stagnating wages of unskilled workers. And too many countries continue to suffer from poor governance, corruption and increasing crime."

It is also observed that:

- Economic globalization is causing severe economic dislocation and social instability
- The technological changes of the past few years have eliminated more jobs than they have created.
- The global competition "that is part and parcel of globalization leads to winner-take-all situations; those who come out on top win big, and the losers lose even bigger."

- Higher profits no longer means more job security and better wages. "Globalization tends to delink the fate of the corporation from the fate of its employees."
- Unless serious corrective action is taken soon, the backlash could destabilize the Western democracies.

The Second National Commission on Labour observed: One of the characteristics of the new economic policy of liberalization is that the policy has concentrated on the private sector and particularly in attracting foreign investment and trade liberalization. The reform process has particularly bypassed the public sector enterprises.

There are some upward trends in wages and productivity and the Second National Commission on Labour observed: "There is evidence to indicate that both real wages and productivity of labour have registered an increases during the 90s. This growth is visible in all segments of the workforce, even among casual workers".

According to the estimates made by Sundaram based on the 50th and 55th rounds of NSSO, the average daily earnings of adult casual labourers in the rural areas increased by 3.59% p.a. for males and 3.19% for females between 1993-94 and 1999-2000. The average real wage earnings per day received by adult casual wage labouers in urban areas increased by 2.94% for males, and 3.91% for females during the same period.

Along with the growth of real wages, there appears to have been an overall growth in the productivity of workers. According to Sundaram's estimates, labour productivity increased, in all the sectors and the aggregate level, at the rate of 6% p.a. In agriculture and allied sectors, it increased a little over by 3.3% p.a. in real terms. In agriculture and allied sectors, it increased a little over by 3.3% p.a. in real terms. In manufacturing, trade, hotels and restaurants and community, social and personal services, the average labour productivity measured by gross value added per worker increased at an annual compound rate of 6.1, 2.8 and 10.1% respectively. In the construction and transport, storage communication sectors the gross value added per worker vntually stagnated."

However, the effect of globalization can not be undennined. Stating this, the Second National Commission on Labour further observed:

"At the same time globalisation has also had negative impacts on a variety of sectors of the Indian economy.

a. Except the IT, telecommunications and entertainment industry, all other traditional industries in India are facing problems. There is np demand for their products and they have had to face tough competition from imported products or products manufactured by MNCs in India.

b. As a result, a large number of such industries are downsizing and some have closed. This has resulted in VRS, retrenchment and closure of many units. A very large number of workers have lost their jobs.

c. Because of global competition and increasing number of mergers and acquisitions (M&A), Indian entrepreneurs have lost controlling interest in their enterprises and because of the general recessionary trends, one seems to be planning new projects, diversions and expansion. There seems to be some degree of pessimism about future prospects of the Indian economy

d. while internal demand is affected, exports too have been affected. They seem to have stagnated during the last few years. Thus imports are growing, without simultaneous increase in exports.

e. There is a general slow down of industrial activities, and Indian manufacturers have not perfonned well. The capital goods industry has been affected very badly and has registered a negative growth.

f. There is a general feeling that India does not enjoy any competitive advantage in manufacturing.

g. Small-scale industries are the worst affected. A large number of them are closed. No new investments are taking place in a big way in this sector.

h. The capital market is almost dead during the last three years and very few new issues have been launched.

i. Service industry is the only industry that is progressing and manufacturing and agriculture have taken back seats.

j. Though India has received foreign investments, the amount is too low as compared to the funds received by China. This is in spite of opening many economic activities for foreign investors. Much of these funds have come for portfolio investment and M&A activities. Proportionately very small amounts have reached India for Greenfield or brownfield investment.

k. A greater number of MNCs are delisting from stock exchanges, and converting into private companies.

l. The new economic policy has neglected the farm and small scale sectors with adverse consequences on the employment situation.

m. Employment is not growing and as a result unemployment is increasing in the country.

n. Participation in and the benefits of globalisation have so far been limited to a small segment of the educated and skilled population and some private sector entrepreneurs. However, the poverty level seems to have come down though income disparities have widened.

o. Even among the educated middle class, a very small section of persons engaged in IT, Telecommunication and entertainment industry are well placed while all others in the traditional industry are working under considerably uncertain circumstances.

p. Thus, jobs are being created only in very narrow fields such as information, communication and in certain informal sector using low technology. Other areas of economic activities, like traditional manufacturing, agricultural and non-farm activities and non-farm activities are not experiencing any increase in jobs. Globalisation led growth cannot be described as a job led growth.

q. Markets are now free, more goods are available, and prices are stable. But the poor are hurt because there is no opportunity for them to earn more income and therefore they have no means to benefit from the availability of goods.

It is also said: " The impact of globalization up to now has been to raise profits, strengthen the corporate and weaken the workforce. But in the new capitalist global order it is the super-rich elite groups, most of them investors in the Third World countries, which are the real beneficiaries. The system has not changed. Rather, it has become mote extreme through the growth of inequality.[14]

Thus, globalization of trade has very effective impact on the wages of the workers. MNCs offer better wage packages to the workers and there will be mobility of workers from one industry to another basing on their skill and wage packages. Nowadays, not the 'supply and demands' in the market is ruling the level of wages, but the 'supply and demand' of the skill of worker determining the wage level. Of course, this is not the rule universally applicable to all the industrial activities.

Social Security for Unorganized Workers in Globalization Era

Workers in the unorganized sector who constitute 93% of our workforce[15] have low earnings and poor working conditions and lack of social security execution it is being vitalized that refer is need for social security programmes, particularly for newtralising some of the negative consequences of the reforms. Besides the case for any sort of changes to labour laws can be strengthened if all workers have atleast a minimum of social security. The state has a role in helping the poor in times of insecurity and in ensuring minimum security for those unable to gain from the post-liberation economic growth process.

The term social security in the developing countries is used in a multi broader sense than in the developed countries,

Amalgams and Jean distinguish between two different aspects of social security protection and promotion. The protective type programmes such as old age pension, widow pension, and survivor benefits period a certain degree of support has so for relied on promotional measures such as self employment and wage employment programmes, general health and education.

There is however, overlapping between the two measures. For example, the national rural Employment guarantee scheme, which is one of the biggest social security progresses for unorganized sector workers, can come under promotional as well as protective measures. Although the coverage is not high, several state Governments have attempted to proved various protective social security measures for the unoraganised poor. Kerala and Tamil Nadu took the lead in proceeding social security. A social security system in the form of the National Social Assistance Programme (NSAP) was introduces in 1995. However, the coverage of the National and the State level programmers is not adequate.

The National Commission for Enterprises in the Unorganized Sector was set up by the UPA Government under the chairmanship of Arjun Sengupta, in September, 2004. The Commission prepared two draft bills.

i) Unorganized Sector Workers Social Security Bill, 2005 and

ii) Unorganized Sector Workers (Conditions of Work and Welfare Promotion) Bill, 2005.

As the name suggests, the first bill attempts to provide social security for the unorganized workers. It provides a model by demarcating clear responsibility of central and state Governments. According to the draft bill, it will cover all workers in the unorganized sector with a monthly income of Rs. 5,000 and below. This category includes self-employed workers (including marginal and small farmers) wage workers including agricultural laborers, and home based workers. It also includes informal workers under the organized sector. It is estimated that around 30 crore workers are eligible under this scheme.

The bill indicates that there will be as national minimum social security for all eligible workers covering four things.

i) Health insurance;

ii) Naturally benefits;

iii) Life insurance; and

iv) Old-age pension.

Every unorganized sector worker is eligible for registration. The registered worker will get a unique social security card. The existing welfare programmes will continue as before.

A national social security fund will be created. The scheme will be financed from the contributions at Rs 11/- a day by workers, employers (wherever identified), and the Government i.e., Rs. 36.5 per worker a day or Rs. 1,095 a month). The Government contribution will be divided between Central Government and state Government in the rate of 3:1 respectively (75 paise per worker by center, and 25 paise per workers by the state governments.)

Similar to the employment Guarantee scheme, the national commission estimated the costs of the minimum social security scheme, If all the 30 crore workers are covered, the constitutions would workout to Rs. 32,850 crore. The share of the central Government will be Rs. 17,548 crore and that of the State Govt. Rs.5,010 crore. This adds up to a total of Rs. 22,558 corre to be spent by Central and State Government, equal to 0.8% of the gross domestic product in 2004-05. If we include administrative and other expenses the Government contribution may not exceed 1% of GDP. Similar to the national EGS full coverage is expected to be reached in 5 years. If 6 crore workers are covered in the first year, it will be Rs. 4,612 crore and Rs. 22,558 crore from the fifth year. The Govt. can contribute to the fund in the form of grants or through tax or cess.

The draft bill also provides an organizational mechanism for implementing the scheme. The commission proposes to create a national security board, state level social security boards, and workers facilitation centers at the local level decided by the state boards.

The second bill, which deals with conditions of work and livelihood promotion, address the issues relating to providing and basic minimum standard on hours work, payment of minimum wages, bonded labour and child labour. The bill also recognizes some minimum entitlements of the workers such as the right to organize, non-discrimination in the payment of wages and conditions of work safety at workplace, and absence of sexual harassment.

The commission wants debate and discussion on the bills before they are introduced in parliament. There are several issuers that need to be discussed.

First, Financial implications have to be discussed. The commission has estimated only the likely amount of funds from the contributions. The costs of providing health insurance, maternity benefits, life insurance and old age pension for the 30 crore workers are not clear from the bill. The government contribution in the first year (Rs 4,512 crore) is not large but in the fifth year it is closer to 1 % of GDP. As the draft says, tax or cess is an option for raising resources for the government. The ambiguity on state Governments' contributions may create problems for the scheme as their finances are in bad shape.

Secondly, the bill seems to be following the targeting approach for identifying beneficiaries. For example, the bill says that it would cover all workers in the unorganized sector with a monthly income of Rs. 5,000/- and below thus may again lead to targeting errors and corruption.

Involving Panchayats

Thirdly, the implementation machinery still looks bureaucratic although decertratisation is mentioned. It in better to involve Panchagati raj institutions more:

Fourthly, legislation alone is not enough. For example, health insur4ance for all the workers will not help if there are no doctors and health infrastructure. Particularly in rural areas hence, spending has to increase at the grass roots level for better delivery systems.

Fifthly, the working of the present welfare boards for workers must be examined Kerala's experience shows that there are problems of sustainability, high cost, meager benefits etc. lesson should be learnt from these experience.

Sixthly the second bill on conditions of workers in equally important. Some regularly institutions are needed without ending up with inspector Raj. Minimum wages have to be fixed keeping in view the increasing needs of the poor. The law should be effectively implemented. Some estimates shows that even if the existing wages may not bring many workers above the poverty line. This is the main reason why we have so many "Workers Poor" in the country. The poor are working but at low wages. The main issue is how to improve the wage rates for the unorganized sector.

93% of the workers in the unorgansed sector do not have any social security in India. The employment guarantee scheme is considered one of the important components of social security for unskilled workers. Apart from these we need protective type social security such as old age pension, maternity benefits and health benefits. Also the conditions of workers in terms of number of hours and provision of minimum wages need attention. In this context, the two bills prepared by the National Commission are important. It should be an important concern of public policy to ensure that a certain minimum measure of social security in the unorganized sector is ensured. The major challenge is to extend social security to 300 million workers covering all states and all groups of workers. As India has no implemented protective social security schemes on a large scale, more debate and discussions are needed for better implementation.

Workers in the unorganized sector have low earnings and poor working conductions. In a liberalized economy the state have to ensure them minimum social security.

Labour-Management Relations in I.T. Sector

The issue before us is whether the Information Technology sector be included in the essential services while emphasizing that there could be no dilution of labour laws in it. They made it clear that labour laws should be implemented in these crucial sectors that need to have uninterrupted service.

There is a need to implement labour laws in the I.T. Sector, where the working conditions were like "a 19th century prison" and the employees working like "slaves". The issue was whether the sector should be treated at par with essential services such as water, power, milk and hospitals or treat as a money making service.[16]

The present tendency is labour laws are applied in the information technology sector. Now it is going phenomena that the I.T. Sector is major component in providing adequate employment in and around the globe. The right to form trade unions, collective bargaining and striking work should exist in the I.T. Sector and that the country's labour laws should be applicable to it. As for the nature of work and services in I.T. Sector was concerned, a comprehensive document would be prepared and placed before central committee for its approval.

The I.T. Sector is an all India issue and the right of trade unions and collective bargaining be ensured. Some vital services needed to be defined in the sector that had facets such as software, hardware and business products and outsourcing. There might be some IT enterprises provided services that could be taken out on the issue of strike the question arose when trade unions wanted to go for such an action.[17]

The trade unions are likely to take a common stand on the union government's move to amend labour laws to provide for contract labour in the I.T. Sector. The proposed changes to the labour laws would have far reaching impact on millions of workers. The changes would make hire and fire easier; retrenchment of employees and closure of industries less cumbersome; and loosen the government control of industries. The union labour industry wants to move the critical amendments to the labour laws with a view to bringing in flexibility to the labour market regulation and thus help India meet the commitments under W.T.O. The multinational firms may therefore, hesitate to invest because of the strict labour laws that do not allow hire and fire. It is therefore argued that relaxing the labour laws would increase job opportunities which may not be helpful to synchronise the disputes between the employers and the employees.[18]

New Labour Laws Needed to meet the Challenges of Globalization

More flexible regime will create more jobs. Making out a strong case for pushing forward labour reforms, Prime Minister Manmohan Singh said the process of doing business with India was to be made "less intimidating, "less cumbersome and less bureaucratic to attract more investment". A more flexible and transparent regime of laws, including labour laws, would contribute to increased employment and, therefore, appropriate legislation were in the interest of labour.[19]

Calling upon industry and labour to work together in removing hurdles to faster economic growth, the Prime Minister said the physical barriers to growth and employment creation were easier to deal with than those created by policies that had outlived their original purpose.

"Many of these are legacies of the past that have no longer much relevance today. Indeed, some of them have become counter productive and may well be hurting the very people they are meant to benefit", he said.

Dr. Singh said the country needed new laws for new times. Laws which provided safety standards catered for the basic needs of workers, took care of their welfare and were flexible enough to create rather than destroy jobs.

"It should be possible for us to sustain growth rates of close to 8-10 per cent for several years provided several impediments to new investment are removed so that we can accelerate the growth process and generate more employment.[20]"

The European Parliament's vote to scrap the opt-out clause from the law that regulates working time is a welcome step towards universalising labour standards across the European Union. Conversely, insistence by Britain's Labour Government on retaining the exemption is nothing but an attempt to legislate

Thatcherite legacy as the norm for the rest of Europe. The European Commission, a body comprising non-elected bureaucrats that favours retention of the opt-out provision, should weigh the adverse implications of such a stance for an enlarged EU and its international negotiating clout. The 1993 Working Time Directive caps working hours for employees other than managerial and executive cadres at 48 per week. Britain, then under a Conservative government, negotiated an opt-out, arguing that the decision to put in long hours should be a matter of individual choice. Germany, France, and Spain obtained relief from the directive for the health sector after the European Court of Justice ruled that the hours employees were on call should be deemed working time even if they did not discharge regular duties. The European Parliament has proposed phasing out the exemption over a three-year span. The decision has been criticized by British business and industry lobbies as a regressive step that would affect competitiveness of the economy and increase unemployment. Trade unions have welcomed the move, saying long hours endanger the health and safety of employees, affect the balance between family and work, and reduce productivity. Significantly, 18 of the 19 members of Prime Minister Tony Blair's party in the European Parliament have backed the withdrawal - in defiance of the British government's wish to continue with the exemption.

The rationale behind the Working Time Directive should be obvious in the context of the growing pressures on industry to cut cost and stay competitive in the global arena. The measure is an important safeguard to ensure that the basic human needs of the working class for leisure and cultural development are protected by statute since it will not be able to earn enough fully to offset the negative consequences of overwork. Moreover, the elimination of unfair trade practices, including the exploitation of cheap labour in developing countries, has been at the top of multilateral negotiations. Western industrialised countries have been strongly advocating the universalisation of labour standards but with limited success. Enforcement of labour regulations globally will help contain unfair competition through sweat labour and at the same time improve the overall quality of life for millions of working people. The European Union's moral credibility to press for such universalisation will be eroded if it countenances in its own jurisdiction measures incompatible with this objective. The current drive to evolve a common labour regime across Europe must succeed.[21]

Challenges Ahead

The country was now facing new challenges in the backdrop of globalization. "Improvement and changes in technology and industry and their application in business enterprises do not wait for you. Your competition is already implementing these and creating new products with better efficiency and better price structure, which undercuts your market share and market viability. It is now estimated that 80 per cent of what we would be using in daily life seven years from now has not been invented yet. Combine this galloping technology with the on-going globalization and it becomes very clear that no business, institution or individual can stand still or depend on the laurels of the past."[22]

Fittest to Survive

Making it clear that only the fittest will survive in the fast changing world. Each worker, institution or business had to re-train, re-educate and re-evaluate the situation everyday. The new era of globalization was posing new challenges for educationists, particularly for institutions of higher learning.

India was being looked at by all the developed countries as a hub to develop technologies. Many were coming forward to establish high technological industries, research institutes so that they can take advantage of the workforce intelligent at low wages compared to their man power, professionals with inherent innovative nature. Indians were considered more intelligent, this was the reason why Indian engineers were preferred in information technology field by the UK and the US.[23]

Base for Social Security in India Even in Globalization Era

The concept of social security is dynamic.

The three contributory production are:

1. Capital

2. Management and

3. Labour.[24]

Labour is the investment of the "Working class for the development and growth of any nation. Hence, adequate social security is the well deserved social night of every worker and his family.

Industrial democracy is the functional ideology of a social democracy. The employer – employees participation with shared responsibility and shared rights, externally controlled by the state, which represents the society is the corner stone of the institutional organization and arrangement in social democracies for the production process.

Social insurance to guarantee social protection to the working class, is a basic necessity for societal survival, justified both in theory and practice.

If the worker is cared and his capacities are channelised for productive issue, the society is truly benefited. If he is uncared and his capacities distilised he becomes socially a liability.

Everyone contributes for the whole and whole society provide for each one; Therefore, to provide for the adequate security of one and all, each individual and family is the functional duty and responsibility of every state and government in its sovereign capacity. Hence comprehensive social security becomes a social policy for a democratic government.

A government is justifiably entitled in exercise its coercive force through appropriate means and measures to obligate the society to share the responsibility to practical sufficient and social security, to all its citizens, more particularly the working class.

The whole system of social security must be designed in a manner that not only everyone is able to maintain a minimum standard of living and does not follow below that minimum but would also help to bridge the gap on economic inequality and remove social disability.

Thus to ensure a sound social system of an egalitarian society, a social security system is needed even in Globalization era.

REFERENCES

1. Venkata Ratnam, C.S., *Globalization and Labour Management Relations–Dynamics of Change*, Response Books, New Delhi, 2001.
2. *Times of India*, February 27, 2002.
3. *The Hindu*, March 1, 2002.
4. *Business World*, March 11, 2002.
5. C.S. Venkata Ratnam, *IJIR*, Vol. 37 No. 4, April 2002.
6. Triska, Dusan., "Privatization: Czecholovakia". *East European Economics*, Fall. Vol. 30(1) pp. 22-27, 1991.
7. Lipton, David and Jeffrey Sachs., "Privatisation in Eastern Europe: The case of Poland". In Vittorio Corbo et al. (Eds). "Reforming Central and Eastern European Economies: Intial Results and Challenges ". World Bank : Washington, D.C, 1991.
8. Bishop, M. and Kay.J., *Does Privatisation Work: Lessons from the U.K.*", London Business School, London, 1988.
9. Venkata Ratnam, C.S., - *Social and Labour issues in Privatization – An Overview*, IJIR, Vol.28 No. 2, Oct 1992.
10. ILO/UNDP., "Privatisation: Its Impact on Labour Relations in ASEAN." ILO: Geneva. ILO. *Social and Labour Bulletin* (various issues)
11. Vulsteke, 1988, Vol.1, pp. 169-72
12. TUC (U.K.), *Bargaining in Privatised Companies*. TUC: London, February, 1986.
13. Colling, T., "Priavatisation and the Management of I.R. in Electricity Distribution". *Industrial Relations Journal,* (Oxford), Vol. 22 (2) summer, pp. 117-129, 1991.
14. *Ibid.*
15. Mahendradev, S., Director, Centre for Economic and Social Studies, Hyderabad, 2005.

16. Uphold labour laws in I.T. Sector CPI (M)-Reported in *Hindu* dt: 26-10-2005.
17. "I.T. Sector should come under labour laws, says CPI (M)-Reported in *Hindu* dt: 27-10-2005.
18. Unions opposed contract labour in I.T. Sector-Reported in *Hindu* dt: 28-10-2005.
19. At the inauguration of the 40th session of the *Indian Labour Conference* (ILC)
20. Aarth Dhar, More flexible regime, will create more jobs – reported in *Hindu*, Dated, 11-01-05
21. For common Labour standards – reported in *Hindu* Dated 28-05-2005
22. *Ibid.*
23. Globalization throws New Challenges – reported in *Hindu*, dated 17-12-05.
24. Srivatsav, S.C. *Social Security & Labour Laws*, 2005.

5

INDUSTRIAL ADMINISTRATION AND ADJUDICATION

From the late sixties onwards, the problem of unemployment and poverty was gradually assuming alarming proportions in India for several reasons. Agricultural growth rate continued to be poor; industrial sector, after exhibiting some buoyancy up to the mid-sixties, had started recording slower growth rates; mobilization of resource for development plans became so difficult that Fourth Five Year Plan had to be postponed; some signs of political instability (although temporary) appeared during this period and, to make things worse there was a severe drought in 1967, baring the weaknesses of country's fragile food security arrangements. All these meant such a deepening of the problem of unemployment and poverty that it shattered the hopes of the nation, air of optimism gave way to an atmosphere of agony and, consequently, the exercises in planning was replaced by the management of crisis. A number of addresses from mid-sixties onwards on the forum of the society were all addressed to these fundamental problem and, on reading those notes, one can easily infer that the professional economists have shared the agony of the people as much as they had shared their hopes during the early years after independence.[1]

Industrial Relations Scenario

The conflict between labour and capital is so fundamental that it can never be ignored and it is impossible to think of a situation where industrial growth occurs in the absence of an institutional and effective mechanism through which conflict in interests of the two parties are balanced. Exceptions to this statement can be found only in history, of nearly two centuries back, when industrial revolution had just started in Europe but the notion of democratic principles was yet to be crystallized. In the recent history, it would be very difficult to find a country situation where democratic values have been completely ignored and the authoritarian state has suppressed the conflict by ruthless laws and physical force. Fortunately, for whatever historical reasons, the democratic values had taken firm roots in Indian polity even before independence and thus the role of industrial relations in promoting industrial growth and attaining other objectives of planned development was vital. For historical reasons again, formal trade unionism in India was nearly three decades old at the time of independence and the urgency of the task of evolving a suitable framework for industrial relations in independent India was felt very early. It is thus not unusual that nearly one-third of the Presidential addresses included in this volume are concerned with problem of industrial relations and other related issues.[2]

Trade Unions and Industrial Relations

In the very inaugural conference at Lucknow, Shri V.V. Giri (1958) had devoted most of his Presidential address to discuss industrial relations and trade unionism in India. With his vast personal experience in the field, he was quite aware that "industrial" peace does not merely signify the absence of industrial unrest, but the active presence of harmonious and good industrial relations generating amity and goodwill between the partners in an industry." Such being his perception, it was only expected that he would be averse to the arrangement of arbitration (by the state machinery) in any collective bargaining and would insist on an internal settlement, except on very special circumstances. But unfortunately the statutory provision on compulsory arbitration prevents such an internal settlement, instead of acting as a safeguard against bypassing the process of collective bargaining. However, far more than the legal and administrative provisions, the most important factor standing in the way of improving the industrial relations in India has been the absence of any trust between the trade union and the employer. One of the ways to build that missing trust was to involve the workers in the affairs of the industry through workers' participation in management.

Shri V.V. Giri (1959) in his second Presidential address discussed the prospects of such participation programme in India and specified two main hurdles against the programme- the basic weakness of the trade unions in India in terms of workers' disunity and the employers' indifference. His hope that these difficulties would gradually disappear was, however, belied as would appear from the fate of the programme even there decades later.

Although industrial relation concern mainly two parties, trade unions and employers, it cannot function in isolation from its political, economic and social environment. It is thus only desirable that an evaluation of the industrial relation policies in India is done in the overall context of Indian society and Professor G.P. Sinha (1979 and 1980) attempts the task in his two Presidential addresses in successive years. In his first oration, he characterizes the crisis in industrial relations in India, not in terms of an irresponsible trade union or rigid attitudes of employers, but as a consequence of the industrial relations policy trying to serve simultaneously many contradictory goals, e.g., technological change and progress but no resistance form the workers, economic stability with the freedom of labour and capital to set wages and prices, industrial democracy, i.e. increasing workers' control over management of enterprise without requiring the workers to bear the risks, and the like. Obviously this is too demanding a situation where scope for behavior modification of the trade unions is extremely limited. A supplementary factor behind the existing crisis in industrial relations in India is the dated perception, particularly of the employers, that the only contribution that healthy relations can make is to avoid stoppage of production process. The associated benefit of improving the production process through higher productivity is generally not thought about by the employers and, to that extent, there is also scope for behavior modification of the employers towards promoting healthy industrial relations.

In most of the discussions on industrial relations, the focus is generally on the work stoppages caused by strikes and the role of trade unions on causing them. Rather surprisingly, the equally disturbing phenomenon of lockouts is overlooked. Professor Rudder Datt (1991) tried to remove this particular gap in the study of industrial relations by analyzing the trend of lockouts in India over the last three decades. In the later half of this period, he observed, the intensity of lookouts has much increased vis-à-vis strikes and the phenomenon is particularly severe in West Bengal. Although economic reasons like industrial sickness were there, one can also notice the emergence of new types of employer militancy during this period, causing those upward trend in lockouts. He, therefore, pleaded for more effective government interventions in this regard "by strengthening the legal framework so as to prevent the malafide action of the employers."

Workers' Participation in Management (WPM)

Planners in India were quite aware about the utmost necessity of establishing industrial democracy as prerequisite for industrial growth. The formal expression of that awareness was embodied in Second Five Year Plan document and since then a number of measures were taken to provide and institutional base for the emergence and growth of industrial democracy in the country. Some of these measures were regulatory in nature in the form of legislations on industrial relations and related issues. In contrast, the ambitious scheme of Workers' Participation in Management was a promotive measure which aimed at 'transforming the attitude of both employers and workers for establishing a cooperative culture which may help in building strong self-confident and self-reliant country with a stable industrial base'. As the concept was new, its operational character had to be evolved over some stages of experimentation, since its beginning in late fifties as a non-statutory schemed. However, up to the mid seventies, the scheme was generally treated with difference by both the workers and employers. Thereafter, some of the enterprises have made efforts to run the scheme and, during the eighties, several economists have tried to evaluate its functioning and suggest ways to improve it. One of the most persistent suggestions arising out of such evaluative exercises is to lend further strength to this scheme by incorporating employee ownership as part of Workers' Participation in Management and Professor D. N. Najundappa (1990) argues for the same strategy after making an exhaustive analysis of the scheme, taking into account its legislative base and working, experience, particularly since mid-seventies. Although specific details about working of the scheme relate to a single case study, the overall working experience suggests that employee-ownership has generally been resorted to when the companies were in red, perhaps to minimize the loss of the private owners, and to evoke sympathy by advancing the case of labour who would be thrown out of employment if the company closes its doors. But even under such trying circumstances, when the labour opts for owing the industry, they do so with a full sense of responsibility and are prepared to make temporary sacrifices in wages in return for expected higher benefits later on. Obviously such display of sense of responsibility by the workers is more related to their joint ownership than to the fact that it is a crisis situation and it thus strongly indicates the positive results that both employers and workers can obtain if employee-ownership is allowed under normal circumstances.

A second pleading for employee-ownership as an effective strategy of workers' participation in management is made by Professor V.M. Dandekar (1989) along with discussing some important financial implications of the scheme in fair details. He also deplores the tendency that employee-ownership has generally introduced till now as a lost resort to prevent plant closures; but, based on the successful experience of the scheme in United States and Britain (not in Western Europe, though), he considers the scheme worth pursuing in India. As regards the financial arrangement, he proposes the utilization of Employee Provident Fund for employee-ownership scheme. Using the data of 500 plus large public limited companies in India, he shows that such funds can cover the entire share of those companies and, thus, necessary funds for the scheme is already there. In view of the fact that the income level of the workers in organized sector is not very low, and they may not be entirely averse to take some risk, employee-ownership scheme may get accepted in near future, causing a new role for employers, workers and trade unions.

Labour problems are of a dynamic character and change in nature and scope from generation to generation. Their growing complexity baffles not only laymen, but the technicians as well. A proper appreciation of these questions will no doubt usher industrial peace and result in economic advancement; and this objective can be facilitated better through a non-political, non-partisan institution, mainly devoted to promote and impartial investigation and study of the subject.

A major prerequisite for industrial progress is the prevalence of industrial peace - a suitable climate in which the industries can thrive. Industrial peace does not merely signify the absence of industrial unrest, but the active presence of harmonious and good industrial relations generating amity and goodwill between the partners in an industry. Good industrial relations, therefore, is indispensable for the successful industrialization of any country.

The need for an effective labour policy to bring about good industrial relations began to assume a definite shape only during World War II. There were, of course, earlier measures "to settle trade disputes. The Trade Disputes Act, 1929, modelled on the British lines, provided Courts of Enquiry and Boards of Conciliation. The Act, if properly implemented in its true spirit, would have served the cause of industrial peace as it did in the U.K. Its failure is entirely due to the non-implementation, in the proper way, of this legislation by the former bureaucratic Governments, which always tried to emphasize on the preservation of law and order more than their desire to settle trade disputes.

During the War period, the Government, in their anxiety to maintain War production, introduced the Defence of India Rule, 81-IA. This Rule prohibited strikes and lockouts and provided compulsory adjudication and compulsory conciliation machinery for the speedy disposal of cases. Such measures had in mind interests other than the establishment or maintenance of good industrial relations. Similar rules were adopted in the U.K. and the U.S.A. also; and it was an inevitable measure during War emergency. In these countries, the workers as well as employers and governments realized that this compulsory method has done its part and further continuation would be more a hindrance rather than a help in establishing industrial peace and good industrial relations. But in India, unfortunately, compulsory arbitration has not only been continued, but a greater emphasis has come to be laid on this machinery than on mutual negotiations or voluntary conciliation.

Everyone agrees that internal settlement, preferably mutual agreement, is the best method of solving differences between the employers and the workers. But, at the same time, some of my trade union friends would like to have compulsory adjudication to remain in the picture as a last resort. So long as compulsory adjudication forms part of the statute book, the employers and workers will hesitate to put their cards on the table and they would give secondary importance to collective bargaining and voluntary conciliation.

It is also important to note that when the workers find that there is an external machinery, which has the final voice in settling a dispute, such as adjudication, they do not have an urge either to strengthen or to place their entire confidence in their trade union organizations, which alone should possess sanctions behind their reasonable demands.

Compulsory arbitration stands as a policeman watching out for signs of discontent, and at the slightest provocation, takes the parties to the Court for a dose of costly and not wholly satisfying justice. The moment the back of the policeman is turned, the parties grow red in face with redoubled determination and the whole cycle of litigation starts all over again, with the proverbial legal delays and continued rancor and bitterness.

It is, therefore, high time that a basic policy with reference to the settlement of disputes must be evolved. The policy of internal settlement - of course with sufficient safeguards, restoring to the parties their self-confidence and inculcating in them a spirit of self government - should be the basis. As aides and safeguards, I would advise, firstly, that the workers and employers should have strong organizations which could effectively speak on their behalf and deliver goods to either side. Further, a Joint Standing Machinery at all levels must be provided in individual factories and in respective industries which should, from time to time, discuss all matters relating to production, welfare and each side trying to understand the views and aspirations of the other. Conciliation Boards and Courts of Enquiry should always be at the disposal of the Government to bring the parties together for settling any issues that may arise. The tripartite and bipartite machinery of Governments, both at the Centre and in the States, must be strengthened and should not be merely ad hoc, but a permanent staff of experts, with a thorough knowledge of the technique of different industries, must be available to the parties for settlement of an actual or apprehended dispute. Lastly, an Industrial Court, on the lines of the British Industrial Courts Act of 1919, be constituted which would effectively advise parties if all other methods of settlement through the machinery indicated above had failed. If this system is persisted and acted upon, the decisions of these Courts, though they may not be statutory in character, can carry successfully the public opinion behind them. Traditions and conventions must be gradually built wherein the parties would accept the decision of such Court as just and practicable. There would naturally be a tendency to accept the conclusions and close the dispute, as otherwise the parties that persist in carrying it on will not have a leg to stand upon.[3]

In the absence of an adjudication machinery in cases of emergency when a situation arises which causes prolonged and serious hardship to the community or threatens some other grave and irremediable consequences, such as complete breakdown of the industry itself, causing widespread unemployment? Emergencies have to be met by emergent measures; even to the extent of invoking ordinances in case where Legislatures are not in session; and appoint, in exceptional circumstances, after hearing the parties involved, tribunal to adjudicate an industrial dispute of a grave nature. But the ordinary industrial law of the land need not provide for such emergency legislation, if the ordinary machinery designed for industrial peace is to produce proper and abiding results. Nothing is lost if this view is accepted and acted upon even as a measure of 'trial and error' for a short time. Keeping interesting in view, it is necessary to evolve a practical solution to the problem of industrial relations, so necessary if India has to find its due place among the big industrial nations of the world.

Tripartite Labour Machinery

In one respect we have borrowed a model from the I.L.O. The I.L.O. has accepted three principal parties for what is called the Tripartite Labour Machinery; its Governing Body, the Central conference and the Industrial and Advisory Committee. In all these bodies, they have representatives of Government, Employers and Workers. The principle of the representation of those three parties in connection with labour problems was endorsed by the Royal Commission of Labour in India (1929-31), which recommended the creation of an Industrial Council consisting of representatives of the three parties.

This was brought home, when the 1935 Act made 'Labour' as a concurrent subject, thereby emphasizing the need to establish some central machinery for coordination of policy. The first Indian Labour Conference, on the tripartite principle, was convened in 1942 with the following main aims and objects.

(i) the promotion of uniformity in labour legislation

(ii) the laying down of a procedure for the settlement of industrial disputes; and

(iii) the discussion of all mattes of all India importance as between employers and employees.[4]

The Triple Pillars of Industrial Socialism

The three pillars of industrial socialism are: (i) an integrated fair wage and bonus policy no longer left to the whims and caprices of the Industrial Courts or adjudicators but springing from voluntary Wage Councils at different levels; (ii) collective bargaining, and (iii) worker participation in management, passing over into profit-sharing. Voluntary collective bargaining is seriously jeopardised today by the State assuming larger and larger responsibility for major wage, industrial peace and welfare decisions. Compulsory arbitration of industrial disputes, in particular, saps the foundations of collective bargaining and the development of self-organization among the working class. As Sri V.V. Giri remarks: 'The spirit of self-confidence and self-reliance, engendered by healthy bargaining has given place to the habit of importunity and litigation. That is bad enough, but what is worse is the deplorable effect that this dependence on a third party has brought about in the outlook and attitude of the parties towards each other. An attitude of suppressed hostility in one party and of unconcealed satisfaction and triumph in the other may lead to transient truce, but not lasting peace.[5]

Labour Administration

There is no reason to think that the maintenance of good industrial relations which is the responsibility of the ministry of the labour is less important than the responsibility that any other ministry holds. The reasons for the same may be the ministry has to take welfare of labour and a paternalistic attitude and the fact that the performance of the ministry is not quantifiable.

Labour administration means public administration activities to translate the labour policy into action. India has ratified a total of 39 conventions adopted at different sessions of the I.L.O. These include conventions on hours of work, unemployment, night work, minimum wage, weakly rest, worker's compensation, forced labour, labour inspection, child labour, underground work, and equal remuneration for men and women for a work of a similar nature. The labour administration in India is mostly rooted in labour laws. There are only a few activities that are not based on laws. They are mostly in the field of workers' education and craftsmen training other than apprenticeship training etc.

The chief labour commissioner's organization has the responsibility to enforce the Industrial Disputes Act, 1948, The Payment of Wages Act, 1936 and rules in respect of mines, Railways and transport services, the Maximum Wages Act, 1948, the contract labour (Regulation and Abolition) Act, 1976, the interstate migrant Workmen (RE & CS) Act, 1979, Payment of

Bonus Act, 1965, Child Labour (Prohibition & Regulation) Act, 1986, Payment of Gratuity Act, 1972, Labour Laws exemption from furnishing and maintaining registers by Certain Establishments Act, 1988, Building and other Construction Workers (RE & CS) Act, 1996, chapter VI(A) of the Indian Railways Act and Hours of Employment Regulations for Railway Employees, Industrial Employment (Standing Orders) Act, 1946, and the Maternity Benefit Act, 1961 (Mines and Circus Rules, 1963) for organizations where the Central government is the appropriate government. The Central Provident Fund commissioner enforces the Employee Provident Fund Act. The Director General of Employees State Insurance Corporation enforces the ESI Act.

The organization of Chief Commissioner (Central) is responsible for prevention and settlement of Industrial Disputes in the Central spheres, enforcement of awards and settlements in the central sphere, and administration and enforcement of the labour laws such as prosecution, claim cases, quasi-judicial functions etc.

The chief inspector of labour is required to file a claim first before the payment of wages authority or minimum wages authority respectively the Payment of Wages Act and the Minimum Wages Act.

Presently the Minimum Wages Act applies only to scheduled employments and as such the same cannot be enforced in non-scheduled employments and therefore it should have to be amended to entry at "Other employments not covered in the schedule" or all schedules are given up. There is a popular perception that the process of conciliation is not effective in dissolving industrial disputes. This perception is only partially correct as the record of conciliation efforts by the central industrial relations machinery shows conciliation has not been as effective in the case of rights disputes, as in the case of interest disputes. The rights disputes over dismissal, denial of regularization from, promotion etc; conciliation should be optional. The party should have the right to approach labour courts and the labour relations commissions straight away.

Industrial disputes not settled in conciliation should go for either voluntary arbitration or by arbitrators maintained by the labour relations commission or adjudication. In the case of essential services like health and sanitation, transport, power and water supply, etc. The disputes should go for compulsory arbitration. The arbitrator should be chosen from eminent persons in industry conciliators, trade unionists and labour judiciary. Labour adjudication in the central sphere as all along been based on adhoc arrangement. Industrial tribunal/labour courts are also not empower either to issue decrease or to initiate contempt proceedings to enforce their awards. The only course available under law to secure implementation of awards/ settlements is prosecution under sec 29 of the I.D. Act by the officers of the Central industrial relations machinery or the state labour departments. As the officers or establishments like the CPWD, defense, department of telecom, archeological survey of India and railways enjoy protection against prosecution U/S 197 of the Cr.P.C.; permission of the employing ministry is necessary to prosecute them. This permission from the employing ministry U/S 197 of Cr.P.C. is seldom granted. The recommendation of the labour commission, in this regarding that all employing ministries be advised to implement awards/sanction prosecution with in one month of the matter being referred to them. Failing which it should be deemed that the sanction has been given. The remedy in the existing law is for the enforcement authority to launch persecution U/S 29 of I.D. Act. This remedy has not proved effectively in which consumes time at every step. If does not empower the courts to ensure the implementation of awards. The implementation of awards of labour courts and industrial tribunals has become as major problem that paralyzes the effectiveness of the Disputes Resolution Machinery and thwarts the basic intentions of the I.D. Act. In the process, the employer management obtains a stay order from the High court concerned and the awards remained suspended till the High Court decides the case or vacates stay order. In 70-80% of writ petition cases employer/management does not get success and the award is upheld but the decision of the High Court comes after 3-5 years and some times of more than a decade. Most of the awards in which employers/ management challenge relate to the regularization, reinstatement backwages etc of large number of workers. And in many times awards in respect of individual workers too or being challenged. After 10 or 15 years, when the employer/Management losses in every court, it is often that the concerned worker has disappeared from the scene. The management involves S.19(6) of the I.D. Act and terminates awards in a clandestine and perfunctionary manner. Otherwise, even though this action of the management is not in conformity with the statutory provision. An award can be terminated U/S 19 (6) of the I.D. Act, of it satisfies the condition that it has been inoperation for a period of 1 years as provided Sec 19 (3).

Here it is necessary to findout that the Hon'ble Supreme Court had directed the government of India to set up a committee consisting of representatives of the ministry of the industry the bereau of public enterprises and the ministry of laws to monitor disputes between ministries and PSUs to ensure that no litigation went to the court or tribunal with out the matter being examined and cleared by the committee for litigation.[6]

The Hon'ble Supreme Court further directed to that every court and every tribunal where such a dispute is raised should first demand a clearance from the committee and in the absence of the clearance, refuse to take further proceedings. The intention of the apex court order is clearly to prevent litigation between department and the agencies of the government.

The National Commission on Labour rightly speaks that if the existing unethical system of continuous denial of Justice is not changed, the workers would loss faith in the law, labour administration and in the labour judiciary. The remedy is essential that the awards is implemented immediately and the payment to the worker should be started on the basis of last salary drawn. This principle would however apply to workers both in the private and public sector organizations. Normally public sector organization wish to prefer appeal against the orders of the labour courts, they should obtain permission of a screening committee to be setup by the appropriate government. It would go alongway in providing relief to the workers if the above recommendation is accepted and the necessity of the disputes of provisions provided in the I.D. Act would never arise.[7]

There should be legislative backup for the simplification of law and procedures through uniform definitions of "appropriate government", "Workmen" / "employee", "employer" etc; enabling provisions to cover all employments especially in unorganized sector under the minimum wages Act. The existing labour laws should have to be five or more groups pertaining to

1. Industrial relation.
2. Wages
3. Social security
4. Safety and
5. Welfare and working conditions etc.

It is also necessary to reduce the number of registers to be maintained and the returns to be submitted. The charges due to globalization, liberalization and privatization and market driven economy require that Indian industry should be competitive both in quality and cost. The voluntary resolution of disputes should be encouraged over the legislative approach of settlement of disputes through adjudication. There should be a legislative framework for voluntary dispute settlement. It is very difficult for the employer to deal separately with multiple unions having different ideologies. If there is a system of recognition of a negotiating agency the employer can negotiate with the recognized negotiating agent or negotiating council.

There must be end to the adhocism in the appointment of presiding officers to the industrial tribunals and there must be a regular cadre of labour adjudicators drawn from experienced Judges and conciliators to improve the quality of adjudication as well as to improve prospects of their professional advancement.

The labour is concurrent subject according to the Indian constitution. There are number of industrial, agricultural and service enterprises in the country. There are differences in priorities in the problems that demand attention. In such circumstances, policies can be evolved and some degree of uniformity in directions and programmes achieved only through frequent and meaningful consultations at high level. Therefore the Indian labour conference is necessary because it is only the high level tripartite forum that exists in India. There is no reason to hold that the workers in the unorganized sector need not be represented at the Indian labour conference forum. The Indian labour conference may look into the following aspects.

(i) To review the labour situation in the country.

(ii) To consider the conventions and recommendations of I.L.O. for adoption.

(iii) To consider legislative proposals of the central government that are referred to it before or after being moved in the parliament.

(iv) To provide a forum for consultation and hearing of complaints regarding the violation of the rights of the labour.

(v) To review the implementation of the programmes drawn up by the central government for the benefit of the labour.

(vi) To coordinate the conclusions and recommendations of standing labour committee.

(vii) To review implementation of its own recommendations.

The standing labour committee should prepare the agenda of the conference and there must be a director general of Indian Labour Conference and the functions should be as follows.

(i) For collection and distribution of information relating to condition of work and life of the labour.

(ii) For examination of the subjects which are proposed to be brought before the standing committee and the conference.

(iii) For preparation of documents on the various items of the agenda for the meeting of the standing committee and the conference.

(iv) For editing the issuing publications in English, Hindi and also the regional languages is dealing with problems of labour.

A tripartite National and state level councils of employment should be set up to monitor and plan problems related to employment such as:

(i) The development and adoption of a employment policy designed to promote full productive and freely chosen employment.

(ii) Co-ordination between employment policy and the overall economic and social policy and development programmes.

(iii) Assessment of the incidence of unemployment and under employment

(iv) Promotion of overseas employment

(v) Development of short term/temporary employment programmes.

(vi) Employment market analysis and man power planning.

(vii) Prevention of discrimination, in employment.

(viii) Monitoring the status of women workers and related matters.[8]

The laws on safety in India for industrial workmen precede the constitution and under the Indian Factories Act, 1981, the District magistrate was designated as the Enforcing agent for safety. Factory inspectors were appointed as early as 1911 even though the factories Act in the present form came into being only in 1948. There are number of laws for the safety of industrial and commercial organizations.

(i) The Factories Act, 1948

(ii) The Indian Explosive Act, 1884

(iii) The Petroleum Act, 1934

(iv) Inflammable Substances Act, 1952.

(v) The Insecticides Act, 1968.

(vi) The Indian Electricity Act, 1910.

(vii) The Indian Boilers Act, 1923.

(viii) The Environment (Protection) Act, 1986.

(ix) The Public Liability Insurance Act, 1991.

(x) The Dangerous Machines (Regulation) Act, 1983.

(xi) The Atomic Energy Act, 1962.

(xii) Building and Other Construction Workers (Regulation of Employment and Conditions of Services as) Act, 1996.

(xiii) Fatal Accidents Act, 1985.

(xiv) Dock Workers (Safety, Health and Welfare) Act, 1986.

(xv) Shops and Establishment Acts of Various States.

(xvi) Plantation Labour Act, 1951.

(xvii) Mines Act, 1952.

Even when we observe the laws, we often do so to avoid getting into trouble with the law, not because we feel that observing laws of safety is a duty we owe to ourselves and other around as. It is perhaps this attitude which was responsible for the holocaust at Bhopal in the right of 2/3 December, 1984. Bhopal, the capital of Madhya Pradesh had a population of 8 lakhs at the time of the accident.

The constitution of India has the bestowed the onus of exploitation and management of mineral resources with the central government and the state Governments. The Industrial Policy Resolution 1956 and the Mines and Mineral (Regulation, Development) Act, 1957 broadly laid down the frame work for the regulation and development of all minerals other than petroleum and Natural Gas the Mining Concession Rules, 1960, regulates the grant of prospecting licenses and mining leases of all minerals other than atomic and minor minerals. The director general of Mines safety (DGMS) under union ministry of labour and apart from administering the mines Act and its subordinate legislation the DGMS also administers other allied laws in respective of mines. The Mines Act, 1952 Coal Mines Regulations, 1957, Oil Mines Regulations, 1984, Mines Rules,

1955 Mines Vocational Trainees Rules 1956 Mines Rescue Rules, 1985, Coalmines Pit Head both rules 1959, and Indian electricity rules 1966 and adding to that there allied legislations in the following way.

1. Factories Act, 1948 Chapter III and Chapter IV
2. Manufacture Storage and Import of Hazards Chemicals Rules 1984 under Environmental Protection Act, 1986.
3. Land Acquisition (Mines) Act, 1985 and the Coal Mines (Conservation and Development) Act, 1974.[9]

The National Labour policy formulated during the 6th plan stated that the working conditions include not only wage structure fixing of minimum wage and protection of income, periods of rest, paid holidays, provision of canteen facility and provision of cretches for children.

As regards the workers participation management in India, the royal commission on labour 1929-31 said as i.e. "we believe that if these committees (works committees) are given proper encouragement and the post errors are avoided they can play a useful role in the Indian industrial system." These recommendation could, however be translated into law only in 1947. The functions that the ID Act, 1947 visualised for the works committees to promote measures for securing and preserving amity and good relations between employer and employees, to that and comment upon matters of common interest or concern and to endeavour to compose any material difference of opinion between the employer and employee.[10]

The Indian Labour Conference in its 17th session held in 1959 discussed the function of the works committees and approved of list of functions which could be assigned to the work committees and a list of function which could not be assigned to the works committees.

In 1975, the government of India formulated a scheme of workers participation in industry at shop floor plant level. In 1977, the government of India introduced another scheme for workers participation. The scheme of workers participation in management was meant for commercial and service organizations having large scale public dealings such as Hospitals, post and telegraphs, railway stations, booking offices, government provident fund and pensions organisitions, road Transportation and Electricity boards, insurance institutions like FCI and Central Warehousing Corporations public distribution system including fair-price shops super bazars, all financial institutions Air and Water transport ports and docks and handlooms and handicrafts export corporations, Municipal Services Corporations, Milk distribution Services, irrigation systems, tourist organization, public hotels and Restaurants and establishment for public amusements etc.

Apart from that, tripartite committee on workers participation is summrised as:

1. The scheme of workers participation in Management should be such as could involve all interest groups in undertaking. It should provide for freeflow of basic information to inculcate responsible responses.
2. Training of workers and managerial personnel in the art of participative management.
3. The objective of any scheme of workers participation should be to develop industrial efficiency, create a sense of involvement in the work process and generate a sense of discipline, democratise decision making process, and foster closure relationship between workers and management.
4. The scheme of workers participation should be such as could create a society which ensured social justice.
5. The trade unions had a very important role to play in protecting and furthering the rights and economic interests of the workers.
6. There should not be any distinction between the public, private and co-operative sectors and adoption of three tier system of participation at corporate level, plant level and shop floor level.
7. Shop floor level issues having commonality amongst

various centers such as common production facilities, storage facilities in a shop, material economy, errors in documents, operational problems, wastage control, hazards, safety problems etc.

The very fact that more than half a century we have been trying to explore and expand the area of mutual contact, co-operation and co-determination between the management and workers surely underlines the extreme importance of the co-operative approach in the course of industrial activity.

The time has come for the government to enact a law to provide for participatory management at all levels keeping in mind the necessity to ensure that the responsibility and freedom to take management decisions are not fragmented to the determent of the enterprises, the social partners or the society at large.

The employment scenario in the country- the unemployment situation is that like a tickling a time bomb. The economy is expanding but it is hardly creating any new jobs.

The new economic policy of internal liberalisation and globalisation have created an atmosphere which is not conducive to expanding employment in the organized private sector. Most of the existing industrial units are shedding what is termed excess labour and in order to be competitive are inducting sophisticated machinery and automation. There are limits to which agriculture can absorb new entrants. Thus, there is a "jobless" growth and the rate of unemployment as measured by NSS surveys has increased after 1991, unemployment increasing from 6.03% in 1993-94 to 7.32% in 1999-00. The NSS data also shows that the growth of employment has come down from 2% per year in the period 1983 to 1993-94 to less than 1% in period from 1993-94 to 1999-2000 and from 2000-2001 to 2005-2006 to less than 0.5%.

This is serious situation and before taking time bomb explodes urgent action will have to be taken to promote the generation of more employment in the country. Otherwise it will result in serious problem of law and order in the country.

Recent Trends

During the last few years, either through VRSs, or through retirement the number of workers is being reduced in both public and private sectors.

National Textile Mills has introduced VRS in 6 units in Tamilnadu and Podichery. Due to that 2006 textile mills are effected. The textile industry is one that has suffered most as a result of the new economic policy. 396 out of the 1850 registered units have been shut down. 3.49 lack of the 9.97 lakhs workers in the industry have been retrenched. During the last one year, 15,000 jobs have been cut between March 2005 to June 2006.

- The hotel industry is also badly affected with business travel as well as tourist traffic going down.
- There is a growth in casual labour in the total employment picture of the last decade.

The general trend of employment in different countries in South Asia, there are some common features summed up as follows.

1. Slow down of economic growth and consequent growth in employment in the organized sector.
2. Casualization of employment in both formal and informal sectors.
3. Non-declining share of the informal sector in the total employment.
4. Stable or rising unemployment rates and persistently high underemployment
5. Increasing incidence of long term unemployment
6. Declining labour force participation rates
7. Low level of education and skills of labour force.

In this connection India is no exception.[11]

Province of Industrial Adjudication

Industrial adjudication was perceived differently by the

varied parties involved in the employer - employee relationship. Government justified it for protecting public interest. Working class welcomed it as they hoped that it would increase their economic status. Trade unions supported it as it provided them a protective shield against the arbitrary decisions of employer. The employer has received it well as he found in it an easily usable device for settling his score with employees in the adjudicatory institutions including the apex court due to the system's legalistic leanings.

Positive industrial peace in tune with distributive economic justice and continuity of active production are the goals sought to be achieved by industrial adjudication. The essence of real justice in the sphere of industrial adjudication is a quick solution and prompt remedy. State provided mechanism was painted as the one ideal for realising those goals and ensuring real justice. State was empowered to establish industrial adjudication machinery by the Industrial Disputes Act, 1947. This legislative measure is not the first to make such a provision. It only reflected the legislative policy that was in vogue even before 1947. The adjudication machinery currently in use is the one established under the Industrial Disputes Act.

The Industrial Disputes Act of 1947, with its successive amendments, is still the sheet - anchor of industrial adjudication law in India. It provided for direct negotiations between employer and employee. The works committee to be constituted under the Industrial Disputes Act is an example. The Works Committee consisting of representatives of employers and employees at the shop or floor level was required to be constituted to promote amity and good relations between employer and employee. The scope of the works committee was so wide and the precise boundaries of its functions are not clearly drawn even though it is generally agreed that matters for joint negotiation such as the terms and conditions of employment are outside the scope of these committees. The fear in the minds of the trade union leaders that it could be used to bypass them is largely responsible for their ineffective functioning.

The Act also provides for Voluntary Arbitration. There is

no doubt that voluntary arbitration is to be preferred to compulsory adjudication. Forgotten conveniently is the fact that voluntary arbitration can thrive only in a setup where a voluntary relationship between the parties is established. Otherwise, it is only an attempt to give another name to the present method of compulsory adjudication and to perpetuate the bitterness among the parties caused by fighting before a third party, more so because, in our country atleast, the line between the scope of adjudication and arbitration is rather blurred.

Conciliation Machinery has to be constituted under Industrial Disputes Act. The object of the conciliation under the Act is to create an atmosphere conducive to settlement of dispute through peaceful means. Under this process. the representatives of the employees and the employer are brought together with a view to persuading them to come to an agreement among themselves by mutual discussions. The conciliator's job is to find the ways by which the parties may reach an agreement. Reaching such agreement is the settlement for their dispute. The conciliation machinery under the Act take cognizance of an existing or apprehended dispute either on its own or when approached by both the parties or by anyone of them. Conciliation in non-public utility service providing institutions is optional whereas it is a must in institutions providing public utility services.

Compulsory Settlement of the dispute is to be resorted to only when the parties fail to settle their dispute by reaching an understanding thereto otherwise. Industrial adjudication, thus, even though a last resort, yet bulges out in the employer - employee relationship. Industrial Disputes Act, naturally, lays emphasis on industrial adjudication on the foundation that the state cannot afford to remain a silent and helpless spectator in the economic warfare. The state on the failure of the parties to resolve the dispute intervenes by adopting a coercive or compulsory process for settlement of disputes. The Industrial Disputes Act provided the blue print for the industrial adjudication by mapping out the machinery to be constituted by the state for that purpose.

The Industrial adjudication machinery provided under the

Act consists of Labour courts and Industrial Tribunals constituted by Appropriate Government and the National Industrial Tribunal constituted by Central Government. They are of ad hoc nature and cannot key note of any dispute on their own. Their doors are opened only by reference by the concerned government to them.

The main objective of the adjudication machinery is to ensure industrial peace by providing a solution to the dispute at the earliest. Another predominant objective is to satisfy e claims of social justice in settling disputes between the employer and employee. As a after of fact, the community has very high expectations from the industrial adjudication, it is looking upon the system to play its role very effectively and purposefully as a social engineering system and to be the architect of the new industrial culture and ethos. An objective assessment of their functioning can only reveal whether industrial adjudication was able to achieve that salutory objective or not.

The legal province of industrial adjudication is demarcated in the Industrial Disputes Act 1947. Industrial adjudication mechanism currently in vogue was attacked both on the theoretical as well as practical considerations. It attracted protests from the professional as the amature; the illiterate as well as the intelligent and from the insiders of the industry as well as the outsiders of the industry. Perusal of the pertinent among them would augur well for formulating a proper base of the vistas of industrial adjudication.

Categories of Disputes

Industrial disputes are broadly categorised into "interest disputes" and "rights disputes." This distinction is virtually made allover the industrialized western world. Broadly speaking, interest disputes relate to the establishment or modification of the existing terms and conditions of employment, which constitute the rights and obligations of the contracting parties, i.e., the worker and employer. Most interest dispute relate to determination or revision of existing wage levels or matters related to them. Rights dispute, on the other band, relate to the application or interpretation of existing clauses in an employment contract the collective bargaining agreement and so on. Most rights disputes usually relate to termination of a worker's services by the employer. Interest disputes are usually settled through negotiation, failing which it involves threatening of industrial action in the form of strikes and lockouts. On the other hand, rights disputes are usually settled by labour courts or arbitrators.

In India, however, even a semblance of such a distinction is not made between the two terms for the purpose of dispute resolution. Both conciliation and adjudication services are available for both types of disputes.

Although any negotiable item can lead to a labour dispute, a large portion of such disputes has been directly related to salaries and other forms of remuneration. Increasingly, the question of termination of employment has been an important factor in dispute settlement. In India, where the definition of industrial disputes has a wide coverage, all disputes relating in employment, tenure of employment and conditions of labour between worker and employers have been conferred with the status of industrial disputes and are legally adjudicable under the Industrial Disputes Act 1947.

Relevant ILO Standards on Industrial Disputes Settlement

The International Labour Organisation has set up international standards related to labour matters including industrial dispute settlement. The ILO Conventions and Recommendations which are relevant to industrial dispute settlement, are as follows:

1. The freedom of association and protection of the right to organise convention, 1948 guarantees to all workers and employers, without distinction whatsoever, the right to establish and join organisations of their own.

   These organlsations have the right to draw up their own constitution and rules to elect the representatives freely to organise their administration and activities. The Convention also provides for the right to affiliate with international organisations.

2. The right to organise collective bargaining convention, 1948 gives to workers' and employers' organisations

protection against acts of interference by each other. It also gives to workers adequate protection against anti-union discrimination of employers.

3. The tripartite consultation (International Labour Standards) Convention, 1976 requires that the member country on ratification shall establish effective means of tripartite consultation on all matters concerning labour issues.

4. The collective bargaining convention, 1981 envisages provision of measures aimed at ensuring rules and procedures for the settlement of labour disputes so that they contribute to the promotion of collective bargaining.

5. Voluntary conciliation and arbitration recommendation, 1951 contemplates that voluntary conciliation machinery appropriate to national conditions be made available to assist in the prevention of industrial disputes. It is provided that this service should be made available free of charge and should lead to expeditious resolution of industrial disputes.

6. The examination of grievance recommendation, 1967 deals with grievances of one or several workers against certain measures or situations concerning labour relations or employment conditions. Where the grievance is not resolved within the undertaking, the recommendation states that there should be possibility of final settlement through agreed procedures.

7. The termination of employment convention, 1982 provides for an appeal against a decision to terminate the employment to an impartial body such as court, labour tribunal, and arbitration.[12]

Prevention of Industrial Disputes

It has been widely recognised that the best way of preventing and resolving industrial disputes is through strengthening bilateral relations between labour and management and the development of a more collaborative and cooperative relationship.

The new era of globalised business has been marked by the adoption of the practice of human resource management by most corporate organisations. This policy is pursued as a strategy to recognise the tremendous importance of human resources as individuals in the new dispensation and the need for maintaining industrial peace. All over the globe, there is talk of eliminating the basis of workplace conflict and promoting cooperation. More emphasis is being placed on cost-cutting and quality improvement. Newer ways of promoting employee commitment, motivation and satisfaction are being developed. HRM has come to form part of a new style of strategic industrial relations, also labelled new industrial relations. There is greater focus on enterprise-based conflict resolution rather than industry based issues. Furthermore, great attention should be paid towards developing more efficacious grievance redressal procedures and also towards developing participatory structures. Greater attention has to be paid towards developing a human resource oriented culture at the enterprise level.

The prompt and equitable settlement of labour disputes is an important basis for sound industrial relations. Industrial conflict resolution has traditionally been the central concern of industrial relations; and this scenario will continue to be so in the globalised economic environment.

Whatever be the central concern of the entrepreneur in the new economic scenario, a professional approach to labour relations would essentially involve development of an efficacious system of industrial dispute prevention and resolution. The paradigm shift that is taking place in labour relations postulates that proactive policies have to be pursued by management for securing commitment on workers. The labour administration institutions and industrial relations executives will have to give tremendous importance to prevention and settlement of labour disputes.

A still greater importance would have to be given to grievance redressal of employees at the enterprise level so that they do not get converted into industrial disputes in a big way. In fact, industrial relations scholars believe that an ideal industrial relations policy involves a judicious mix of mechanisms to promote effective grievance redressal, collective bargaining and joint consultation - these three issues being intimately interwined with each other.

There is now a growing recognition for greater imagination and experimentation to find new and effective means to resolve disputes, and governments are showing a greater concern for effective labour dispute resolution as the success of economic reforms would depend on ensuring industrial peace and harmony.

Nature of Reference

Access to industrial adjudicatory justice cannot be demanded by a disputant party as of right. It is the discretion of the appropriate government to refer or not to refer an industrial dispute - collective or individual - for adjudication by the adjudicatory body. Discretionary reference was preferred to direct access. The panorama of discretionary reference, especially its objective; its criticism and its persistence, is to be considered for a proper understanding of the amplitude and magnitude of the discretionary power of reference conferred on the government.

Total state intervention in the labour - management relations is a historical legacy. State regulation served the interests of labour better than collective industrial action through trade unions as trade unions in India, it was felt, were not strong enough to protect the interests of its members. The State emphasised that it pursuing democratic socialism cannot be a mute spectator when the interests of the weaker sections like workforce are trampled upon. Such reasoning and philosophy deepened the roots of an era of virtually uncontested State intervention which was reflected in the power vested for making or not making the reference of industrial disputes for adjudication.

India moved into the successive five - year plan period with such philosophy and with the legacy of colonial legal framework of industrial relations pursued the same labour policy. The off-shoot of such preference of labour policy is to confer on the state threshold control over industrial relations in the shape of power of reference.

The reference making power has been vested in the government under the Act to ensure speedy settlement of industrial disputes. Inexpensive and quick resolving of industrial conflicts is the raison D'etre for the creation of special procedure for the settlement of industrial disputes under the Industrial Disputes Act. The Supreme Court in *State of Bombay Vs K. P. Krishnan* in 1952 observed that the object of the Act is to provide a cheap and expeditious machinery for decisions of all industrial disputes by referring them to adjudication and thereby avoiding industrial conflicts arising out 9f frequent lock-outs and strikes. The government's reference making power was intended to facilitate the realisation of that objective.

Such avowed objectives led to the conferment of wide, uncanalised and unregulated discretionary power of reference on the appropriate government either to refer or not to refer the industrial disputes for industrial adjudication under the Act to the authorities constituted for that purpose.

Reference to Whom?

The Industrial Disputes Act, 1947 confers power on the appropriate Government to refer industrial disputes for resolution. Normally for settling any dispute, industrial dispute is not an exception, the method of 'negotiation' is the first resort. In this method the parties to the dispute sit face to face, negotiate and resolve the dispute. If the dispute could not be resolved by negotiation between the employer and workmen, machinery for settlement of industrial disputes should be provided. To achieve this end, provision for constituting various authorities endowed with the power to settle industrial disputes is made under the Industrial Disputes Act.

The authorities constituted under the Act reflect the philosophy of 'conciliation' and 'adjudication'. In the conciliation method, an entirely outside agency will be using its influence and good offices for making the parties agree for settlement. In the adjudication method, an entirely outside agency, though constituted by the Government, will be judging the relative merits and demerits of the contentions of both the parties at logger-heads and gives its decision which is final and by which both the parties are bound whether they like it or not. According to section 10 of the Act, the industrial dispute may be referred by the appropriate Government to the authorities constituted under the Act. The following are the authorities constituted for that purpose.

A. Boards of conciliation.

B. Labour Court.

C. Industrial Tribunal.

D. National Industrial Tribunal.

E. Court of Inquiry.

Industrial Relations Machinery

Broadly speaking, rules or procedures dealing with industrial disputes in our country have evolved mainly two types of machinery. They are, first, machinery for direct settlement of industrial disputes and second, machinery for third party settlement. While tIl1e former comprises both statutory and voluntary measures such as mediation, works committees, grievance procedure, collective bargaining, etc., title latter consists of purely statutory measures like conciliation, adjudication and voluntary arbitration. Both the methods are followed in settling industrial disputes. Similarly, the machinery set-up for ensuring industrial hormony consists of (i) consultative machinery, and (ii) conciliation or arbitration machinery. The consultative machinery now exists at almost every level, i.e., at level of undertaking, industry, state and the national. It aims at bringing the parties together for mutual settlement of differences in a spirit of cooperation and good will At the undertaking level there are the wage boards and industrial committees; at the state level there are the labour advisory boards and at the national level there are the Indian Labour Conference and the Standing Labour Committee. The Bombay Industrial Relations Act, 1946 and the Industrial Disputes Act, 1947 have provided three important statutory methods for settlement of industrial disputes, namely, conciliation, adjudication and voluntary arbitration.

Mediation

Mediation is a process available to the parties-involved in contract negotiations by which an outside party is called in by union and management to help them reach a settlement. The neutral mediator does not ultimately resolve the dispute, but instead tries to move the parties toward agreement by maintaining communication and suggesting alternative solutions to dead-locked issues. The mediator's function is to-provide a positive environment for dispute resolution by drawing on extensive professional experience in the field of labour management interaction. The mediator must possess thorough knowledge of the issues, and an ability to innovate solutions to problems. The mediator must be an effective communicator, know the importance of timing and most of all, have the cenfidence and trust of the parties. A mediator must possess attributes such as integrity, impartiality and fairness.

Conciliation

Boards of Conciliation

Section 5 of the I.D. Act deals with the establishment of Board of conciliation. The powers of the Boards are spelt out in section 11 of the Act while the duties of the Boards are enunciated in section 13 of the Act. The essence of these provisions in the Act is given below:

Establishment

- Appropriate Government may constitute Boards of Conciliation as occasion arises.
- Official gazette notification has to be issued.
- Constituted for promotion of settlement of industrial disputes.
- Consists of Chairman and 2 or 4 members as the Govt., thinks fit. The Chairman shall be an independent person.
- Other members shall be in equal number representing the parties at dispute.

- They shall be appointed on the recommendation of the respective parties.
- If the recommendation is not forthcoming, the Govt., may appoint at its discretion to represent that party.
- It can act if there is prescribed quorum even if there is no Chairman or other member.
- If the government notifies the vacancy of the post of Chairman or any member, Board cannot act till the vacancy is filled.

Powers

- It can follow the procedure it thinks fit subject to rules.
- It has the powers of a civil court like compelling attendance, inspection of documents, entering premises etc.
- The members shall be deemed to be public servants.

Duties

- It can take note of any industrial dispute on reference by appropriate Govt., according to Section - 10.
- On reference, it shall investigate and do all that is necessary for bringing out a fair and amicable settlement.
- If settlement is arrived at, report with memorandum should be sent to appropriate Govt.
- If no settlement is arrived, it should report to the appropriate Govt., the facts, the steps taken and the reasons which accounted for non - settlement.
- It must also send its recommendations for determination of the dispute.
- Report should be submitted within 2 months from the date of reference of the dispute. The period may be extended by the appropriate Govt., or with the consent of the parties in writing. The extension by appropriate' Govt., should not exceed 2 months in aggregate.

- The report should be signed by all members and dissent, can be recorded according to section 16 of the Act.
- On receipt of the report, if the appropriate Govt., does not refer the dispute to court on tribunal, it should communicate the reasons to the parties when the dispute is in a public utility service.

Statutory provision for the conciliation machinery in the country was made for the first time in the Trade Disputes Act of 1929, which provided for the setting up of Boards of Conciliation by the government for settling industrial disputes. On the recommendation of the Royal Commission on Labour, the Trade Disputes Act of 1929 was amended in 1938 to provide for the appointment of conciliation officers. The Industrial Disputes Act and other state enactments authorise the government to appoint conciliators (sometimes called mediators) charged with the duty of mediating in and promoting the settlement of industrial disputes. A conciliation officer may be appointed for specific area or for specific industries in a specific area or for one or more industries either permanently or for a limited period.

The appropriate government may also constitute a board of conciliation for promoting the settlement of industrial disputes. Such a board consists of an independent chairman and two or four other members, representing the parties to the dispute. The appointment of the conciliation officer has become a normal feature whereas the constitution of the boards have rarely been resorted to. The conciliation machinery can take note of the existing as well as apprehended disputes either on its own or on being approached by any party to the dispute. While conciliation is compulsory in all public utility services, it is optional in non-public utility services. In conciliation, the ultimate decision rests with the parties themselves but the conciliator may offer a solution to the dispute acceptable to both the parties and serve as a channel of communication. The parties may accept his recommendation for settlement of any dispute or reject it altogether.

If conciliation fails, the next stage may be compulsory adjudication or the parties may be left to their own choice.

Broadly speaking, the conciliators bring the contending parties to a conference table and endeavour at least to narrow the gulf of difference between them by removing the sources of friction and tension, and help them to find common areas of agreement. They have no power to decide the disputes or pass a final or binding order on the parties. In cases where a settlement is arrived at, they can record the settlement and in cases of failure of the conciliatory negotiations, they can only send a failure report to the appropriate government. It should be noted that they are required under the Act to conclude their proceedings within 14 days while boards are allowed two months, unless the parties agree for a further extension of the time limit. A memorandum of settlement will be binding on the parties for six months from the date of its signing or for such period as may be agreed to between the parties. Even after the expiry of such period, the agreement remains in operation until one of the parties, which is unwilling to continue it, gives a notice for its termination. Under Section 22(1), the Act prohibits a strike or a lock-out during conciliation proceedings and also seven days after the conclusion of such proceedings. Settlements can also be arrived at by the parties when a dispute is pending before the labour court or industrial tribunal. Moreover, such settlements can be included in the awards of the labour court/ industrial tribunal in order to give them a legal status. These are called "consent awards".

Undoubtedly, conciliation has brought about a successful resolution of a large number of conflicts. But it has been subjected to several criticisms. First, considerable delays are usually involved in conciliation proceedings. Second, the parties to the dispute many times do not attend conciliation meetings on the prescribed dates. Third, it is alleged that most conciliation officers lack training and competence in conciliation work. Fourth, conciliation is treated as a preliminary step leading to adjudication through the labour courts or tribunals. In such a state of affairs, the parties do not feel strong urge to arrive at a settlement. The National Commission on Labour was in favour of a more basic rearrangement of conciliation work in order to bring about a qualitative change in the set-up. It observed that conciliation can be more effective if it is freed from outside influence and the conciliation machinery is adequately staffed. The independent character of the machinery will inspire greater confidence and will be able to evoke more cooperation from the parties. The conciliation machinery should, therefore, be a part of the proposed Industrial Relations Commission. This transfer will introduce important structural, functional and procedural changes in the working of the machinery as it exists today. There is need for certain other measures to enable officers of the machinery to function effectively. Among these are: (1) Proper selection of personnel; (2) Adequate pre-job training; (3) Periodic in-service training.[13]

Other suggestions which may be considered to facilitate speedy disposal of cases are: (i) the conciliation officer should hold conciliation proceedings in the concerned factory instead of calling the parties of his office; (ii) he should have the statutory power of enforcing attendance of the parties before him on the prescribed date; and (iii) he should dispose of the cases within the time limit as far as possible.

After examining the demands of the complaining party and the comments of the opposite party, the conciliation officer decides whether he should intervene or not. Once he decides to intervene he intimates to the parties the date of commencement of the proceedings and requests them to attend a joint conference. On the date fixed for the commencement of conciliation proceedings, the representatives of both parties meet at the place fixed by the conciliation officer. He may hold a meeting with each party separately. If the dispute admitted in conciliation is not resolved during the conciliation proceedings, the conciliation officer submits a failure report to the competent authority. The authority after scrutinising the failure report and the confidential note submitted by the conciliation officer, may refer or refuse to refer the dispute to the industrial tribunal or labour court, as the case may be, for adjudication. If the parties at the time of conciliation proceeding so desire, the industrial dispute is referred for voluntary arbitration to the persons unanimously agreed to by them.

Adjudication

Adjudication means a mandatory settlement of industrial disputes by labour courts or industrial tribunals or national tribunals under the Industrial Disputes Act or under any other corresponding state statutes. The government generally refers an industrial dispute for adjudication on failure of conciliation proceedings. By and large, the ultimate legal remedy for the settlement of an unresolved dispute is its reference to adjudication by the appropriate government. The Industrial Tribunals and Labour Courts set up by the State Governments and Union Territory Administrations are also utilised by the Central Government far adjudication of industrial disputes and disposal of applications under Section 33 c(2) of the Industrial Disputes Act, 1947 in the central sphere. Section 10 of the Industrial Disputes Act lays down the conditions and circumstances under which the appropriate government can make or refuse to make a reference of an existing or an apprehended industrial dispute to the respective tribunals or courts for adjudication. There are two requirements to be adhered to by the government before exercising its discretionary power. Firstly, it has to arrive at a subjective opinion as to whether an industrial dispute exists or is apprehended. Secondly, even after it has come to such a conclusion, it has to consider the expediency of making such reference. In other words, the existence of, or the apprehension about, the existence of an industrial dispute does not necessarily follow that the government is bound to refer it. The decision or the act of making reference is purely an administrative act and not judicial or quasi-judicial. This principle is firmly established by several cases decided so far.

The adjudication machinery has exercised considerable influence on several aspects of conditions of work and labour management relations. "The adjudication has been one of the instruments for improvement of wages and working conditions and for securing allowances for maintaining real wages, for standardisation of wages, bonus, and introducing uniformity in benefits and amenities. It has also helped to avert many work stoppages by providing an acceptable alternative to direct action and to protect and promote the interests of the weaker sections of the working class, who were not well organised or were unable to bargain on an equal footing with the employer[14]." As against these advantages, various criticisms leveled against the system of adjudication are:

(i) considerable delay is caused in the termination of adjudication proceedings which generally makes the proceedings ineffective;

(ii) adjudication is sometimes discriminatory as the power of reference vests in the government;

(iii) adjudication is quite expensive because in cases of failures in tribunals, the employees invariably prefer a writ in the High Court and/or an appeal to the Supreme Court; and

(iv) adjudication has inhibited the growth of trade unions, prevented voluntary settlement of industrial disputes and growth of collective bargaining; and

(v) adjudication has failed to achieve industrial peace.

The courts may adopt any procedure that it deems fit. It has all the powers conferred upon the civil courts under the Civil Procedure Code, 1908 in respect of enforcing the attendance of any person and examine him or her on oath, compel the production of documents. Section 36 of the I.D. Act does not allow the appearance of legal practitioners before conciliation officers but permits them before the adjudicating authorities with the consent of the opposite party and permission of the adjudicator. When a case is referred by the government, the parties involved can submit their respective written statement of claims. The power to determine who pays the costs of the proceedings shall lie in the hands of the court. The Act does not make provision for appeals or revisions against the order of the adjudicatory authorities. The aggrieved parties, therefore, have to seek constitutional remedies.

The courts or tribunals are expected to hold proceedings Judiciously, and where a matter has been referred by the government, it shall, within the period specified in the order, submit its award to the appropriate government. In case of proceedings against dismissal and discharge, if the labour court grants reinstatement of any worker and the employer prefers an appeal, the employer shall be liable to pay full wages last drawn by the worker during the pendency of such proceedings. What is important to note is although there is a provision for a labour court, it is government which refers the matters to this forum. Individuals are not in a position to directly approach the court except in cases of contravention of provisions of Section 33 providing for non-alteration of conditions of work during the pendency of proceedings. In such cases, the worker may approach the adjudicatory authority directly.

However critical one may be about the system of industrial adjudication, the fact remains that its contribution to the development of industrial jurisprudence and industrial harmony in our country has been remarkable. Apart from the adjudicatory authorities under the Act, different High Courts and also the Supreme Court of India have laid down definite principles and broad guidelines on industrial matters. Adjudication has, by and large, succeeded in bringing out some measure of industrial peace. Industrial adjudication has endeavoured to resolve the disputes with a pragmatic approach keeping in view the socio-economic requirements of society, and also the social welfare philosophy of industrial relations enshrined in the Directive Principles of the Constitution of India.

Labour Court

Section 7 of the Act deals with the establishment of labour courts. The powers of the labour courts are spelt out in sections 11 and 11 A of the Act while the duties of the labour court are enunciated in section 15 of the Act. The essence of the provisions in the Act is given below.

Establishment

- Appropriate Govt., may constitute one or more labour courts.
- Official gazette notification has to be issued.
- Constituted for adjudication of industrial disputes relating

to matters in the second schedule and such other functions as may be assigned and also matters referred in third schedule provided it is not likely to affect more than 100 workmen.

- Consists of one person only to be appointed by appropriate government. Only the following are qualified to be the presiding officers of labour courts.
  a) Judge of High Court
  b) Has been a District or Additional District Judge for 3 years.
  c) held any Judicial Office for atleast 7 years.
  d) Presiding Officer of a lower court constituted under any Provincial Act for atleast 5 years.
- The following are disqualified to be the presiding officers under the Act.
  a) who is not an independent person
  b) who has attained the age of 65 years.
- The following are the matters set - out in the second schedule of the Act over which the labour court can adjudicate.

The Second Schedule

Matters within the Jurisdiction of Labour Court

1) The propriety or legality of an order passed by an employer under the Standing Orders;
2) The application and interpretation of Standing Orders;
3) Discharge or dismissal of workmen including reinstatement of, or grant of relief to workmen wrongfully dismissed;
4) Withdrawal of any customary concession or privilege;
5) Illegality or otherwise of a strike or lock-out; and
6) All matters other than those specified in the Third Schedule.

Powers

a) It can follow the procedure it thinks fit subject to rules.

b) It has the powers. of Civil Court like compelling attendance, inspection of documents, entering premises etc.

c) The Presiding Officer shall be deemed to be a public servant.

Duties

a) It can take note on any industrial dispute only on reference by appropriate Govt., according to Section - 10 of the Act.

b) It shall hold proceedings expeditiously.

c) It should submit its award to the appropriate Govt., within the time specified in the order of reference.

- The Award shall be signed by the Presiding Officer.
- It has the power to grant appropriate relief including reinstatement. No limits whatsoever on its powers.
- It must confine consideration to those matters referred only.

Labour court is the prime institution established for settlement of referred industrial disputes.

Industrial Tribunal

The constitution of Industrial Tribunal is dealt in section 7-A of the Act and its power and duties are dealt in sections 11-A and 15 of the ID Act. The essence of these provisions is given below:

Establishment

1) Appropriate Govt., may constitute one or more Tribunals.

2) Official Gazette notification has to be issued.

3) Constituted for adjudication of industrial disputes relating to any matter specified in the Second Schedule or Third Schedule and performing such other functions as may

be assigned.

4) Consists of one person only to be appointed by appropriate government.

5) Only the following are qualified to be the presiding officer tribunal:

   a) Judge of High Court.

   b) Has been District & Additional District Judge for 3 years.

6) The appropriate Govt.. may appoint two persons to be 'ASSESSERS' to advise the tribunal.

7) The following are disqualified to be the presiding officer according to section 7C of the Act.

   a) who is no an independent person

   b) who has attained the age of 65 years.

The Industrial tribunal can adjudicate not only on matters mentioned in the Second schedule in the Act but also on matters that are set out in the third schedule in the Act on reference by the appropriate government:

The Third Schedule

Matters within the Jurisdiction of Industrial Tribunals

1) Wages, including the period and mode of payment;
2) Compensation and other allowances;
3) Hours of work and rest intervals;
4) Leave with wages and holidays;
5) Bonus, profit sharing, provident fund and gratuity;
6) Shift working otherwise than in accordance with Standing Orders.
7) Classification by grades;
8) Rules of Discipline;
9) Rationalization;

10) Retrenchment of workmen and closure of establishment; and

11) Any other matter that may be prescribed.

Powers

a) It can follow the procedure it thinks fit subject to rules.

b) It has the powers of a Civil Court like compelling, attendance, inspection of documents, entering premises etc.

c) The presiding officer shall be deemed to be a public servant.

Duties

a) It can take note of any industrial dispute only on reference by appropriate government according to Section - 10.

b) It shall hold proceedings expeditiously.

c) It should submit its award to the, appropriate Gov1., within the time specified in the order of reference.

- The Award shall be signed by the Presiding Officer according to section 16 of the Act.
- The Tribunal has the power to grant appropriate relief including reinstatement. No limits whatsoever on its powers.
- It must confine consideration to those matters that have been referred to only under section 10.

Industrial Tribunal is the most important authority for settlement of industrial disputes.

National Industrial Tribunal

Section 7-8 of the Industrial Disputes Act provided for the constitution of National Industrial Tribunal by the Central Government. Its power are enlisted in section 11 -A while the duties are stated in section 15 of the Act. The essence of these provisions in the Act is given below.

Establishment

- Central Gov1., may constitute one or more National Industrial Tribunals.
- Official Gazette notification has to be given.
- Constituted for adjudication of industrial disputes which in the opinion of the Central Govt., involve questions of national importance or industries situated in different states are likely to be affected by such disputes.
- Consists of one person only to be appointed by the Central Govt.,
- Only a Judge of a High Court is qualified to be the presiding officer.
- The Central Govt., may appoint two persons to be 'assessors' to advise the tribunal.
- The following are disqualified to be the presiding officers according to section 7 - C.

a) who is not an independent person,

b) who has attained the age of 65 years.

Powers

a) It can follow the procedure it thinks fit subject to rules.

b) It has the powers of e Civil Court like compelling attendance, inspection of documents, entering promises, etc.

c) The Presiding Officer shall be deemed to be a Public Servant.

Duties

a) It can take note of any industrial dispute only on a reference by the Central Government according to Section - 10.

b) It should held proceedings expeditiously.

c) It should submit its award to the Central Govt., within the time specified in the order of reference.

d) The Award shall be signed by the presiding officer according to section 16 of the Act.

e) It has the power to grant appropriate relief including reinstatement. No limits whatsoever on its powers.

f) It must confine consideration to these matters referred only as per section 10 of the Act.

The National Industrial Tribunal is constituted with the avowed object of providing adjudicatory mechanism for settlement of industrial disputes which are not confined to the geographical boundaries of any state. In such an event, there is the possibility of different industrial tribunals rendering different solutions to similar problems. To ensure uniformity in such resolution of disputes, it is essential that they are adjudicated by a single authority. That authority is the National Industrial Tribunal. There can be disputes of national importance and to tackle such disputes, a higher level of authority has to be constituted. Hence the establishment of National Industrial Tribunal. The significant role it is expected to play cannot be under stated. It is the most important compulsory adjudicatory authority under I.D. Act.

Courts of Inquiry

Section 6 of the Act deals with courts of Inquiry, to be established by the appropriate Government for investigation into industrial disputes. Their powers are dealt in section 11 and the duties are stated in section 14. The gist of these provisions is given hereunder.

Establishment

1) Appropriate Govt., may constitute courts of inquiry as occasion arises.

2) Official Gazette notification has to be issued.

3) Constituted for inquiring into any matter appearing to be connected with or relevant to an industrial dispute.

4) It may consist of one independent person or such number of persons as the appropriate Govt., thinks fit.

5) If it consists of more than one, one of them shall be the chairman.

6) If there is quorum, it can function even if there is no chairman or other member.

7) If the Govt., notifies the vacancy of the post of chairman or any member, court can not act till the vacancy is filled in.

Powers

a) It can follow the procedure it things fit subject to rules.
b) It has the powers of a Civil Court, like compelling, attendance, inspection of documents, entering premises etc.

c) The members shall be deemed to be public servants.

Duties

a) It can take note of any industrial dispute only on reference by the appropriate Govt., according to Section - 10.

Voluntary Arbitration

Voluntary arbitration in India was introduced and experimented for the first time in the textile industry of Ahmedabad as far back as 1920 under the initiative and guidance of Mahatma Gandhi. He said: "We should not resort to law courts but should have all disputes settled by private arbitration. Since then this has been followed by the Millowners' Association and Textile Labour Association of Ahmedabad. There are other firms such as Bata Shoe Company, TISCO at Jamshedpur, Aluminium Industries at Kerala, etc. which provide for voluntary arbitration for settlement of differences arising out of their agreements. The. BIR Act recognised arbitration and the machinery was set up by the state. In various five year plans, there has been specific mention of voluntary arbitration. The Industrial Disputes Act, 1947 as originally passed, did not contain any provision for voluntary arbitration. In 1956, this Act was amended and a new section (Section 10-A) was inserted in the Act, providing for voluntary reference of disputes to arbitration.

The main ingredients of voluntary arbitration are:

(i) the industrial dispute must exist or be apprehended;

(ii) the agreement must be in writing;

(iii) the reference to voluntary arbitration must be made before a dispute has been referred to under S.1 0 to a labour court, tribunal or national tribunal;

(iv) the name of arbitrator/arbitrators must be specified; and

(v) the arbitrator or arbitrators shall investigate the dispute and submit to the appropriate government the arbitration award signed by the arbitrator or all the arbitrators, as the case may be.

The principle of voluntary arbitration was incorporated in the Code of Discipline, Industrial Truce Resolution of 1962, and also in the various five year plans. The National Arbitration Promotion Board (NAPB) was set-up by the Government of India in 1967 to strengthen the system of voluntary arbitration in our country. The Board consists of representatives of employers' and workers' organisations, public undertakings and central and state governments. Model principles were drawn up by the NAPB by tripartite consent. These principles broadly lay down the circumstances under which individual as well as collective disputes can be referred to voluntary arbitration. In 1972, the Board decided that voluntary arbitration would form the next step for resolving industrial disputes when mutual negotiations and conciliations have failed. Many state governments and union territories also have set up Arbitration Promotion Boards.

Voluntary arbitration is one of the recognised and democratic ways for settling industrial disputes. It is the best method for resolving industrial conflicts and is a close supplement to collective bargaining. It not only provides a voluntary method of settling industrial disputes, but is also a quicker way of settling them. It is based on the notion of self-government in industrial relations. Furthermore, it helps to curtail the protracted proceedings attendant on adjudication, connotes a healthy attitude and a developed outlook; assists in strengthening the trade union movement; and contributes for building up sound and cordial industrial relations. Thus, it is the functioning of democracy in industry and inculcates some degree of union-management accommodation.

Despite the utmost significance of voluntary arbitration, it is unfortunate that this system could not make significant progress in our country due to several reasons. As observed by the NCL, "voluntary arbitration has not taken root in spite of the influential advocacy fort in different policy making forums. Factors which have contributed to its slow progress are:

(i) easy availability of adjudication in case of failure of negotiations;

(ii) dearth of suitable arbitrators who command the confidence of both the parties;

(iii) absence of recognized unions which could bind the workers to common agreements;

(iv) legal obstacles;

(v) the fact that in law no appeal was. competent against an arbitrator's award;

(vi) absence of a simplified procedure to be followed in voluntary arbitration; and

(vii) cost to the parties, particularly workers.

With the growth of collective bargaining and the general acceptance of recognition of representative unions and improved management attitudes, the ground will be cleared, at least to some extent, for wider acceptance of voluntary arbitration. The NAPB may then have a better chance of success in the task of promoting the idea. The NAPB should pay special attention to preparing and building up suitable panels of arbitrators. Moreover, the success of this enlightened approach depends upon the faith and trust, and the will and dignity, which employers and employees lend to its implementation. Hence, all participants in the process, viz., trade unions, employers, personnel executives, and the arbitrators themselves, have an equal stake in an orderly, efficient and constructive arbitration procedure. Certain impediments which come in the way of effective implementation of arbitration practices. are to be removed.

One of the main factors which acts as a hurdle to the maintenance and promotion of industrial peace at present is the increasing resort to adjudication machinery in preference to voluntary arbitration and conciliation. The State Governments should take all necessary measures to encourage settlement of disputes through voluntary arbitration and conciliation. There should be a clause in every settlement and agreement for reference of disputes arising over their interpretation or violation, to arbitration. It should also provide that there will be no strike or lockout over the question of interpretation of collective agreements. It is now increasingly felt in certain circles that there is too much intervention by the government machinery which prevented creation of a proper atmosphere for meaningful collective bargaining. But to quote the NCL, "The requirements of national policy make it imperative that state regulation will have to co-exist with collective bargaining". However, it has recommended for a shift in emphasis in favour of collective bargaining.[15]

Incidental Matters

The authorities to whom the reference was made by the appropriate government for promoting settlement of industrial dispute will follow the procedure and submit their decision, called award. Some authorities will submit the memorandum of settlement that was arrived between the parties. The award and settlement, as the case may be, will be submitted to the appropriate government. The award or settlement is submitted to the appropriate government because the dispute was referred by it and it is natural that it should receive decision rendered. The parties to the dispute would not receive the award directly but it will be submitted to the appropriate government.

The Industrial Disputes Act also laid down the procedure that the appropriate government laid down the procedure that the appropriate government adopts after the award submitted by the concerned authority to the appropriate government. That procedure states and deals with their binding force, their operation or in operation etc. Thus detailed provisions relating to the awards and settlements are specified in the Act. In accordance with these principles, the adjudicatory process is put to use for finding and promotion of a solution to the industrial dispute that defined the same. No matter was left for conjucture of the parties. These are discussed under the public of Govt. controls over judicatory process.

Judicial Response to Labour Management Relations – Recent Trends

Vanishing rights of workmen - a comment on *Indian drugs & pharmaceuticals Ltd. V R.k. Shewarmani*[16]

It is said that history repeats itself. The developments in industrial jurisprudence prove that it is true. The employer - employee relationship in the era of laissez faire was that of hire and fire. It is back with a bang. Referring to industrial relations in laissez-faire era the Supreme

Court in *Glaxo Laboratories v. Labour Court* observed[17]:

In the days of laissez-faire when industrial relations was governed by the harsh and weighted law of hire and fire the management was the supreme master, the relationship being referable to contract between unequals and the action of the management treated almost sacrosanct.

But now, the courts have increasingly come to the rescue of the employers by delivering judgments, which take us back to the era of hire and fire. While the decision of the Supreme Court in *T.K.Rangarajan v. State of Tamil Nadu*[18] cut the roots of workers rights, the present decision shaves of whatever little was left. There is no doubt that the pronouncement of the court that the workers do not have "moral, equitable or legal right" to strike have actually caused the vanishing of the workers rights. An analysis of the decision of the case at hand illustrates that the era of hire and fire is back.

The respondent-employee a medical representative of the appellant company was transferred from Delhi to Eluru in the

State of Andhra Pradesh by order dated 17.6.1989. Allegedly the employee did not join duty at the transferred post and, therefore, he was charge-sheeted twice, once on 27.9.1989 and again on 12.12.1989. While these two charges were pending consideration in departmental proceedings, action in terms of rule 30A of the Industrial Drugs & Pharmaceutical Ltd. Conduct Discipline & Appeal Rules, 1978 (in short the Rules) was taken. Rule 30A was introduced by way of an amendment w.e.f 30th March 1990 on the basis of a decision taken by the board of directors on 24.4.1990.This rule reads as follows:"30(A) Notwithstanding anything contained to the contrary in any other rules, the services of any employee shall be terminated by the company if:

(a) His post is abolished;

(b) He is declared on medical ground to be unfit for service in the company; or

(c) He *remains on unauthorised absence for thirty days or more.*

The decision in case of clause (c) could be taken only with the prior approval of a screening committee of two directors/ executive director to be constituted for the purpose by the chairman and managing director.

The employee took the stand that since he had already been charge sheeted and enquiry was going on, the employer could not bypass the enquiry and take action on the basis of amended rule 30(A). The employer being not satisfied with the reply and keeping in view the unauthorized absence terminated the services of the respondent-employee under rule 30(A).

The respondent-employee not only questioned the termination order but also challenged the validity of the amended rule 30(A) in the High Court. The court set aside the termination order. Legality of this decision of the High Court was challenged in an appeal filed by the appellants in the Supreme Court. The Supreme Court reversed the decision of the high court and thereby upheld the validity of the termination order.

In order to support its decision the court stated that since rule 30(A) was prospective in effect and that the period of absence related to a period subsequent to the date of introduction of the rule, the termination was valid as per rule 30(A). It is submitted that this conclusion by the court is erroneous. It is very clear from the facts of the case that the employee was facing a departmental enquiry for allegedly not joining duty at the transferred place. Thus during the time that the departmental proceedings were being conducted the employee was kept out of employment. Under such circumstances how could the employee go back to work without answering the charges? And, therefore, he *remained out of employment* due to the compulsions of the departmental proceedings. The absence of the employee from work is to be considered from the date on which he did not report for duty at the transferred place and for which a departmental enquiry was being conducted. It is not a case where pending the enquiry the employee was asked to report for duty and the employee failed to join duty. Had it been a case where the employee joined duty pending the enquiry and the employer introduced rule 30(A) and meanwhile the *employee remained on unauthorised absence for more than thirty days* thereafter the employer would have been justified in initiating action as per the rule. It would then have been a case of prospective application of a rule. However, in the instant case rule 30(A) were introduced w.e.f. 30th March 1990 and was implemented with retrospective effect, i.e., action was taken for a period of absence, which related to the time when the departmental enquiry was in progress. The view of the high court that rule 30 (A) had no application as the two departmental proceedings were already pending and those related to periods prior to coming into effect of rule 30 (A) is correct under the facts and circumstances of the case. It is obvious from the facts of the case that the employer brought about the amended rule not with a *bonafide* intention but with the ulterior motive of terminating the services of the employee.

In order to buttress its decision the court has referred to the decision in *Pyare Lal Sharma* v. *Managing Director and Ors*[19]. In this case the services of Pyare Lal Sharma was terminated under regulation 16.14 of Jammu & Kashmir Industries Employees Service Rules & Regulations, which was similar to rule 30(A).

Regulation 16.14 as amended on 20.4.1983 stood as follows:

The services of an employee shall be terminated by the company if:

(a) His post is abolished; or

(b) He is declared on medical grounds to be unfit for further service; or

(c) If he remains on *unauthorised absence*; or

(d) If he takes part in active politics.

The court while commenting on the regulation said[20]:

It is basic principle of natural justice that no one can be penalised on the ground of a conduct, which was not penal on the day it was committed... The notice served on the appellant was thus illegal and as a consequence the order of termination cannot be sustained and has to be set aside.

The ratio of this decision is not applicable to the facts and circumstances of the present case. In *Pyare Lal Sharma* the facts show that the employee had an on going fight with the management and, therefore, the management devised a method to remove him from service by amending the regulation and inserting one more additional clause for his removal. The gravity of the situation in both the cases differs. Whereas the conduct of the employee in *Pyare Lal Sharma* was such that any management would have dismissed him from service, in the present case the only fault of employee was that he allegedly did not report for duty and for which he was facing a disciplinary enquiry. Despite the conduct of the employee in Pyare Lal Sharma the court was lenient in favour of the employee. It said:[21]

This case has a chequered history. From 1976 onwards there has been continuous litigation and mistrust between the parties. The facts which we have narrated above go to show that Sharma has equally contributed to this unfortunate situation. In view of the facts and circumstance of this case we order that 60% of the wages to be paid to Sharma.

In *Pyare Lal Sharma* the court not only put the employee back in service but also allowed him backwages. Looked at from this background, in the present case, the employee did deserve some compassion from the court. The court has committed a grave error in considering the period of absence as that relating to a period subsequent to the date of introduction of the amended rule, when the fact was that the employee was facing a departmental enquiry and therefore was out of employment (during the time of -amendment of rule 30(A)).

The constitutional validity of a rule similar to the above rules was challenged in *Central Inland Water Transport Corporation Ltd.*[22] case also. Rule 9 (i) of the Central Inland Water Transport Corporation Ltd. Service Discipline and Appeals Rules of 1979, though not similar in wording, was similar in its effect. Rule 9 (i) was as follows:

Termination of Employment for acts other than misdemeanour:

(i) The employment of a permanent employee shall be subject to termination on three months' notice on either side. The notice shall be in writing on either side. The Company may pay the equivalent of three months notice basic pay and dearness allowance, if any, in lieu of notice or may deduct a like amount when the employee has failed to give due notice.

The court while holding rule 9 (i) as being opposed to public policy and ultra vires article 14 of the Constitution held:[23]

No apter description of Rule 9 (i) can be given than to call it "the Henry VIII clause". It confers absolute and arbitrary power upon the corporation.

The court while quoting from its earlier decision[24] remarked on the above rule thus:

[A] naked 'hire and fire' rule, the time for banishing which altogether from employer-employee relationship is fast approaching. Its only parallel is to be found in the Henry VIII clause so familiar to administrative lawyers.

The court further said:[25]

A clause such as Rule 9 (i) in a contract of employment affecting large sections of the public is harmful and injurious to the public interest for it tends to create a sense of insecurity in the minds of those to whom it applies and consequently it is against public good. Such a clause, therefore, is opposed to public policy and being opposed to public policy it is void under section 23 of the Indian Contract Act.

The court in the Instant case could have tested rule 30(A) on the basis of the above remarks and held the rule as invalid.

The proponents of globalisation no doubt will welcome this sort of interpretation by the judiciary. Judiciary is in fact making labour laws flexible. Decisions of such nature will fasten the burial of workers rights. The company can afford to dispense with the services of an employee. It will find hundreds of others. An employee cannot afford to lose his job because if he does so, there are not hundreds of jobs waiting for him. The courts while upholding the termination of the services of an employee must be guided by the principle adopted in awarding a death sentence that is, '*rarest of rare cases*'. After all confirming the termination order of an employee is, in a sense, equal to awarding a death sentence. Termination of employment has far reaching consequences not only on the individual employee but also on his family. While deciding issues relating to termination, courts must be guided by Krishna Iyer J's remark-"*Social justice is the signature tune of the constitution of India and this note is nowhere more vibrant than in Industrial jurisprudence.*[26]

It seems that through such decisions the court is favouring the values fostered by liberalisation. Unfettered freedom to the employers in the guise of flexibility would mean destruction of level playing field for labour and undermining industrial democracy. The Supreme Court has created a wealth of industrial jurisprudence in this country by responding to the plight of workers. Its decisions have effect not only on the individual concerned but also on the society at large. Many a time the government has been compelled to modify the law in tune with the judgment of the court. The courts should evolve a consistent Judicial policy in resolving Industrial Disputes.

Posner understands the concept of pragmatism and examines its implication in terms of philosophical theory on the one hand and everyday application on the other. We know the famous dictum of Holmes: "The life of the law has not been logic: it has been experience." In support of this, Posner narrates how Holem's theory of contract law has come to occupy as the core of pragmatic adjudication and an example of legal pragmatism and makes twelve generalizations regarding legal pragmatism among which, systemic consequences and reasonableness seem to be very prominent. From Holmes Posner moves to Marshall, declaring the latter as pragmatic judge and concluding that influential judges tend to be pragmatic judges and that in the twenty first century America there is no alternative to legal pragmatism.

The point that is well brought out is that one can determine the pragmatic approach of the courts only through their decided cases. What makes the court to go away from the beaten track or find legaslation unacceptable is the emergent situation. According to the Posner an 'emergency' rightly or wrongly trumps the law! and courts do this as a way of crisis prevention through pragmatic adjudication. In support, *Bush* v. *Gore's* decision is quoted as an excellent example of pragmatism in the application of law. In India, the courts and judges have been pragmatic to interpret law to sustain the democratic ideals and constitutional values. The theme of "every day pragmatism" could very well be accepted in India. This pragmatism is squarely applicable to labour law and policies particularly in the post-globalisation era.

Contract of Employment and Management Prerogatives[27]

The traditional relationship between 'Master and Servant' was formerly governed by common law and not by statute.[28] The common law conferred upon the master an unfettered right to: hire and fire" the servant. The relationship was essentially contractual. This was clearly not justifiable. Consequently, the employer was under an obligation to pay wages for the work done by the employee former. The employer, however, could get rid of an unwanted employee any time by dismissing him from service. The dismissal was unilateral like character as the employer could terminate the contract whether or not the employee was agreeable to that course. The employers in industries often exercised their power to dismiss the workman capriciously and arbitrarily.

The social consequence of their vindictive acts was disastrous for workmen besides affecting production and the law an order situation Employees, therefore, reacted swiftly against the capricious actions. But in the absence of community support, the unionized activates were firmly curbed by the state from time to time. The court also aggravated the situation by giving judgments which favored more the employers than the workman.[29]

The shift, however, came in the policy of the government which gradually favoured the employees since 1926. The post-1946 legislation and decisions flowing there under had the effect of curbing the management's power to dismiss workmen to such an extent that one wonders if an actual practice, anything is left of the traditional right of the employer. Nomerous cases have gone to the Supreme Court during the last 44 years to determine the contract of employment. The court has evolved various principles for the betterment of the economic and social conditions of workmen.[30]

In the epoch making judgment, the Supreme Court[20] held that the rule empowering the corporation to terminate services of its employees giving notice of a specified period or pay in lieu of notice period is opposed to public policy and violative of articles 14 and 16 of the Constitution, being against the public policy in terms of section 2 of the Contract Act.

The alarming increase in the number of disputes relating to service matters led to the sotting up of tribunals under article 323-A of the constitution (42nd Amendment Act of 1976). Clause (1) of article 323-A empowers Parliament to make laws for adjudications or trial by tribunals in respect of recruitment and conditions of service of persons appointed to public services under clause 2(d). the administrative Tribunals Act 1985 was accordingly enacted to deal with service matters. The Act provides for establishment of the Central Administrative Tribunal. It empowers the tribunal exercise powers, authority and jurisdiction of all courts. It excludes jurisdiction of all courts except that of the Supreme Court under article 16 of the Constitution. Be that as it may, the appointment, promotion and disciplinatary actions of government service hence been the subject matter of litigation and requires special treatment.

Judicial Trend in the Liberalized Era

In *West India Steel Company Ltd. vs. Azeeza*[31] Trade Union leader obstructed work in the factory for five hours protesting against deputation of workman to work in another section. It was held that a worker inside the factory is bound to obey the reasonable instructions given by his supervisors and carry out the duties assigned to him. The mere fact that such worker is a Trade Union leader does not confer on him any immunity in that regard A trade union leader has no right in law to share managerial powers and he cannot dictate any worker individually or to the workmen generally about the manner in which they have to do their work or discharge their duties. A Trade Union can espouse the case of the workers and can resort to lawful agitations for conducting their rights but officials of Trade Union are not entitled to order a workman to stop his work or otherwise obstruct the work of the establishment. Where officials of a Trade Union obstruct the work the management is justified in proceeding against such worker and deal with him effectively.

A trade union leader or an office-bearer of the union has no immunity from misconduct.[32]

Organizing the unorganized is the creed of trade union workers. The strike, the boycott and the picket lines are the primary weapons of organized labour. Unionization and collective bargaining would have little value without the right to use these economic weapons Under the Trade Union Act, 1926 it is possible for the workmen to unite and bargain collectively, which goes to satisfy a basic need of workmen, the natural human desire to participate in decisions affecting their lives as workingmen. The Trade Unions Act however puts certain limitations on trade union activities. The lawful activities of trade unionism found in Section 15 of the Act. Trade unions have the right to declare strikes and to do certain, acts in furtherance of trade disputes. They are not liable civilly, for such acts as Trade Unions Act permits, but there is nothing in that Act which apart from immunity from criminal conspiracy allows immunity from any criminal offences.[33] Sections 17 & 18 of the Trade Union Act grant certain exemptions to members of a trade union, but there is no exemption against either an agreement to commit an offence or intimidation, molestation or violence, where they amount to an offence. Therefore a concerted movement by workmen, by gathering together either outside or inside the industrial establishment, within the working hours is permissible when it is peaceful and does not violate the provisions of law, but when such a gathering is unlawful or commits an offence then the exemption is lost[34]

Non-Violent Concerted Absence from Duty

In connection with certain demands made by a registered trade union, another registered federation wrote a. letter to various trade unions of cine workers not to report for shooting work at the studio of a particular company. In a suit filed by the company, the civil court, by an interim order, restrained the said federation and the union from, inter alia, acting upon the said letter. Keeping in view, that no intimidation or coercion was resorted to and that the letter was written by the federation to propagate its ideas and to lend support to the just demands of the employees, a Single Judge of the Bombay High Court held that such a conduct or act on the part of the federation was protected by Section 18. Therefore, the Single Judge set aside the said part of the Civil court's order[35]

Suit Against Blocking Ingress to and Egress from the Factory

In *Simpson & Group Companies Workers and Staff Union vs Amco Batteries Ltd*[36] case, pursuant to a character of demands submitted to the respondent company by the appellant union, the State Government had initiated conciliation proceedings. However, during the pendency of the proceedings the appellant union, with a view to pressurize the management to concede to its charter of demands, resorted to various tactics including prevention of free movement of men and material from and to the respondent's factory. The respondent company instituted a suit to prevent such activities on the part of the workmen. Subsequently, it declared a lock-out due to the said circumstances. The trial court passed an ad-interim order restraining, the members of the appellant union from interfering with the free movement of men and material into and from the respondent's factory and from endangering the life of persons. The said ad-interim injunction was impugned in appeal. Rejecting the appellant' s contention that the impugned order weakened the bargaining power of the union to arrive at a settlement on its charter of demands, a Single Judge of the Karnataka. High Court observed that physical interference or duress with the free movement of the executives, contractors, staff, suppliers and other public, or physically obstructing the free movement of cars/vehicles and lorries carrying raw materials, intermediaries, end products into and out of the Respondent's factory could not be justified as a trade union right or a fundamental right under Article 19(l)(c) of the Constitution of India. The Single Judge further. observed that the conduct of the workmen in blocking the passage of men and material of the respondent company did not enjoy immunity under Section 18 of the Act.

The early combination cases, especially Strike cases, in which labour combinations were held as criminal conspiracies are based on the theory that labour combinations are organised for committing the crime of conspiracy. The string of criminal conspiracy was ultimately removed by way of provision of immunities against civil and criminal proceedings under the Trade union Act of 1926 in Indian in line with immunities provided under the English Trade Disputes Act 1906. The Judicial trend in 70's and 80's was positive to some extent in protecting the different types of strike actions of the trade unions, but in the liberalized era it could not tolerate even non-violent actions of the trade union leaders like interference of free movement of executives, contractors, staff, suppliers etc.

Right to Strike as a Fundamental Right

It is an established fact that there is no fundamental right to go on strike under our constitution. Despite the Shah-Lakshmanan Bench's attempt in *T.K. Rangarajan v Government of Tamil Nadu.* and Others to draw sustenance for its claim - that there is no fundamental right to strike - from the Supreme Court's earlier judgments, dating back to the 1960s, the question whether the right to strike can be construed as part of the freedom of expression has not been legally settled.

Right to Strike

The recent observation of Shah, J., of the Supreme Court to the effect that 'no fundamental statutory or equitable moral right to strike exists with the government employment', which though ostensible directed against the labour in general, has virtually sirred up a hornet's nest, against this obiter dicta and prominent human rights activist also denounced the same. Even the then Attorney General of India, Soli Sorabjee, Decried these comments in no uncertain terms and also desired mischief. True to the maxim adversity has its own sweet fruit this has concertedly for the vindication of their long cherished rights of collective bargaining and for making a forceful demand to the ruling classes to work, as a Justiciable and constitutionally protected, if not a fundamental right in this background, it would be worthwhile here to go in some detail into the historical and legal particulars concerning the right to the strike.

However, the right to strike has been statutorily recognized, though not positively and directly but in an indirect manner, by the labour statutes in the country. Chapter V of the Industrial Disputes Act, 1947 (Act 13 of 1947) entitled 'Strikes and Lock-outs' provides for the essentials of these two rights – one for the workmen and the other for to ensure social justice to both employers and employees and advance the progress of industry by bringing about the existence of harmony and another thing that the Act is generally interpreted as a social welfare defines 'Lock-out' 2(q) defines 'strike'. Sections 22 and 23 deal with specific and general prohibition of strikes and lock-outs, section 24 and section 25 prohibits any sort of financial and other aid to such illegal endeavours. in doing so, chapter V of the Industrial Disputes Act lays of the right to strike. Then section 18 of the trade Unions Act confers possible action for damages, etc. arising form the breach of contract not treated as a breach of contract enabling the employer to terminate the contract of service merely on the basis.

Moreover, in a catena of decisions, the various high courts

in India as well as the Supreme Court itself have adverted to and positively affirmed the right to strike insofar as workmen are concerned. Chinnappa Reddy, J., then judge, Andhra Pradesh High Court (later elevated to Supreme Court) had most emphatically asserted to positive nature of this right by saying:

> The right to strike is labour's ultimate weapon and in the course of a hundred years it has emerged as the inherent right of every worker. It is an element which is of the very essence of the principle of collective bargaining and as stated by an eminent English judge (Lord Denning in Morgan v. Fry (1968) 3 WLR 506 at 516) the right to strike is an implication read into the contract by modern law as to trade disputes, the nature of the contract by modern law as to trade dispute conformity with the provisions of statute providing for such abridgment or taking away.

In *Kameshwar Prasad and Others vs. State of Bihar and Another* (1962), the Supreme Court's Constitution Bench held that the Bihar State Conduct Rules, insofar as it prohibited strikes, was valid, since there was no specific fundamental right to resort to strike. In this ease, however, counsel did not press the question of right to strike, and the Bench made just one statement on the right to strike ironically, in the same case, the Bench struck down the rule in the conduct rules which sought to impose a blanket ban on all demonstration. The Bench held that banning a peaceful demonstration would be violative of fundamental rights Apparently the Bench did not consider the issue whether the right to peaceful demonstration and non-violent strike can be separated at all, as a strike was a means of demonstration and one to register a protest. In fact, the entire judgment in this case was on the question of the right to demonstrate rather than strike work.

In *Radhey Shyam Sharma vs. The Post Master General Circle, Nagpur* (1964), another Constitution Bench considered the challenge to the Essential Service Maintenance Ordinance (1960) and concluded that the ordinance was only with respect to any "illegal" strike, meaning thereby that a strike can also be legal, if proper notice was given by the employees. In both these cases, the Supreme Court concluded there was no fundamental right to strike, by its superficial reading of Article 19(1)(a) guaranteeing the freedom of speech and expression. Apparently, this ruling requires re-examination, as subsequent rulings of the court have considerably expanded this Article. Freedom of the press, for instance is implied in this article as per the court's ruling.

In *All India Bank Employees' Association vs. National Industrial Tribunal & Others* (1962), the Constitution Bench specifically held that even a very liberal unions, could not lead to the conclusion that trade unions had a guaranteed right to an effective collective bargaining or to strike either as part of collective bargaining or otherwise. But this did not consider the question why the right to strike cannot be construed as a fundamental right with reasonable restrictions on its proper exercise. The bench concluded that the right to strike was not a concomitant right of the right to form associations that is strike was not a means to achieve all the objectives of the union. The question whether right to strike is a fundamental right was not examined in the case.

The Shah-Lakshmanan Bench seems to have failed to take note of two key cases that highlight the importance of the right of strike. In the *Gujarat Steel Tubes Case (1980),* concerning the mass dismissal in his employees, Justice V.R. Krishna Iyer in the Supreme Court held that a strike might constitute an infraction of law, but it might still not be a justification of the extreme punishment of mass dismissal. In his view, a large number of people participating in a strike would be passive strikers, as against the actual conspirators, and therefore, they ought not to be punished with dismissal, which would be disproportionate to the nature of illegality committed by them. The facts of the case are similar to the recent Tamil Nadu government employees' case, which resulted in the present judgment. In the *B.R. Singh case (1989),* which dealt with the Trade Authority of India's dismissal of certain employees without referring the dispute to the Tribunal for resolution under the Industrial Tribunal Act, former Chief Justice of India Justice A.M. Ahmadi, who wrote the judgment, found that the strike was justified because the workers were denied reinstatement without the dispute having been referred to the Tribunal as required under the law.

Though temporary suspension of work is lockout, the relationship between the employees and an employee continues. A mere refusal to provide work does not amount to lock out, unless such refusal is prompted by some dispute with workers. It is not permanent closure of business but only a temporary suspension of it only means the refusal of management to continue to employ the workers.

It is well-settled, as pointed out by the Supreme Court, in *Express Newspapers V. Their Workmen,*[37] that a lock-out involves merely the closing of the place of business, and not of the business itself This distinction is also the test of the difference between a lock-out and a closure, as the latter involves the closing down of the business itself.

In *Feroz Din Vs State of West Bengal,*[38] the Court interpreted the definition of a "lock-out" to mean 'the employer's refusal to permit any:. number of persons employed by him to attend to their duties, without effecting a termination of service.

In *Singareni Collieries Col. Ltd V. Their Mining Sirdars,*[39] it was. held. that the words "any number" of persons, used in Ssec.2(j). should be interpreted to mean more than one person In this case, it was held that there cannot be .a lock-out when only one person is affected by the employer's action.'

In *Swadeshi Industries Ltd. v Their Workmen*[40] it was held that when the employer claims' that the concerned workmen were, employed in the public utility services of the establishment, the burden of proving the same is on the employer.

In *Municipal Committee, Pathankot v. Industrial Tribunal, Punjab,*[41] the Court held that a failure to observe the provisions contained in Section 23 renders the strike illegal. The genuineness of the workmen's demands cannot justify a strike which is otherwise illegal.

As observed by the Supreme Court in India *General Navigation and Railway Co. Ltd. v. Their Workmen,*[42] the Act has not made any distinction between an illegal strike which is justifiable and one which is . not. The Court is concerned with the legality or otherwise of the strike. .

In *Balarpur Collieries v. Presiding Officer, Central Government Industrial Tribunal*[43], the workmen of 'a colliery had, gone on a strike during the pendency of a reference to the Tribunal. The Court held that 'this was sufficient ground to hold that the strike was illegal, as it was in contravention 'of Section 23(b), The challenge on the ground of a violation of section 25(c) was not justified as the strike was not in breach of a matter covered by a settlement, though it may have occurred during the pendency of the agreement.

In *Workers of Motor Industries Co. v. Motor Industries Co. Ltd.*[44] the Court had to consider a situation wherein the workmen had gone on strike despite a settlemeot which provided that they would not go on strike without giving four days' notice The Court held that not with stand the Standing Orders, and the settlement mentioned above, the strike was not illegal as being m contravention of Section 23(d), as the subject-matter of the strike related to workman's suspension, and was not "in respect of any of the matters covered by' the settlement".' Going on' strike without notice in violation of the settlement may render the, liable under Section 29 of the Act, but will not make the strike illegal under Section 23(c).

Some Other Cases that Reflected the Changing Attitude of Judiciary in Globalization era:

In India *Tourism Development Centre v. Presiding Officer, Labour Court)*[45]. Delhi High Court held that While modifying the punishment of dismissal of a workman, the Labour Court Must consider his past conduct.

In *Purafil Engineers, Pune v. Shaikh Anwar Abdul Rahman,*[46] held that Object of the Labour Laws is not to harass and extract money from the employers.

Adjudication and not writ petition will be proper to determine the validity and fairness of a settlement.

- All issues including that of a 'workman' are to be decided together by the Labour Court. The High Court will not interfere in the findings of the Labour Court while exercising jurisdiction under Articles 226 and 227 of the Constitution of India.[47]

- Unless there is a request to decide issue pertaining to enquiry, the Labour Court/Tribunal has no duty to advise the management.[48]
- An employee raising dispute after 13 years about his termination will not he tenable.[49]
- Whether an employee is a 'workman' or not under the Industrial Disputes Act is to be adjudicated by the Labour Court and not by the High Court.[50]
- It is for the Labour Court and not the High Court to adjudicate on f acts whether an employee who has been discharging supervisory functions is not a 'workman'.[51]
- Burden of proof lies upon the workman to establish that he has worked for 240 days before his termination.[52]
- The Labour Court should not have interfered in the punishment of dismissal of a workman against whom the charge of misappropriation has been proved in the enquiry.
- Denial of employer-employee relationship by the employer will not be tenable when it is not properly pleaded and also the employer has not sent any reply to the letters of the workman demanding his reinstatement with full back wages.[53]
- Courts should interfere in the administrative decisions of the employer in imposing punishment only when the punishment is illogical or suffers from procedural impropriety or is shocking.[54]
- Unlike Civil Courts, the Labour Court or the Industrial Tribunal is not vested with the power-to decide any question as' a preliminary issue hence the request of employer to this aspect has been incompatible with the scheme of Industrial Disputes Act and the Rules.[55]
- Burden of proof lies upon the employees and not the employer when they allege that their resignations were

not voluntary but obtained under coercion and duress.[56]

- The Burden of proof to have worked for 240 days in the preceding 12 calendar months lies upon the workmen claiming their wrongful termination.[57]
- The award of the Labour Court except answering the additional issues it would not be proper hence deserves to be quashed and is hereby quashed.[58]
- While adjudicating an industrial dispute, the Labour Court has to confine its powers to the terms of reference and in case any party wants modification, amendment or alteration it has to approach the appropriate government.[59]
- When the Labour Court did not frame any issue as to whether the workman is a casual employee or a permanent employee for the purpose of awarding consequential reliefs and in the absence of such finding, no direction can be given for the back-wages and continuity of service.[60]
- The Industrial Tribunal having passed an award without hearing the unions or the workers whereas it is just and proper to afford an opportunity to the Unions and the workers to highlight their grievances and their suggestions before the Tribunal and for that purpose the award has to be set aside and the matter remanded to the Tribunal.[61]
- The Industrial Tribunal has rightly rejected the dispute of the probationer alleging violation of the principles of natural justice whereas even during the probation period, his performance remained unsatisfactory.[62]
- An Industrial Tribunal has to confine its jurisdiction only to that dispute which has been referred and can not travel beyond the terms of reference.[63]
- If the Industrial Tribunal decides to interfere with the punishment, it should adhere to the principle of proportionality.[64]
- In absence of domestic enquiry, the employer has the right to satisfy the Industrial Tribunal about validity of

its action in terminating its employee.[65]

- While awarding reinstatement by setting aside termination, the Labour Court has to give the reasons in support of its award.[66]

Ideal Industrial Adjudicatory Process

Ideal industrial adjudicatory process, which is of universal application, is not in existence. Expecting such a system is wishful thinking akin to the wish of having the moon in the hands. It is because the ideal industrial adjudicatory process largely depends upon the factors operating within the geographical limits of a Nation largely and it is shaped by factors operating beyond the National Frontiers to a minimum extent. Thus, each country has to determine what is ideal for industrial adjudication in its own way suitable to its industrial scenario.

The philosophy guiding the establishment of ideal industrial adjudicatory system is determined by the political, social and particularly economic policies of any nation. They provide the foundation on which the superstructure of industrial adjudicatory process is built. The four pillars that influence the shaping of that process are:

1. Globalisation's Impact and International standards
2. State of economic development of a Nation with particular emphasis on Industrial development.
3. Working community characteristics and the extent to which they require protection in the light of their collective bargaining strength
4. Protection of consumer's interests.

Keeping these four forces in perspective and operating within the Nation's socio, political and economic policies, which are dynamic, the values that should go into and constitute the core of the industrial adjudicatory process are to be determined. Such value system is the ideal one. The values that guide the formulation of an ideal industrial adjudicatory system are to be ascertained for shaping such a system. The most important values are free play, social justice, accommodation and judicial review. Moreover arbitration being made compulsory for certain kinds of dispute resolution will lessen the work of adjudicatory mechanism.

REFERENCES

1. See Editorial note by T.S. Papale, P.P. Ghosh and Alakh N. Sharma., Labour Employment and Industrial Relations in India, Indian Society for Labour Economics, B.R. Publishing Corporation, Delhi, 1993.
2. *Ibid.*
3. V.V. Giri., Beginning of an era - (See Editorial note by T.S. Papale, P.P. Ghosh and Alakh N. Sharma., *Labour Employment and Industrial Relations in India,* Indian Society for Labour Economics, B.R. Publishing Corporation, Delhi, 1993.)
4. C.N. Vakil - the role of the labour economist - (See Editorial note by T.S. Papale, P.P. Ghosh and Alakh N. Sharma, *Labour Employment and Industrial Relations in India,* Indian Society for Labour Economics, B.R. Publishing Corporation, Delhi, 1993.)
5. R.K. Mukharjee., *Role of Labour in Democratic Socialism.* - (See Editorial note by T.S. Papale, P.P. Ghosh and Alakh N. Sharma., *Labour Employment and Industrial Relations in India,* Indian Society for Labour Economics, B.R. Publishing Corporation, Delhi, 1993.)
6. Order : dt. 11.10.1991 in civil appeal No's 2058-59 of 1988 in the case of ONGC Vs Collector or Central excise.
7. Chalapathi Rao. P.V., *Labour Management Relations and Collective Bargaining,* Anmol Publications Pvt. Ltd, New Delhi, 1995.
8. Chaturvedi. S.M., *Labour and Industrial Law,* Central Law Agency, Allahabad, 1995
9. Kothari. G.M, Kothari, A.G., *A Study of Industrial Law,* N.M. Tripathi Private Limited, Bombay, 1987.
10. Bhattacharya. S. Joshi, *Labour Law Digest* (1966-69) Law Publishing House, Allahabad, 1970.
11. Giriappa. S., *Issues in Labour Problems (A case study in fishing plantations and Crop cultivation),* Ajanta Publications, Delhi, 1990.
12. See the ILO reports 1948, 1951, 1967, 1976, 1981 & 1982 and also Mitra. N. L., Toil in Distrust. *J.I.L.I.* Vol. 31; 2, 1989.
13. Report of the NCL, p. 323.

14. Report of the NCL, p. 325

15. Report of the NCL, P 327.

16. (2005) 6 SCC 76

17. (1984) 1 LLJ 16

18. (2003) 6 SCC 581

19. 1989 (3) SCC 448

20. Id. at 456

21. Id. at 457

22. Central Inland water Transport Corporation Ltd & Another v. Brojonath Ganguly and Another, AIR 1986 SC 1571.

23. Id. at 1614

24. West Bengal State Electricity Board v. Desh Bandhu Ghosh, AIR 1985 SC 722 at 723

25. Supra note 7 at 1615

26. Punujab National Bank V. Ghulam Dastgir, 1 *LLJ* 1978 SC 321

27. Harish Chandar, *Contract of employment and management prerogatives*, Vijaya Publications, New Delhi, pp. 322, 1993.

28. Tej Bahadur Sapru, *Encylopedia of General Act and Code of India*, Vol. VI p.2 (1959).

29. Srivastava. S.C., *Industrial Disputes and Labour Management Relations in India* 391 (1984).

30. Central Inland Water Transport Corporation Ltd., V. Vrajo Nath Ganguly, A.J.R. 1987 S.C. 1571

31. (1990)2 LLJ 133 (Kerala)

32. (Palani Vs. Bajaraj Textiles, 1991 LLR 456 Mad)

33. (AIR 1935 Nag 149 at p.154)

34. (AIR 1963 Cal 407 (SB)

35. (Federation of Western India Cine Employees vs Fima laya Pvt. Ltd. (1981 Lab IC 1220)

36. (1992 Lab IC 414)

37. (1962 II LU 227 Sc)

38. (1960 I LU 244 Sc)

39. (1967 II LU 465)
40. (A.I.R. .1960 S.C. 1258)
41. (1971 II LU 52 Punj.)
42. (1960 I LU 13 S.C.),
43. (AIR 1972 SC 1216)
44. (AIR 1969 SC 1280)
45. 2000 LLR 262 (Del HC)
46. (2000) 84 FLR 144, (2000) LLR 268 (Bom HC)
47. Manager Air Control Engg. Company Ltd. v. Kanaiyalal Ghusabhai Kunvaria, 2000 LLR 592 (Guj HC).
48. Management of Triplicane Urban Co-operative Society Ltd. v. The Presiding Officer, Principal Labour Court, 2000 LLR 1228 (Mad HC).
49. Management of Indian Iron and Steel Company Ltd. v. Prahlad Singh (2001) 1 5CC 424: AIR 2001 SC 69: 2001 LIC 26: 2001 LLR 157 (SC).
50. L.K.P. Merchant Financing Ltd. v. Government of National Capital Territory, Delhi, 2003 LLR 367: 2003-I LLN 1044: 2003 (97) FLR 460 (Del HC).
51. L.K.P. Merchant Financing Ltd. v. Government of National Capital Territory, Delhi, 2003 LLR 367: 2003-I LLN 1044: 2003 (97) FLR 460 (Del HC).
52. N.S. Ravichandran v. Management of Thanthal Periyar Transport Corporation, 2003 LLR 380:2003-I L LJ 729: 2003-I L L N 415 (Mad HC).
53. Creative Garments v. Kunwar Prasad, 2003 LUR 424 (Born HC).
54. United Commercial Bank v. P.C. Kakkar, (2003) 4 5CC 364: AJR 2003 SC 1571: (2003) 2 LU 181: (2003) 2 SUR 445: 2003 LLR 436: 2003-I LLN 825 (SC).
55. Novapan Industries Ltd. v. S.K. Murthy, 2003 LUR 569: 2003 (97) FUR 342 (AP HC).
56. B.C.C.L. v. Presiding Officer, Central Government, 2003 LLR 618: 2003-II LU 92 (Jhar HC).
57. Bharat Coking Coal Ltd. v. Presiding Officer, Central Government

Industrial Tribunal-II, Dhanbad, 2003 LLR 954: 2003 (98) FUR 718 (Jhar HC).

58. L.S. Sharma v. Presiding Officer (I) Uttar Pradesh Ghaziabad, 2003 LLR 1021: 2003 (98) FUR 922 (All HC).

59. Mahaveer Conductor v. Nand Kishore, 2003 UUR 1167: 2003 (99) FUR 354 (Raj HC).

60. Kattabomman Transport Corporation v. Labour Court, 2004 LLR 246: 2004 (100) FLR 580 (Mad HC).

61. T.C.M. Employees 'Union, Kalamassery v. T.C.M. Ltd., 2004 LLR 285: 2004-I LIJ 280 (Ker HC).

62. Vasant C. Hanhad v. Chairman, Oriental Insurance Company Ltd., 2004 LLR 372: 2004-I CLR 791 (Guj HC).

63. Metallurgical Engineering Consultant (I) Ltd., Ranchi v. State of Bihar, 2004-I LU 793 (Jhar HC).

64. Muriadih Collery of Bharat Coking Coal Ltd. v. Bihar Colliery Kamgar Union through Workmen, 2005 LLR 1085 (SC).

65. S. Chandraiah v. The Presiding Officer, Additional Industrial Tribunal, 2005 LLR 1172 (AP HC).

66. Kamla Nehru Memorial Hospital v. The Presiding Officer, Labour Court, Allahabad, 2006 LLR 5 (All HC).

6

NATIONAL LABOUR COMMISSIONS' REPORTS ON LABOUR MANAGEMENT RELATIONS – A REALISTIC STUDY

The state having realised the importance of employer-employee relationship started controlling and balancing the relationship so as to enable the economy to survive. This era was marked by employee friendly labour legislations, popularly known as welfare legislations. The social welfare legislation is in tune with the objectives laid down in part IV of the Constitution. The rapid industrialisation that took place after independence led the government to take steps for labour protection. Laws relating to minimum conditions of employment, wages and other monetary benefits, social security and industrial relations were enacted towards ensuring labour protection.

The First National Labour Commission was set up in December 1966 to examine the ways and means of extending the labour welfare measures beyond the organised sector. The recommendations of the First National Labour Commission covered issues like recruitment agencies and practices, employment service administration, training and worker's education, working conditions, labour welfare, housing, social security, wages and earnings, wage policy, bonus to workers and employers and industrial relations machinery.

The recommendations of the First National Labour Commission were sought to be implemented through amendments to existing labour laws as well as by identifying the areas where fresh legislation would be necessary. Examples of the former are amendments to labour laws like the Workmen's Compensation Act, 1923 (for removal of wage ceiling for coverage) and the Industrial Disputes Act, 1947 (mainly in respect of the unfair labour practices). The Employees State Insurance Act,1948 (for enhancement in the wage limit for exemption from payment of employees' contribution), Factories Act, 1948 (for making penalties more stringent for violation of safety requirements and provision of welfare facilities) and the Employees' Provident Funds and Miscellaneous Provisions Act, 1952 (enhancement in the rate of contribution and making default of dues a cognizable offence). New legislations that were enacted in the light of the recommendations made by the First Labour Commission, include the Contract Labour (Regulation & Abolition) Act, 1970, Equal Remuneration Act, 1976 and Child Labour (Prohibition & Regulation) Act, 1986.

Market economics and pressure from world capitalists forced the governments including India to open up its economy to the benefit of private and global investors. And since then the cry for labour law reforms started in India. The pro reformers felt that the employee friendly labour laws are an obstacle in business. The Government of India meanwhile appointed the Second National Commission on Labour to investigate the whole question of rationalisation of the existing labour laws in the organised sector so as to make them more relevant in the changing economic conditions under the impact of globalisation. Though the report and the suggestions for labour law reform have been submitted to the government, it has not gone ahead with its implementation due to political compulsions. Suggestions for labour law reform by the commission have invited criticism from workers representatives. Welfare laws still exist. It is the economic scenario, which has undergone change. Weare yet to change the laws to suit the needs of the changing economic scenario.

First National Labour Commission 1969, Regarding Industrial Relations

The Royal Commission on Labour was appointed as far

back as 1931. The Labour Investigation Committee (Rege) reported in 1946. Since independence industrial landscape has undergone a thorough change, Necessity was felt for a fresh and comprehensive review of the labour situation in the, country. Consequently, the National Commission on Labour, headed by Dr. Gajendragadkar, was appointed in December, 1966. The Commission submitted its report in August, 1969. The terms of reference of this Commission were:

(i) to review the change in the conditions of labour, since independence' and to report on existing conditions of labour,

(ii) to review the existing legislative and other provisions intended to protect the interests of labour, to assess their working and to advise' how far these provisions serve to implement the Directive Principles of State Policy in the Constitution on labour matters and the national objectives of establishing a socialist society and achieving planned economic development,

(iii) to study and 'report in particular on:

(a) the levels of workers' earnings, the provisions relating to wages, the need for fixation of minimum wages including a national minimum wage, the means of increasing productivity, including the provision of incentives to workers;

(b) the standard of living and the health, efficiency, safety, welfare, housing, training and education of workers and the existing arrangements for administration of Labour welfare – both at the center and in the states.

(c) the existing arrangement for social security.

(d) the state of relations between employers and workers and the role of trade unions and employers' organizations in promoting healthy industrial relations and the interests of the nation.

(e) the labour laws and voluntary arrangements like the

code of discipline, joint management councils, voluntary arbitrations and Wage boards and the machinery at the center and in the states for their enforcement.

(f) measures of improving conditions of rural labour and other categories of unorganized labour and

(g) existing arrangements for labour intelligence and research and

(h) to make recommendations on the above matters.

Conditions have to be created for promotion of collective bargaining. The most important condition is statutory recognition of a representative union as the sole bargaining agent.

Collective bargaining cannot exist without the right to strike or lock-out. But other forms of labour protests such as 'go-slow', and 'work-to-rule' may be treated as unfair labour practices under the Standing Orders.

For the first time, a 30 day limit is proposed to be placed on any legitimate strike in non-essential industries, while for 'essential' industries, the Commission has provided a self-contained Code and machinery which, it claims, will make strike wholly unnecessary.

The Commission feels that the Government cannot be final authority to decide whether an issue should go for arbitration or not, and has suggested modification of the present system of joint consultative machinery for Central Government employees. It has, however, stated that prohibition of strikes would be justified if an effective alternative for settlement of unresolved disputes is provided.

While recognizing the validity and relevance of strikes and lock outs in certain situations the NLS has suggested the imposition of some restrictions including a limit on the duration. In essential industries, the right to strikes or lock-outs should be made redundant by requiring the IRCs to adjudicate when mutual negotiations fall and parties do not agree to arbitration. A compulsory strike notice and a strike ballot open to all members of the union have also been recommended by the NLC.

Having recognized the legitimacy of strikes and lock-outs, in certain given situations, the NLC has left it to the IRC to terminate the strike/lock-out even before the prescribed period after considering the motion in that behalf from the appropriate Government. The penalties which have been provided for unjustified strikes, or lock-outs, would, in the Commission's opinion, ultimately avoid strikes and lock-outs and in due course, persuade the parties to settle their differences by negotiations.

Conciliation can be more effective if it is freed from outside influence and the conciliation machinery is adequately staffed. The conciliation machinery should be a part of the proposed Industrial Relations Commission. With the growth of collective bargaining and the general acceptance of recognition of representative unions and improvement in attitudes, the grounds will be cleared for wider acceptance of voluntary arbitration.

The Commission is of the view that '*gheraos*', apart from their adverse effects on industry and the economy of the country, strike at the very root of trade unionsim. It depreciates resort to '*gheraos*' which invariably tend to inflict physical duress on persons affected and endanger not only industrial harmony but also create problems of law and order. If such means are to be adopted by labour for realization of its claims, trade unions may come into disrepute. It is the duty of all union leaders therefore to condemn this form of labour protest as harmful to the interests of the working class itself.

'*Gherao*' cannot be treated as a form of labour protest since it involves physical coercion rather than economic pressure. It is harmful to the working class and in the long run may effect National interest.

In certain essential industries where cessation of work may cause harm to the community, the right to strike may be curtailed but with the simultaneous provision of an effective alternative to settle the disputes. Every strike or lock-out should be preceded by a notice.

The present arrangement for appointing adhoc industrial

tribunals should be discontinued. An Industrial Relations Commission on a permanent basis should be set up at the Centre and one in each State for settling 'interest' dispute.

The Commission, in making its most important recommendation regarding the setting up of IRCs at the State as well as at the National level, has been motivated by the desire for insulating the settlement machinery against political pressure.

The National Industrial Relations Commission should be appointed by the Central Government for industries for which that Government is the appropriate authority. Each State should have an Industrial Relations Commission for settlement of disputes for which the State Government is the appropriate authority. The proposed IRCs will be high powered bodies independent of the executive. The main functions of the National and State Industrial Relations Commissions will be (*i*) adjudication in industrial disputes, (*ii*) conciliation and (*iii*) certification of unions as representative unions.

The IRCs will have both judicial and non-judicial members. The judicial members including presidents of the National/ States IRCs, are to be appointed from among people eligible for appointment as Judges of High Courts.

The Conciliation Wing of the Commissions will consist of conciliation officers with the prescribed qualifications and status. There will be people with or without judicial qualifications in the cadre of conciliators. The functions relating to certification of unions will vest in a separate wing of the National State IRC.

Standing Labour Courts should be constituted in each State. Members of the Labour Court will be appointed by Government on the recommendations of the High Court. Labour Courts will deal with disputes relating to rights and obligations, interpretation and implementation of awards and claims arising out of rights and obligations under the relevant provisions of law or agreements as well as disputes in regard to unfair labour practices and the like.

Works Committees may be set up only in units which have

a recognized union. The Union should be given the right to nominate the worker-members of the Works Committee.

When managements and unions are willing to extend cooperation in matters they consider to be of mutual advantage, they set up a Joint Management Council.

Grievance Procedure should be simple and have a provision for at least one appeal. The procedure should ensure that it gives a sense of (*i*) satisfaction to the individual worker, (*ii*) reasonable exercise of authority to the manager, and (*iii*) participation to unions. A formal grievance procedure should be introduced in units employing 100 or more workers. A grievance procedure should normally provide three steps: (*a*) submission of a grievance by the aggrieved worker to his immediate superior, (*b*) appeal to the departmental head, and (*c*) appeal to a bipartite grievance committee representing the management and the recognized union.[1]

Labour in Public Sector

Suitability of the candidate and his availability for at least 5 years should be the criteria for selection for a senior position in a public undertaking. At the supervisory level, recruitment has to be on an all India basis since the quality of personnel is a crucial factor. The claim for preferential treatment to 'sons of the soil' in appointments in regional establishments has been described as 'plainly inconsistent with the philosophy of one citizenship'.

'We thought', the Chairman qualified 'that it would be unwise to shut our eyes to the hard facts and realties of life'. In his view the Commission has formulated recommendations that may be reasonable and fairly worked out within limits. For example, in certain unskilled categories of employees, it would be convenient to the employer for several reasons to employ local labour. Where there is a choice between two persons who are equally qualified, the local person will get the preference.

Government (Industrial) Employees

In case of Government industrial employees engaged in essential services, the prohibition of strike would be justified.

Such prohibition of strike, however, have to be accompanied by the provision of an effective alternative for settlement of unresolved disputes. This will lead to settlement of disputes by negotiations and agreements. All the same, there will be need for a statutory arbitration machinery.

There should be a wider scope for discussion in the Joint Consultative Machinery on all matters which can be brought within its purview. The limited scope provided in a Joint Consultative Machinery for arbitration is a deficiency which should be removed if the industrial employees of Government are to be treated on the same footing as other industrial employees. A Pay Commission should be appointed immediately to review the wages and other conditions of service of industrial employees of Government.[2]

Unorganised Labour/Contract Labour

A stricter regulation of contract work than at present is called for. The general direction of policy should be towards abolition of contract labour in due course.

Construction Workers

The possibility of introducing a decasualisation scheme should be explored to ensure greater security of employment of construction of workers. Mobile dwellings should be provided for construction workers at work sites.

Casual Labour

There should be a better regulation of conditions of casual labour. If employment is discontinued for a short period and the worker is re-employed, this short period should not be treated as a break in services. After a casual worker completes a stipulated period of service he should be allowed the same benefits which a regular worker enjoys.

Workers in Shops and Commercial Establishments

Working conditions in shops and commercial establishments are at present governed by State enactments. The Central Government should enact a comprehensive legislation for the purpose. It should be applicable to units which have a stipulated minimum number of workers or have an annual turnover above a stipulated limit.

A better understanding of the problems of different categories of unorganized labour is essential to the formulation of suitable ameliorative measures. Detailed surveys about the conditions of work in these employments should be undertaken.

The Commission's Report was placed on the table of both Houses of Parliament by the Minister of State for Labour, Employment and Rehabilitation, Mr. Bhagwat Jha Azad. While submitting the Report to the Union Labour Minister, the Chairman of the Commission described the recommendations as 'crucial' and expressed the hope that the report would furnish rational guidelines for the country's industrial development and growth for the next 25 years.

The recommendations of the Commission in regard to a sound industrial relations system have been under discussion with the representatives of employers and workers' organizations. In pursuance of a suggestion made by the Union Minister of Labour and Rehabilitation at a Conference of Trade Union Organisations, held in May, 1971, the INTUC, the AITUC and the HMS have been having mutual discussions amongst themselves to evolve an agreed consensus on the question of recognition of unions and the dispute settlement machinery. At the 27th Session of the Indian Labour Conference held in October, 1971, they asked for and were given, six months time to conclude their discussions. Meanwhile, however, following the declaration of emergency, the representatives of employers 'and workers' organizations met on December 5, 1971 and adopted a declaration pledging their support to the maintenance of uninterrupted production in an atmosphere of industrial peace. At a subsequent meeting of the representatives of the employers 'and workers' organizations, a Working Party of Employers and Workers was constituted to formulate concrete measures to (1) give effect to the declaration of the workers 'and employers' representatives at the meeting held on December 5, 1971 and (2) suggest the outlines of a suitable machinery which would ensure speedy settlement of industrial disputes.

The Working Party was informed by the workers 'representatives that they had already covered considerable ground in their discussions and had come to a tentative agreement in respect of the basic questions of trade union recognition and the mechanism of dispute settlement. The participating trade union organizations - INTUC, AITUC and HMS - have also agreed to set up a National Trade Union Council to eliminate inter-union rivalry and promote healthy trade unionism[3].

Laws on Industrial Disputes and Trade Unions—Outlines of Suggested Changes

One of the items included for consideration at the National Labour conference held on 17th and 18th September 1982 related important industrial relation issues - Further amendments to the I.D. Act, 1947 and T.U. Act, 1926. The conference referred this item for detailed examination to a committee under the chairmanship of Shri Sanat Mehta, Minister of Finance and Labour, Gujarat, in which State Governments, central workers and employers' organisations, who participated at the conference were represented. The committee gave certain recommendations on the issues referred to it and these were unanimously adopted at the conference. The committee convened a second meeting of this committee on the 18th September 1982 to consider the various suggestions in item of 4 of the Agenda, which are not covered by the recommendations of the committee. It was decided at that meeting that the convener of the committee would prepare a note indicating a draft outline of the manner in which the recommendations already made by the committee could be translated in the form of legislation.

The note was prepared by the convener at the request of the committee which is not to be taken as the views of the ministry of labour on the various issues. It also covered the left over items of the relevant memorandum of NLC. This was considered at the subsequent meeting of the committee held on the 10th December and 20th December, 1982. In the light of the outcome of the discussions on the various items covered in the note the committee agreed to recast the outline of the suggested changes on the lines indicated below.

I. Industrial Relations Acts

- Industrial Relations commissions,
- Standing Labour courts and
- Procedure for settlement of Individual and collective disputes.

The national labour conference had recommended setting up of Industrial Relations commissions, both at the center and the state level as the machinery for resolution of Industrial disputes, in the same manner and with the same functions as recommended by the national commission on labour. The national commission had recommended that the Industrial Relations commissions will be an authority Independent of the executive and the main functions would be

(a) Conciliation;

(b) Adjudication in Industrial disputes; and

(c) Certification of unions as representative unions.

The president of the Commission would have judicial qualifications and experience and there would be judicial and non-judicial members to assist him. The non-judicial members would be persons eminence in the field of industry, labour or management. The judicial members should be persons who are eligible for appointment as judges of a high court. The conciliation wrong will consists of conciliation officers with or without judicial qualifications.

The committee recommends that the proposed new legislation shall prescribe for setting up of Independent Industrial relations commissions and the constitution, setup, qualifications of chairman, members, the supporting officers and staff shall be on the same lines as given in the recommendations of the National Commission on Labour. The Law has to reflect the exact position and Government may work out the details in consultation with the state Governments.

The procedure for settlement of individual disputes would

be by a simple grievance redressal procedure with built-in grievance arbitration. In the respect of collective disputes where collective bargaining fails, the normal means for settlement would be by arbitration. Where arbitration is not acceptable to the parties they can approach the conciliation wing of IRC which would mediate with a view to help the two parties to arrive at a bipartite settlement. The adjudication wing of I.R.C will deal with issues where a conciliation wing is not in a position to sort them out. The decision of the adjudicator would be final and binding on the parties.

The certification wing would deal with all matters connected with registration of unions and identification of negotiating agent and other issues specifically referred to it.

Standing labour courts would also function at the center and at the states under the overall supervision of Industrial relations commissions. These would deal with disputes relating to rights and obligations, interpretation and implementation of awards and claims arising out of rights and obligations under the relevant provisions of law or agreements as well as disputes in regard to unfair labour practices and the like, vide recommendation No. 192 of the National Commission on Labour.

The labour courts would have powers for executions of the decisions of the I.R.Cs, Arbitrators, settlements and rights due under the statues, directly, in the same manner a collector is authorised to collect revenues. The courts would be provided with mamlatdars/Tahsildars, bailiffs and other staff with powers of revenue recovery and power as available to judicial courts for suction of properties so that the money released can be made available to the beneficiaries by the courts directly.

Collective Bargaining Agent

Statutory provision may be made for having a collective bargaining agent at the unit/industry level and the question as to who would be the agent would be decided by the check-off system. The check-off system would operate on the basis of a written authorization which would be valid for a period of 3 years given by every employee to the employer under intimation to the union concerned. The trade unions have to abide by a new code of conduct for being eligible to compete for check-off and recognition as collective bargaining agent and no craft/ category-wise union would be eligible to benefit from check-off or recognition. There would be sole collective bargaining agent, wherever feasible; failing which a composite—bargaining council with proportional representation subject to a minimum membership. The percentages of membership for qualification as sole agent or for inclusion in the council would be laid down by the I.R.Cs. Keeping in view the conditions of the industry, the area of operation, including the extent of unionnisation in that undertaking/industry. The recognition once granted would be valid for an initial period of 3 years and this status will continue till it is successfully challenged by others or when the recognized union violates the code of conduct. The disqualification arising out of violation of the code would operate for specified period.

The above recommendations can be given effect to by having a new chapter in the Industrial Relations Act on collective bargaining agent. The criteria for selection as a sole bargaining agent or as a member of the collective bargaining council has to be on such lines as indicated below.

(i) Where there is only one eligible registered union in a unit / industry it shall be certified as the sole bargaining agent, provided it has a minimum percentage of membership as the IRC may prescribe.

(ii) Where there is more than one registered union in a unit/industry, the union with the maximum support, which shall not be less than 40 percent for a unit-wise union, or 25 percent for an Industry-wise union, shall be certified as the sole bargaining agent.

(iii) Where the conditions stiputated in (i) and (ii) above are not satisfied, the registered trade unions in the unit / industry with a minimum membership as decided by the I.R.C, depending on the extent of unionsation in the unit/industry, may constitute a composite bargaining council for the unit/industry chosen from among the eligible registered trade unions in the unit/industry.

(iv) The trade unions certified as collective bargaining agent or as members of collective bargaining council may give a written undertaking to abide by the prescribed code of conduct as a pre-condition for being considered for certification and for continued functioning as the agent/member of the council.

Method of Determining the Representative Character of Trade Unions

The verification of membership of every registered trade union/industry would be carried out by the certificating wing of the IRC and for this purpose the IRC will rely on the check-off particulars available with the employer. Initially for a period of 6 months from a specified date every registered trade union in the unit/industry would have the facility of check-off. After the results of verification are known only the recognized union/unions will continue to have that facility. Every union/unions certified as collective bargaining agent/members of the collective bargaining council will continue to have the status still it is successfully challenged, after an initial period of 3 years.

Rights of Collective Bargaining Agent and Other Unions

A recognized unions, including members of the council, should alone have, among other things, the right to sole representation for entering into collective agreements on wages and other terms of employment and conditions of service of workmen, right to call for a strike in accordance with the procedure prescribed, right for continued availability of check-off, right for representation in all bipartite and tripartite committees/councils, right to discuss all matters with the employer and to inspect by prior agreement the place of work of any of its member and the right to seek and receive information relevant for collective bargaining purposes.

All registered trade unions will have the right to represent the cause of their workers on all matters connected with individual disputes.

Check-Off

The recommendation is that each employee will be free to indicate to the management, the union of which he is a member and authorize the management in writing to recover from his wages the union subscription and remit it to the union. The check-off authorization by the employees would be valid for a period of 3 years.

The Payment of Wages Act, 1936 has already been amended so as to provide that deductions made, with the written authorization of the employed persons, for payment of fees payable by him for the membership of any trade union registered under the Trade Unions Act, 1926 would constitute valid deductions. All disputes relating to check-off will be decided by the IRC.

Code of Conduct

Trade Union Organisations

The recommendation is that only such trade union organisations should be eligible for recognition as collective bargaining agent, who qualify according to a fresh code of conduct to be laid down a list of unfair labour practices is now given in fifth schedule to the I.D. Act, 1947 (yet to be brought into force). What is now required is to spell out certain positive attitudes the trade unions should adopt so that the members and office-bearers of the trade unions function with a sense of dedication in the cause of the unit/industry. Some of the aspects that could be brought in the proposed code are....

(i) Every employee in an industry or unit shall have the freedom and right to join a union of his choice. No coercion shall be exercised in this matter.

(ii) There shall be unreserved acceptance of an respect for, democratic functioning of trade unions.

(iii) There shall be regular and democratic elections of executive bodies and office-bearers of trade union.

(iv) Casteism, communalism and provincialism shall be

enchewed by all unions.

(v) The trade union shall made every member conscious of his duties and impress on them the need to work with dedication and sincerity.

(vi) The trade union shall not encourage it members to participate in sympathetic strikes, bandhs etc which have nothing to do with any of workers grievances.

Employers

The committee has also recommended that there shall be a code of conduct for employers. The following could form part of such a code.

(i) The employer shall not declare any lock-out, closure, or lay-off or retrenchment, except in accordance with the procedure laid down in the Act and prior consultation with the recognized collective bargaining agent.

(ii) All schemes of rationalization, automation and the like shall in the first instance be discussed collective bargaining agent / bargaining council.

(iii) The employer shall not violate the terms and conditions of service of the workers.

(iv) The employer shall faithfully implement the provisions of all labour laws.

(v) The employer shall accept arbitration when unions offer settlement of disputes.

Whenever the employer/union violates the code the IRC shall impose appropriate punishment including suspension or cancellation of recognitions in the case of trade union appropriate deterrent fine in the case of employers.

Arbitration

The committee had recommended that all individual disputes shall be settled by a simple grievance redressal procedure with built-in-grievance arbitration. Government had already amended the I.D. Act, 1947 to provide for a system of grievance settlement machinery. Thus provisions can be further augmented by providing that whenever are individual remains still aggrieved by the award of the grievance machinery he will have on automatic right to invoke arbitration and every industrial establishment having 50 or more workmen will have a mutually acceptable grievance arbitrator. In dealing with an individual dispute the arbitrator will have the same powers as are available under section 11 A of the I.D. Act, 1947 and the arbitrator shall also call for fresh evidence for deciding all issue in the interest of securing the ends of justice. He may also have powers for grant of interim relief by way of subsistence allowance to individual workman, subject to conditions of non-employment elsewhere during the pendency of the case in arbitration.

The committee had recommended voluntary arbitration also in respect of collective disputes as the normal means of settling disputers wherever collective bargaining fails. Further, the award of the arbitrator including the grievance arbitration award shall be a speaking award, and it shall be final and binding on all parties and shall not be called in question in any court except on grounds of the arbitrator having acted without jurisdiction or on grounds of perversity.

Strikes and Lockouts

Procedure for strikes and Lockouts

The NLC had recommended that every strike whether in an industry classified as essential or not shall be preceded by a strike ballot in which all the workers in the establishment are allowed to participate and resort to strike may be made only if the results of the ballot show that not less than 60 percent of the workers support the strike.

At present the only requirement before going on strike, and that too in relation to public utility services, is serving of a notice. The law may provide that only a certified collective bargaining agent or a member of the composite bargaining council shall have a right to serve a notice of strike. Further the notice will be served only in furtherance of a collective demand and after mutual discussions had failed, and arbitration has been refused by the employer prescribed and the results of the ballot show that 60 percent the workmen of the of the union/ industry support the strike. The strike ballot would be supervised by the IRC.

No Lock-out could be declared by an employer unless collective bargaining has failed and the union has refused arbitration and it is otherwise permissible under the law and this should be proceeded by a decision taken at the highest level of the establishment. However exception could be made in cases of extreme violence for purposes of protecting life and property.

The labour courts would be the authority to decide whether a strike or lock-out is legal and while doing so the court shall take into account the circumstances which led to it and the views of the collective bargaining agent, the employer and the appropriate Government. For getting a decision on this, the collective bargaining agent, the employer and the Government can approach the labour court directly.

Every workman would be free to file an application before the courts for strike / lock-out period wages and the labour court can decided the admissibility of wages as an incidental matter and thereafter proceed to compute the same and order payment.

(i) ***Go-Slow***

The present definition of the term 'strike' in the I.D. Act, 1947 does not cover 'go-slow'. The definition of the term 'strike' shall include 'go-slow' on the lines provided in Maharashtra Act.

(ii) ***Public utility services***

There is no need for a separate concept as public utility services.

(iii) ***Settlement and awards***

When a settlement is arrived at as between employer and the collective bargaining agent / council or there exists a conciliation settlement, such settlements may prescribe a period of validity, which may not be less than 3 years, and no union, workman or management shall challenge the settlement during the period of validity of the settlement.

All awards shall remain in force for a period of 3 years or such longer period as indicated in the award or settlement and this may apply also arbitration awards.

(iv) Section 25-M and 25-N Chapter VB – Lay-off and retrenchment

The existing provisions on lay-off will continue, as far as the procedure concerned, no workman shall be laid off by his employer except with the previous permission of the authority specified by the appropriate Government.

Sections 25-M and 25-N may also be restructured on the same lines as the revised section 25-0 Incorporated in the Industrial Disputes (amendment) Act, 1982, so that the sections provide for (i) giving notice in writing (ii) holding of enquires (iii) guidelines for authorities to follow before granting or refusing to grant permission and (iv) a provision for appeal against the orders of the specified authority.

(v) Chapter V-A

Chapter V-A and Chapter V-B may be integrated further the integrated chapter will apply to all activities irrespective of whether they are factories, mines or plantations. So that the employer in every industrial establishment employing 100 or more workmen would have to obtain prior approval for lay-out, retrenchment and closure.

(vi) Definition of the term 'retrenchment'

The term 'retrenchment' may be redefined so that in addition to what is already provided in the Act, the term may not include;

(a) Voluntary abandonment of service without intimation.

(b) Compulsory retirement according to the provisions of standing orders or contract employment by giving notice after the minimum prescribed years of service, and not for reasons of disciplinary action.

The representatives of the state Governments did not want any change in the existing definition. The representatives of the employers had their own views on what is meant by retrenchment and the chairman agreed to incorporate their views as such. No such views have been received.

(vii) ***Regulation of conditions service by Government certain circumstances***

Wherever there is an Industrial Dispute and the employer and workmen are unable to come to any settlement on matters in dispute, be it in an industry covered as an essential services under the essential services and Maintenance Act or otherwise, after the disputes is seized in conciliation, arbitration or adjudication, the IRC may issue an order requiring the employers, workmen, or both to observe, for such period as may be specified in accordance with that order certain terms and conditions in relation to their workmen. This would be purely an interim measure and would cease to operate once there is a settlement or the adjudicator gives an interim or final award in the dispute.

(viii) ***Protection of legitimate trade union activities***

A specific provision as may be made in the law to the effect that the office-bearers of a union and unions certified as bargaining agent/member of council would have protection from acts such as dismissal, termination of employment, changes in conditions of service and connected matters as long as they are office-bearers and for a further period of 3 years immediately after relinquishing such office. This protection would, however, not be available to an office-bearer where he commits a proved misconduct.

(ix) ***Definition of the term "employer"***

The term "employer" may be redefined as :

"Employer includes, where the owner of any undertaking

in the course of or, for the purposes of conducting the undertaking, contracts with any person for the execution by or, under the contractor of the whole or, any part of any work which is ordinarily part of the undertaking the owner of the under taking.

The labour secretary, Maharashtra would make available to the employers the details of the case laws indicating what the term 'ordinarily' means.

(x) Notice of change: Section-9A

The Act may provide that every objection to a notice of change raised by the bargaining agent / council and not sorted out would be an industrial dispute and the procedure accepted for resolution of collective disputes would be followed.

(xi) Time limit for raising disputes and filing application under sec. 33C (2)

It was decided that no time limit is necessarily for raising of disputes. To check old and state case being the subject matter of reference to labour courts the law may provide a time limit of 12 months for filing applications. This can be waived where the applicants satisfy the authority that they had sufficient cause for not making the application within such period, and the maximum period for admitting delayed applications shall be 3 years.

(xii) Unfair labour practices

The list of unfair labour practices in the schedule of the I.D. Act has to be reviewed particularly in the context of the 'code of conduct'. All complaints of violations of the provisions of chapter VI and the fifth schedule to the Act may be treated as offences which IRCs may decide as courts and for this purpose the provisions of section 30 of the Maharashtra Recognition of Trade Unions and Prevention of Unfair Labour Practices Act shall be adopted. It was also accepted that to check double proceedings the provisions of section 59 of the Maharashtra Recognition of Trade Unions and Prevention of Unfair Labour Practices Act shall also be adopted.

Trade Unions Act, 1926

It was agreed that with the coming into force of a new Industrial Relations (I R) Law, Industrial Relations Committees (IRC), as the authority, the functions of the Registrars of the trade unions would done by the certification wing of the IRC. And the powers that are necessary have to be redefined in that context. The committee made the following recommendations on some aspects relating to amendments to the Trade Unions Act, 1926 as listed in the memorandum.

(i) Provisions for delegation of powers from center to state. At present there is no provision for delegation of powers to state Governments units or its officers by the Central Government as appropriate Governments, is concerned. No uniform procedure is followed in respect of registration of trade union whose of objects are spread over more than one state. The present arrangement which emanates from powers delegated to State Governments under the constitution needs to be specifically spelt out in the Act itself. The committee recommends that a provision on the same lines as in sect 39 of the I.D. Act be made in the T.U. Act, 1926.

(ii) The IRCs while dealing with trade union will have powers to review their decisions and what should be the nature of this and other provisions could be left to the IRCs to formulate.

(ii) Item (h) of section 6 of the Trade Unions Act, 1926 provided that the values of trade union applying for registration provide for the manner in which members to the executive and the other office-bearer of the trade union shall be appointed and removed. In the absence of a stipulation for a minimum tenure for office-bearership, certain office-bearers continue in officer indefinitely and election to office-bearership are never held. The committee recommends that the rules should provide a limit of two or three years.

(iv) In the interest of better management of funds of Trade Unions, auditing of the accounts of the funds of Trade Unions should be conducted by outsiders where the total membership of the union is 300 or above. In other cases they may choos an auditor from among the persons included in the panel of auditors maintained by IRCs and Government, would bear the expenses for audit.

(v) The mode, frequency, need etc connected with operation of sec: 28(4) of the Act for dealing with returns would be left to the IRCs discretion.

(vi) The Act does not provide penalty for failure to maintain accounts. In the absence of this, the position relating to maintenance and scrutiny of accounts are not proving effective. The suggestion is to make these punishable with fine (the fine being a maximum of Rs. 2000.

(vii) Registration of central organisation of workers and employers. The central organisations of workers and employers including federation would also get themselves registered as trade union and registration would with reference to the number of unions affiliated to them. The representative of the HMS (K) while agreeing to this mentioned that he is not component to be a signatory to this recommendation and his note of dissent recorded.

The Indian industrial relations system along with the adjudicatory process under the Industrial Disputes Act, 1947 has been subjected to great criticism from time to time. The present dispute settlement procedure is not providing the right of self-determination by the workermen. This is against trade union solidarity. The employer was never voluntarily forthcoming to mitigate the dissatisfaction. It is the government which has to decide whether any industrial dispute is apprehended and whether it is a fit case for reference to the authorities and whether The award given by me authorities ought to be enforced or not. That power is generally said-to be exercised *malafidely* and under political motivation. The employer always has the-ways and means to influence the government personnel as well as the government policy. and actions. Neither the policy nor actions found favour with the concerned and industrial unrest has prevailed in most of our industries.

The First National Commission on Labour was appointed in 1966 to explore a suitable alternative to the multifarious labour problems. The Commission submitted its report famously

Known as NCL Report. It made several recommendations. Commenting on the present adjudicatory machinery, the commission suggested that there should be an Industrial Relations Commission at the centre as well as in the states which will adjudicate industrial disputes, conciliate and also certify trade unions as representative unions. Before the dispute is actually handled by such a commission it could well be processed through Joint management councils, code of discipline, grievance machinery etc. The government reacted positively to the recommendations and implemented many of the recommendations by either bringing out legislation or making necessary amendments to augment the change.

The most important problem is to decide whether to continue with the present system of dispute settlement machinery wedded to the philosophy of adjudication or should there by a switch in favour of collective bargaining. Unable to choose, the government persisted in continuing with the old machinery only. The suggestion given by the National Commission on labour for setting up of Industrial Relations Commission even if it is accepted, may not bring in the desired result and may prove a flop 'in the times to come because of certain basic reasons. Firstly, the commission will be a further addition in the functioning of adjudicatory machinery already existing. After the Negotiations failed, if the parties do not want arbitration, then the commission will help in conciliating the dispute. If that does not bring any result then IRC itself will adjudicate. Appeal from that might lie either to High Court or Supreme Court. This means that one more step is added making the parties still more difficult resulting in more and more delay in the disposal of cases.

This report was actively considered by the labour ministry and consultation and, interaction on the recommendations with the worker's representatives, employers' organisations, experts has also been initiated long back. These far reaching recommendations by the second national commission on labour awaits imp1ementation. Its implementation needless to say, would go along way in making the industrial adjudicatory process more effective and efficient.

Report of Second National Commission on Labour—A Realistic Appraisal

The Second National Commission on Labour (NCL), under the Chairmanship of Hon'ble Shri Ravindra Varma, was set up on 15.10.1999 to suggest rationalization of existing laws relating to labour in the organised sector; and to evolve an "umbrella" legislation for ensuring a minimum level of protection to the workers in the unorganized sector.

Main Recommendations of the Second National Commission on Labour

I. *Approach to Review of Laws*

1. The impact of globalisation can already been seen in many fields. Competitiveness cannot be acquired without harmonious relations in the industry. The requirement today among the employers and employees is to develop a mindset that looks upon each other as partner and to develop a work culture that new technology and the context of globalisation demand.
2. Labour laws are not the only cause of our unsatisfactory economic development. This, however, does not mean that we do not believe in the need for changes both in laws and attitude.
3. There is an imperative need to evolve a new work culture. The wages have to be looked upon as incomes that are earned through hard work. Individual worker's attitude to work has to include pride in maximizing his own productivity to repay his debt to the society and pride in his commitment to excellence reflected in the quality of work. We must be concerned at the moral culpability of 'short charging' or 'working less' and accepting the same payment.
4. The managements can make contribution to improve work culture. For maintaining high level of work culture, the arrangement required to be established include fair wages, equitable profit sharing, participatory management and opportunities to interact.

5. We have maximum number of holidays. A study reveals that out of seven days an average govt. servant works for three days. If the Government offices are closed all economic activities dependent on government departments come to a standstill. There should be three national holidays. In addition there can be two more holidays and ten restricted holidays in a year.

6. The attitude to hours of work should not be rigid, but hours of work put in beyond nine hours a day and 48 hours a week must be compensated by payment of O. T. wages.

7. For meeting the demand of hire and fire, it is necessary to create social acceptability for change and the social institutions that can take care of the consequences. A fundamental change of this kind has to be preceded by the evolution of socially accepted consensus on new perceptions of jobs, evolution of a system of constant upgradation of employability through training and setting up of social security including unemployment insurance.

II. Review of Laws

1. Whatever be the employment limit, there are certain provisions like maternity benefit, child care, workmen's compensation, medical benefits and other elements of social security and safety which must be applicable to all workers, irrespective of the employment size of the establishment, or the nature of its activity.

2. The Government may either lay down a list of such highly paid jobs who are presently deemed as workmen or fix a cut off limit of remuneration which is substantially high enough, in the present context, such as Rs. 25,000/- p.m. beyond which employees will not be treated as ordinary "workmen". Supervisors would be kept out of definition of 'workers' and would be clubbed along with managerial and administrative employees.

3. The existing set of labour laws should be broadly grouped into four or five groups of laws pertaining to (i) industrial relations, (ii) wages,

(iii) social security, (iv) safety, and (v) welfare and working conditions and so on.

4. The provisions of all laws be judiciously consolidated into a single law called the 'Labour Management Relations Law'. However, we would carve out a section of these workers who are employed in establishments with an employment size of 19 and below, for a different kind of dispensation. We also recommend the repeal of the Sales Promotion Employees (Conditions of Service) Act, 1976 and other specific Acts governing industrial relations in particular trades or employments and also specific laws.

5. Changes in labour laws should be accompanied by well defined social security package.

6. Definition of certain terms such as worker, wages, establishment, etc. should be common in all the labour laws.

7. "Go slow" and "work to rule" are forms of action which must be regarded as misconduct.

8. In socially essential services like water supply, there may be a strike ballot and if the strike ballot shows that 51 % of workers are in favour of a strike, it should be taken that the strike has taken place, and the dispute must forthwith be referred to compulsory arbitration.

9. We are recommending a ceiling on the total number of trade unions of which an 'outsider' can be a member of executive bodies. Trade Unions of workers in the unorganised sector should be registered even where there is no employer employee relationship.

10. Federations or Central organisations of workers should be subject to the same discipline as primary trade unions. Craft or caste-based trade unions should not be entitled to any privileges, immunities or rights.

11. We recommend that the negotiating agent should be selected for recognition on the basis of the check off system. A union with 66 % membership be entitled to be accepted as

the single negotiating agent, and if no union has 66 % support, then unions that have the support of more than 25 % should be given proportionate representation on the negotiating college.

12. Secret ballot is logically and financially a difficult process in certain industries. Check-off system has the advantage of ascertaining the relative strength of trade unions. Check-off system should be made compulsory for all establishments employing 300 or more workers. For establishments employing less than 300 workers also the check-off system would be the preferred mode. Recognition once granted, should be valid for a period of four years, to be coterminous with the period of settlement.

13. All establishments employing 20 or more workers should have standing orders or regulations. Employers of establishments employing 50 at more workers will discuss and decide the standing orders in consultation with the negotiating agent. In case no understanding is reached, the matter shall be decided by the certifying officer appointed by the appropriate govt. Refusal to go for training, which must be at the employers' cost and the employer's time, may be included as, an act of misconduct under the standing orders if such refusal is without valid reasons.

14. A Grievance Redressal Committee for organisations employing 20 or more should be constituted.

15. Prior permission is not necessary in respect of lay-off and retrenchment in an establishment of any employment size. However, in cases of establishments employing 300 or more workers if the lay off is continued for more than 30 days, post facto permission of the appropriate govt. shall be required. The provisions of Chapter VB pertaining to permission for closure should be made applicable to all establishments to protect the interests of workers in establishments which are not covered at present by this provision if they are employing 300 or more workers. All dues of the workers have to be first settled as a precondition to retrenchment or closure. In case of retrenchment, the profit making units shall be

required to pay 60 days wages as compensation for every completed year of service and the establishments which are making losses will have to pay 45 days wages as compensation. In case of closure, the units which have been incurring losses continuously for three years or more will pay 30 days wages for every completed year of service as compensation and the establishments which are not making losses but want to close down shall pay 45 days wages as compensation. Units employing less than 100 workers will have to pay 50% of the amount mentioned above as compensation for retrenchment and closure.

16. The provision for permission to close down an establishment employing 300 or more workmen should be made a part of Chapter VA, and Chapter VB should be repealed. A sixty days notice will be required to be given or wages will be required to be paid in lieu of notice for retrenching or closing down.

17. Labour courts, Lok Adalats and Labour Relations Commissions (LRC) shall form the adjudicatory system to deal with all matters. The labour court will function under the supervision of LRC. The conciliation function will remain with the executive. Officials of labour departments at the Centre and the State who are of and above the rank of Deputy Labour Commissioners/Regional Labour Commissioners with ten years experience in the labour department and a degree in law would be eligible for being appointed as presiding officers of labour courts.

18. All matters pertaining to individual workers be determined by recourse to the grievance redressal committee, conciliation and arbitration/ adjudication by the labour court. The union having at least 10% membership amongst the workers of an establishment shall only have the right to represent cases of individual workers.

19. We recommend that a strike should be called only by the recognised negotiating agent and that too after it had conducted a strike ballot amongst all the workers, of whom at least 51 % support the move to strike. For declaring lock

out, the decision should be taken at the highest level in the management. No strike or lock-out should be declared without giving 14 days' notice. In case of illegal strike, the workers shall lose three days' wages for every day of illegal strike. For illegal lock out, the employer shall pay three days wages for every day of such lock out to the workers.

20. The time has come to legislatively provide for a scheme of workers participation in management. It may be initially applicable to all establishments employing 300 or more persons. For the smaller establishments, a non-statutory scheme may be provided.

21. Small Entrepreneurs (Employment Relations) Act that we have recommended, seeks to cover all aspects of employment including wages, social security, safety and health, bonus and so on (which will be a composite law and will apply to all establishments employing 19 workers and below).

22. Contract labour shall not be engaged for core production/ services/activities. However, for sporadic seasonal demand, the employer may engage temporary labour for core production/service activity. We are aware that off loading perennial non-core services like canteen, watch & ward, cleaning, etc. to other employing agencies has to take care of three aspects - (1) there have to be provisions that ensure that perennial core services are not transferred to other agencies or establishments; (2) where such services are being performed by employees on the pay rolls of the enterprises, no transfer to other agencies should be done without consulting, the negotiating agent; and (3) where the transfer of such services do not involve any employee who is currently in service, the management will be free to entrust the service to outside agencies. The contract labour will, however, be remunerated at the rate of a regular worker engaged in the same organization doing work of a comparable nature or if such worker does not exist in the organization, at the lowest salary of a worker in a comparable grade, i.e., unskilled, semi-skilled or skilled. The principal employer will also ensure that the prescribed social security and other benefits

are extended to the contract worker. No worker should be kept casual or temporary for more than two years continuously.

23. The minimum wage payable to anyone in employment, in whatever occupation, should be such as would satisfy the needs of the worker and his family (consisting in all of 3 consumption units) arrived at on the Need Based formula of the 15th Indian Labour Conference supplemented by the recommendations made in the Judgment of the Supreme Court in the Raptakos Brett & Co case.

24. The Commission recommends that every employer must pay each worker his one-month's wage, as bonus before an appropriate festival. Any demand for bonus in excess of this upto a maximum of 20 % of the wages will be subject to negotiation. Wage ceiling for coverage of workers and for calculation of bonus be raised to Rs. 7500 and Rs.3500 respectively.

25. Central Government may notify the National Floor Level Minimum Wage. Each State/Union Territory should have the authority to fix minimum rates of wages, which shall not be, in any event, less than the National Floor Level Minimum Wage when announced.

26. There is no need for any wage board, statutory or otherwise, for fixing wage rates for workers in any industry.

27. We would recommend consolidation of all laws of the kind and the enactment of a general law relating to working conditions at the work place. For safety, we recommend an omnibus law with different rules for different activities (such as factories, mines; construction, etc.). There should be no restriction on employment of women worker during night hours, if there are at least 5 women workers working in the establishment during that time and the employer provides for their safety and transport. There should be no exemption from labour laws for export processing or special economic zones. Appropriate Govt. may grant exemptions under the laws in case of extreme emergency or hardship. Normal amenities like canteen, drinking water,

washing facilities, be prescribed under the law. Help of local bodies, or NGOs may be sought in this regard. All establishments employing 20 or more workers must provide crèche.

28. We have provided for equal wages for equal work for female workers under the composite law on wages. The other provisions of Equal Remuneration Law should be suitably incorporated either in law on wages or on working conditions. The simplification of returns and registers required to be maintained by the employers should be pursued.

29. Every large State and groups of small States should set up Institutions for training and research in labour matters. V. V. Giri National Labour Institute will help the State Governments in their effort to transform the caliber of labour administration.

30. All matters needing adjudication including under Workmen's Compensation Act or claims or disputes relating to Social Security will be determined by labour courts with provision for appeal to LRCs. Collective disputes between the negotiating agent and the employer, if not resolved bilaterally or in conciliation or arbitration should be dealt with by the LRCs. This will need considerable increase in the number of labour courts and setting up of labour commissions will also increase the demands for high level labour adjudicating functionaries. We recommend an all India Labour Judicial Service which in the new dispensation will be viable and necessary. Equally important is the need for constituting an All India Labour Administrative Service which will enable exchange of officers between centre or state.

III. Unorganised Sector

1. We have to address the question as to what is the minimum that the Umbrella legislation for workers in the Unorganised Sector should ensure. There should be a policy framework that ensures the generation and protection of jobs, access to jobs; protection against the exploitation of poverty and lack of organisation, protection against arbitrary or whimsical

dismissals; denial of minimum wages and delay in payment of wages, etc. The system of Welfare should include access to compensation for injuries sustained while engaged in work; provident fund; medical care; pensionary benefits; maternity benefits and childcare shelter and old age support.

2. The law should be capable of being implemented and monitored easily. It should include machinery for disposal of claims and complaints at a place that is closer to the place of work with expeditions.

3. The system of social security must be such that the worker can make commensurate contribution to the cost, consistent with as many as of his needs as possible.

4. To meet these crucial requirement the Commission has proposed the constitution of unorganised sector workers board with constituent bodies that will extend to the level of Panchayats. An indicative bill for the workers in the unorganised sector to ensure their minimum protection and welfare has been appended in the report.

IV. Social Security

1. The term 'workman' may be replaced by the term 'employee' so as to make the Workmen's Compensation Act applicable to all categories of employees. The Workmen's Compensation Act should be converted from an employers' liability scheme to a social insurance scheme.

2. The provisions of maternity benefit should be extended so as to be applicable to workers in the organised sector. In the unorganised sector women workers need separate legislations for maternity benefits.

3. Running of medical services by ESIC parallel through national health service needs to be reviewed in the current context when public as well as private medical services have increased. Corporation has to take a decision to dealing employment injury and maternity benefits from medical benefits and extend these benefits through out the country. It has been strongly urged that the benefit structure of ESI be unpacked

and provision be made for extension of the scheme for one or more benefits separately or in separate groups.

4. The P.F. Act be made applicable to all classes of establishments, subject to such exceptions as may be considered necessary for specified reasons.

5. The Task Force on Social Security has recommended that the employment threshold should be brought down to 10 immediately, to 5 during the next 3-5 years, and to one within a short time frame thereafter. The Commission agrees with these suggestions.

6. Provision may be made in the EPF Act to enable the organisation to frame different schemes with different contributory and benefit packages.

7. The Payment of Gratuity Act may be integrated with the EPF Act and converted into a social insurance scheme.

8. An integrated insurance scheme providing for gratuity, unemployment should be for benefits, layoff and retrench compensation may be evolved. An unemployment insurance scheme could play a substantial role in coping with unacceptable levels of unemployment resulting from the implementation of the structural adjustment programmes and other economic reforms.

9. Welfare funds (under the Ministry of Labour) can be transformed into instruments of social security by expanding the coverage of the funds; broadening the range of benefits; modifying the financial arrangements for providing benefits and decentralising the administration of the funds.

10. It is the responsibility of the State to provide a basic level of subsistence by an appropriate social security measure to those who have no employment and no source of income. The Central Government should consider introducing a National Scheme of Unemployment Relief to the unemployed persons subject to a means test.

11. The social security system envisaged by the Commission comprises of four tiers, (a) Social assistance programmes,

financed from the exchequer and wholly based on tax revenue, (b) Schemes which are partly contributory and partly subsidised by the State, (c) Wholly contributory social insurance schemes; and (d) Voluntary Schemes.

12. It is high time that a national policy on social security is formulated and a national plan to achieve the objectives set out in this policy. It is necessary to create a small but strong agency in the Central Government which will be concerned with the horizontal and vertical coordination of social security planning, monitoring and review.

13. We strongly recommend the constitution of a high-powered National Social Security Authority, preferably under the chairmanship of the Prime Minister of India. The functions of the Authority will be mainly to formulate the National Policy on Social Security and to co-ordinate the Central and State level programmes. We would suggest a Department of Social Security within the Ministry of Labour.

V. Women & Child Labour

1. Childcare is a major investment in the protection and development of human resources. The mechanisms of childcare should be multi-dimensional. Labour legislation should include provisions for creches where there are 20 or more workers irrespective of the gender of the worker. If it is found that individual enterprises are not in a position financially to run their own creches, enterprises may jointly establish and operate them. Another possibility is that *Panchayats* or local bodies or local tripartite groups run creches, and employing units are asked to make a proportionate contribution to the costs.

2. The approach of the Study Group on Women and Child Labour has been that the child, the child's welfare and the child's future should be central to our programmes, and to our laws. Children are the future of our society, and our economy. Every child should have the opportunity to develop his or her skills and potential, to participate both as a citizen and as a worker. The Commission endorses this

approach.

3. The only way to prevent child labour is to recognise that the rightful place of children is in school, not in the workplace or in the house. So, the first step is to ensure compulsory primary education for all children.

4. The implementation of the present Act depends entirely on the State's bureaucratic machinery. It assumes that the bureaucracy, poorly staffed and ill-equipped as it is today, will be able to ensure that children do not work in hazardous processes and occupations, and conditions of work in non-hazardous settings will be upgraded.

5. We are proposing an indicative law on child labour which would replace the existing Child Labour (Regulation and Prohibition) Act 1986.

VI. Skill Development

1. The study group appointed by us has recommended a new modular approach to vocational training, which will aid multi-skilling, impart skills attuned to the needs of the labour market, and in consonance with the latest technology. We endorse these recommendations.

2. We recommend that an independent regulatory authority be constituted by the Government, whose functions shall, among other things, include setting standards for skills required for a particular competency, standards for programme implementation and standards for accreditation of institutions imparting training programmes for skill development and retraining.

3. For better matching of demand and supply of marketable skills, a labour market intelligence system needs to be set up.

4. We recommend that ITIs need to run market-driven courses; review, and if necessary, revise curriculum every 5 years to keep it contemporary.

5. Further, to ensure effective involvement of industry in the

training process, we recommend that some ITIs may be selected, on a pilot basis, for development into Institutes of Excellence. They should be managed jointly with the industry.

6. Vocational education should be integrated at the school level.[4]

Need to Establish Industrial Relations Commission

I. *Industrial Relations Commission*

(i) The present arrangement for appointment adhoce industrial tribunals should be discontinued. An Industrial Relations Commission (IRC) on a permanent basis should be setup at the center and one each state for settling 'interest' disputes. The IRC will be an authority independent of the executive.

(ii) The National Industrial Relations Commission should be appointed by the Central Government for Industries for which that Government is the appropriate authority. The NIRC would deal with such disputes which involve questions of national importance or which are likely to affect or interest establishment situated in more than one state. Its scope should be broadly the same as that of National Tribunals under the I.D. Act, 1947.

(iii) Each state should have IRC for settlement of disputes for which the state Government is the appropriate authority.

(iv) The main functions of the National / state IRCs will be (a) adjudication in industrial disputes (b) conciliation and (c) certification of unions as representative unions.

(v) The Commission should be constituted with a person having prescribed judicial qualifications and experience as its president and an equal number of judicial and non-judicial members : the non-judicial members need not have qualifications to hold judicial posts, but should be otherwise eminent in field of industry, labour or management judicial members of the National Industrial

Relations commission, including its president should be appointed from among persons who are eligible for appointment as judges of a High Court.

(vi) The conciliation wing of the commission will consist of conciliation officers with the prescribed qualifications and status. There will be persons with or without judicial qualifications in the cadre of conciliations. Those who have judicial qualifications would be eligible for appointment as judicial members of the commission after they acquire the necessary experience and expertise others could aspire for membership in the non-judicial wing.

(vii) The functions relating the certification of unions will vest with a separate wing of the national / state IRC.

(viii) The commission may provide arbitrators from amongs its members / officers incase parties agree to avail of such services. The commission may permit its members to serve as chairman of central / state wage boards / committees, if chosen by appropriate Government for such appointment.

(ix) After negotiations have failed and before notice of strike / lockout is served the parties may agree to voluntary arbitration and the commission will help the parties in choosing a mutually acceptable arbitrator. Alternatively, either party may, during the period covered by the said notice, approach the commission for naming as conciliator within the commission to help them in arriving at a settlement.

(x) In essential industries / services ; when collective bargaining fails and when the parties to the dispute do not agree to arbitration, either party shall notify the IRC with a copy to the appropriate Government, of the failure of negotiations where upon the IRC shall adjudicate upon the dispute and its award shall be final and binding upon the parties.

(xi) In case of non-essential industries / services following the failure of negotiations and refusal by the parties to avail of voluntary arbitration, the IRC after the receipt of notice of direct action (but during the notice period) may offer to the parties its good offices for settlement. After expiry of the notice period, if no settlement is reached the parties will be free to resort the direct action. If direct action continues for 30 days it will be incumbent on the IRC to intervene and arrange for settlement of the dispute.

(xii) When a strike or lock-out commences, the appropriate Government may move the commission to call for the termination of the strike / lock-out on the ground that its continuance may affect the security of the state, National economy or public order and if after hearing the Government and the parties concerned, the commission is so satisfied, it may, for reasons to be recorded, call on the parties to terminate the strike / lock-out and file their statements before it. There upon, the commission shall adjudicate on the dispute.

(xiii) It should be possible to arrange transfer of cases from the National Industrial Relations Commission to the state Industrial Relations Commission and vice-verse under certain conditions.

(xiv) (a) The commission will have powers to decide to pay or with hold payments for the strike / lock-out period under certain circumstances.

(b) If during the pendency of the strike or thereafter, the employer dismissed or discharges an employee because he has taken part in such strike, it would amount to unfair labour practice and on proof of such practice, the employee will be entitled to reinstatement with back wages.

(xv) All collective agreements should be registered with the IRC.

(xvi) An award made by the IRC in respect of a dispute raised by the recognized union should be binding on all workers in the establishments and the employers.

II. ***Labour Courts***

(xvii) (a) Standing labour courts should be constituted in each state. The strength and location of such courts will be divided by the appropriate Government.

(b) Members of the labour court will be appointed by the Government on recommendation of the High Court. Generally the Government should be able to choose from a penal given by the High Court in the order in where the names are recommended.

(xviii) (a) Labour courts will deal with the disputes relating to rights and obligations, interpretation and implementation of awards and claims arising out of rights and obligations under the relevant provisions of law or arrangement as well as disputes in regard in unfair labour practices and the like.

(b) Labour courts will thus be the courts where all disputes specified above will be tried and their decisions implemented. Proceedings instituted by the parties asking for the enforcement rights falling under the aforesaid categories will entertained in that behalf appropriate powers enabling them to execute such claims should be conferred on them.

(xix) Appeals over the decisions of the labour in certain clearly defined matters may lie with the High Court within whose jurisdiction/are a the court is located.[5]

The Commission studied at length the factors that are necessary to improve the competitiveness of an industry and economic activities, to ensure a regime of harmonious industrial relations to ensure increasing opportunities of employment, to ensure at least a minimum level of protection and welfare of workers in all sectors of economy organized as well as unorganized.

The Commission felt that "Globalization has become a dominant future of the world economy over the last decade, as more and more nations are becoming integrated into the global economy through trade and capital flows." It also observed "globalization means different things to different people, and so, we have many definitions. We are, basically concerned with economic globalization which tries to integrate different economies of the world by removing barriers to trade and allowing free foreign investment across the national boundaries, free flow of private portfolio capital and international labour migration."

The Commission has also pointed out the salient features of economic reforms and said

1) "The government opened major sector of the economy which were so far reserved for the public sector to the private sector.
2) Foreign investment was invited in all these sectors.
3) All restrictions on the entry of private sector into the field of infrastructure and strategic industries were removed.
4) These is more freedom for financial institutions.
5) Banks can also approach capital markets for raising funds
6) The government wants to reduce its investment in the public sector enterprises.
7) Import restrictions have been reduced.
8) Subsidies are being cut, tax rates are being reduced and the entire fiscal system is being streamlined.
9) There is a free pricing of shares and more powers are given to the SEBI."

All these steps were initiated to tune the Indian initiative towards globalization and free access to foreign enterprises to Indian markets and also to enhance competitiveness to Indian entrepreneurs. The Commission has made detailed study of impact of globalization on Indian economy.

In its Report the Commission has made a detailed study of other important aspects of unorganized sector, social security measures, skills, measures of labor administration, workers participation in management, employment scenario in the country, review of wages and wage policy.

The Commission has paid more attention to the problems of

workers in the unorganized sector. For the first time, the commission was asked to propose an umbrella legislation for workers in the unorganized sector.

But the Commission expressed the difficulty in identifying or defining the unorganized sector for the lack of a single or primary criterion or characteristic by which the sector could be defined. The commission observed "it has often been pointed out, and perhaps universally accepted, that there are areas in the unorganized sector where it is difficult to identifying an 'employer' and hence, an employer -employee relationship,which the law can attempt to channalise or influence by defining rights and responsibilities and building up a system of social security on a contributory basis.

"The First National Commission on labour has also attempted to identify the problems of unorganized sector. It defined the unorganized sector as that part of the work force who have not been able to organize in pursuit of a common objective because of constraints such as (a) casual nature of employment (b) ignorance and illiteracy (c) Small size of establishments with low capital investment per person employed (d) Scattered nature of establishments and (e) superior strength of the employer operating singly or in combination. The commission mentioned some of the categories of unorganized labour such as:

(i) Contract labour including construction workers

(ii) Casual labour

(iii) Labour employed in small scale industry

(iv) Hand loom/Power loom workers

(v) Beedi and Cigar workers

(vi) Employees in shops and commercial establishments

(vii) Sweepers and Scavengers

(viii) Workers in Tanneries

(ix) Tribal labour and

(x) Other unprotected labour

The Commission also listed some of the characteristics of unorganized labour such as:

(a) Low scale of organization

(b) Operation of labour relations on a casual basis or on the basis of ship or personal relations.

(c) Small own accounts (household) enterprises or micro enterprises.

(d) Ownership of fixed and other assets by self.

(e) Risking of financial capital by self

(f) Involvement of family labourness

(g) Production expenditure distinguishable from house hold expenditures and use of capital goods

(h) Easy entry and exist

(i) Free mobility within the sector

(j) Use of indigenous resources and technology

(k) Unregulated or unprotected nature

(l) Absence of fixed working hours

(m) Lack of security of employment and social security benefits.

(n) Use of labour intensive technology

(o) Lack of support from government

(p) Workers living ill shins and squatter areas

(q) Lack of housing and access to urban services

(r) High percentage of migrant labour.

According to one view the organized sector can be distinguished from the unorganized by the presence of legal protection, size of establishments, capacity of the workers to organize themselves in union and the systematic manner in which production processes are organized in perceptible patterns.

It is also said all workers who are not covered by the existing social security laws like Employees State Insurance Act, Employees Provident Fund and Miscellaneous Provisions Act, Payment of Gratuity act and Maternity Benefit Act can be considered as part of the unorganized sector. Some of sectors come under unorganized sector are apprentices, casual and contract workers, home based artisans and a section of self employed persons involved in jobs such as vending, rag picking and rickshaw pulling. Domestic workers, sex workers, plantation workers, scavengers, agricultural workers, construction workers, migrant labour and those who perform manual and helper jobs also come in the category of unorganized sector workers. Workers who depend directly or indirectly on natural resources that are open or common property based are also included in the unorganized sector provided

a) that it does not include any such person who is subject to the three armed forces Acts or prison services.

b) and that they are not employed as permanent workers in

- factories "as defined under Factories Act
- plantations as defined under Plantations Labour Act, 1951
- Mines as defined under Mines Act 1952.
- Ships and commercial establishment as defined by the different State Acts.

The study group of the commission has listed some of the important characteristics of employment or conditions in the unorganized sector they are:

(ii) It is in general a low wage and low earning sector.

(iii) Women constitute an important section of the workers in this sector.

(iv) Family labor is engaged in some occupations.

(v) Economic activities, which engaged child labour fall within this sector.

(vi) Migrant labour is involved in some sub-sectors.

(vii) Presence of piece rate payment, home based work and contractual work in this sector.

(viii) Direct recruitment is on the decline.

(ix) Some kinds of employment which are seasonal

(x) Most jobs are, in the greater part, on casual basis.

(xi) Workers are not often organized into trade unions.

(xii) There are many co-operatives of self-employed workers.

(xiii) Debt bondage is common in such sector

(xiv) Health hazards exist in a majority of occupations.

Some of the labour legislations are applicable to the workers in the organized sector. The Factories Act., the Minimum Wages Act, The Equal Remuneration Act., the Payment of Wages Act., the Industrial Disputes Act., the Workmen's ompensation Act., the Payment of Gratuity Act are applicable to the workers in the unorganized sector where there isan identifiable employer employee relationship. In some of the employments or avocations, contractors are engaged and this resulting in a situation in which the principal employee does not come into the picture as in building construction activity, beedi rolling, mining or quarrying and various other occupations. These workers are sometimes covered under more than one law e.g. the contract labour (Regulation and Abolition) Act as well as under one specific law or another. However, the commission observed, "... the benefits and facilities prescribed under these laws are derived to them in most cases". Some of the legislations which provide social security to the organized workers are extended to the workers in the unorganized sector also.

Social Security

The Commission examined many aspects of social security relating to labour. The commission also considered the need to recognize' social security as a fundamental human right. The commission felt that "the responsibility to provide social security will be primarily that of the state, and it will be left to individual citizens to acquire higher levels of security through assumption of responsibility and contributory participation." The Commission also agreed with the view of the Task Force on Social Security which recommended that wage ceiling and employment threshold can and should be uniform with a provision for raising the wage ceiling and its eventual removal and lowering employment threshold and its ultimate removal, "Referring to the social security benefit under Workmen's Compensation Act, the Commission recommended that "The Workmen's Compensation Act should be converted from an employees liability scheme to a social insurance scheme, its coverage should be progressively extended to more employments and classes of employees and the restrictive clauses in schedule II of the Act should be removed." Special attention is also paid on application of Maternity Benefit Act and accepted that "there are many classes of establishments where women are being employed increasingly to which the Maternity Benefit Act is not applicable. For women in the unorganized sector, the commission felt that "so far as women in the unorganized sector are concerned, there is undoubtedly a need for a separate legislation for providing maternity benefits". The coil1mission while accepting the observations of the study group on social security, held that "the benefit structure of ESI scheme be unpacked, and provision be made for extension of the scheme for one or more benefits separately or in groups". The study group also suggested that immediate steps. are to be taken to extend the scope of the Act for the purpose of employment injury benefit and maternity benefit throughout the country.

The committee also opined that the management of the ESI scheme should be professionalized.

Regarding Provident Fund Schemes, the Commission felt that "The PF Act be made applicable to all classes of establishments, subject to such exceptions as may be considered necessary for specified reasons, The Commission suggested that "appropriate provisions be made ill the Act to enable the organization to frame different schemes with different contributory and benefit packages for application to different classes of establishments, employees and persons. This is particularly necessary to make the Act applicable to self - employed people." It is also suggested that the "EPF A should have its own mechanism for investment or its balances; investment patterns should be liberalized and government may consider assuring of indexed bonds for investment of PF balance." It is felt that "Proposals to integrate the Payment of Gratuity Act with the Employee Deposit linked scheme and also to introduce unemployment insurance scheme as part of the scheme should be implemented soon". It suggested, "the Payment of Gratuity Act " may be integrated with the EPF Act and converted into a social insurance scheme.

The commission felt that "the insurance companies be required to develop two or more plans providing coverage for the major risks faced by people leaving it to individuals to choose from among them according to their capacity."

Review of Laws

The Commission also reviewed the existing labour laws and it felt that the existing set of labour laws should be broadly grouped into four or five groups of laws pertaining to (i) industrial relations, (ii) wages, (iii) social security, (iv) safety and (v) welfare and working conditions and so on. The provisions of all laws are judiciously consolidate into a single law called 'Labour Management Relations Law.' It also suggested many legal reforms related to labour.

Women & Child Labour

The commission also made the following recommendations on women and child labour. It is felt that the childcare is major investment in the protection and development of human resources. The mechanism of childcare should be multi-dimensional. Labour legislation should include provision for creches where there are or more workers irrespective of the gender of the worker. It is found that individual enterprises are not in a position financially to run their own creches; enterprises may jointly establish and operate them. Another possibility is that panchayats or local bodies or local tripartite groups run creches, and employing units are asked to make a proportionate contribution to the costs.

The Commission endorsed the approach of the study group on women and child labour and said that the child, the child's welfare and the child's future should be central to our programmes, and to our laws. Children are the future of our society, and our economy. Every child should have the opportunity to develop his or her skills and potential, to participate both as a citizen and as a worker.

1. The only way to prevent child labour is to recognize that the rightful place of children is in school, not in the workplace or in the house, so, the first step is to ensure compulsory primary education for all children.

2. The implementation of the present Act to prevent child labour depends entirely on the State's bureaucratic machinery. It assumes that the bureaucratic, poorly staffed and ill-equipped as it is today, will be able to ensure that children do not work in hazardous processes and occupations, and conditions of work in non-hazardous settings will be upgraded.

Skills Development

The study group appointed by the commission has recommended a new modular approach to vocational training, which will aid multi-skilling, impart skills attuned to the needs of the labour market, and in consonance with the latest technology. The Commission endorsed the views of the study group in this direction.

Labour Administration

The Commission made the following recommendations affecting labour administration:

1. Those who lead and 'man' the Ministry should have the highest degree of competence, vision, empathy, tact, skills in the arts of persuasion and inducing introspection and activating social and group consciousness. These qualities should govern the recruitment and placement of officers and staff at every level, and every department of the Ministry of Labour, in the Centre as well as States.

2. A Central Labour Relations Commission should' be set up 'for Central sphere establishments and State Labour Relations Commission should be set up for establishments in the State.

sphere. Above the Central and State labour relations commissions, there will be the National Labour Relation Commission to hear appeals against the decisions of the two other commissions.

3. To make conciliation effective, it is necessary to improve the status and competence and caliber of conciliation officers through proper recruitment, training and placement. A Labour and judicial service can be formed.

Some of the other important recommendations of the Commission are:

1. The Government of India should appoint an expert committee to study the pros and cons of the national minimum wage and make suitable recommendations for construction of such current national minimum wage.
2. The involvement and mediation of local bodies including village panchayats in the enforcement of the rates and payment of wages is important. The state government should specify minimum wages for an unskilled category of worker and these wages should be the same for all industries.
3. It is important to redefine the role of the employment exchanges to meet the new challenges.

Thus, the Second National Commission recommended on many labour issues to reform the existing labour situation in India and also suggested an umbrella legislation to workers working in the unorgairized sector.

Moreover, the setting up of special labour courts as suggested by the commission, is a, unique feature. because it shall have the judicial functions of interpretation after enforcement of all labour laws, awards and agreements. The commission also called for setting up of a mutually accepted grievance procedure by the management for settlement of day-to-day grievances. Some of the suggestions have been acted upon and some are not acted upon. The setting of IRC as recommended by the commissions was not acted upon by the government and the government persisted in continuance with the Industrial adjudication machinery only. This left the state of affairs as it is and no perceptible improvement was found in the industrial adjudication scenario.

REFERENCES

1. See the First National Labour Commission 1969's Report.
2. *Ibid.*
3. Biswanadh Ghosh, *Industrial Relations of Developing Economy* (With Particular reference to India), Himalaya Publishing House, Mumbai, 2001.
4. See Second National Commission on Labour Report.
5. Supra, note 4.

7

CONCLUSION AND SUGGESTIONS

Typically the focus of labour legislation in India has been on the procedural aspects rather than on the substantive ones. This is reflected in the legislative mandate to industrial establishments to religiously and rigorously comply with the laws through returns, registers, notices et cetera. There are too many of these procedural compliances. However, the substantive rights granted to the workers are very limited. To cite an instance randomly, under the Industrial Disputes Act, workers do not get any substantive right against retrenchment or layoff. What is provided is merely a procedural requirement that notice to employee and the appropriate Government, and in case of establishments employing more than 100 workers a prior permission from the Government. This permission is also deemed to have been granted if the government does not grant the permission within 60 days. The only substantive right which a worker gets is that of monetary compensation. There are scores of similar instances of laws whose focus is on procedural compliances rather than substantive rights. The problem of the scarcity of substantive rights is compounded by the existence- or non-existence - of a delaying, dysfunctional and dismal labour judiciary which is tottering on the brink of a collapse. Thus, an inescapable inference which we can draw is that we have too many procedural provisions and too little substantive rights, thereby setting at naught the very spirit of legislation.

Apart from the above two major areas, there are other issues which warrant a passing reference if not an engaging elaboration:

Firstly, there is the problem of definitions. There are as many definitions of a term as there are legislations.

For example, the terms 'workman', 'employee', 'wages', to name a few have been defined separately by different Acts. True, this may be because of the different purposes and focus of the Acts, but this has led to a host of definitions leading to confusion. Wherever possible common and comprehensive definitions can be arrived at. There some more terms which we are still struggling to define. A random instance is the definition of 'industry'. Even after 50 years of the existence of the Industrial Disputes Act we have not been able to define the term 'industry' comprehensively.

Secondly, there is the problem of legislative domains. Under the Constitutional scheme of federal distribution of powers, the legislative domains of the Centre and the States are clearly spelt out. But labour is a concurrent subject, thereby allowing both the Centre and the States to legislate on the topic. Though the judiciary has evolved mechanisms in the form of doctrines of 'pith and substance' and 'colourable legislation', the possibility of the laws belonging to the Centre and the States working at cross-purposes cannot be discounted.

Thus, the crisis facing the labour legislative machinery is two-fold. One internal to it, and another external to it. Internally, there are too many laws but they are disparate and disjoined. Externally, there is an utter lack of co-ordination between the various actors in the process viz. The legislating body, the enforcing body and the interpreting body i.e. the labour judiciary.

Labour legislations seek to regulate every aspect of the employment right from the stage of recruitment to separation. The Employment Exchanges (Compulsory Notification of Vacancies) Act seeks to regulate the recruitment process by requiring certain establishments to notify the vacancies in that establishment. The Industrial Employment (Standing Orders) Act seeks to regulate the service conditions of employees. The wage legislations like Minimum Wages Act and Payment of Wages Act regulate the wage aspects of employment. Legislations like Payment of Bonus Act and Payment of Gratuity Act govern the fringe benefits. The Factories Act and various Shops and Establishments Acts regulate the working conditions of workers. The Factories Rules elaborately and painfully spell out details such as the level of illumination, canteen requirements et cetera. The Industrial Disputes Act stipulates a machinery for the avoidance and settlement of disputes. It also lays down the conditions under which workers may be retrenched or laid-off.

Various social security legislations like ESI Act, PF Act, Workmen's Compensation Act et cetera are aimed at providing security to the worker and his family in contingent circumstances. So, practically every aspect of employment is legislatively regulated. Thus, the protected few are heavily protected.

Historically, the history of labour legislation can be broadly divided into two phases viz. Pre-independence and post-independence. During the pre-independence phase, labour legislation was largely the product of the protection of the colonial power's commercial interests. Another factor which contributed in no small measure to labour legislation was the desire on the part of the powers that be to import into India legal principles developed in England through case-law in the form of Acts by codifying those principles. During the post-Independence era, labour legislation was guided more by the lofty tenets of Socialism and the ideal of a welfare State. During, both these phases the development of labour has been unnatural in the sense that it did not evolve from within but was imposed from above. The development of labour law in India has not been co-terminus with industrial development. In most of the developed countries the development of labour law has been in response to the pressing needs of those times. Workers fought for their rights and got them. Labour law evolved there in response to the needs. But in India labour laws have been enacted in response to the needs of the working class as perceived by the powers that be.

However, laws enacted for a different age, for a different technology and for a different workforce no longer serve the needs of a new generation.

If laws are seen as an instrument to ensure the equitable

distribution of power within a society then labour laws in India have categorically failed. Though we have a large number of enactments, it is a matter of common knowledge that they failed to deliver the promised goods. Sheer quantity of Acts do not ensure equitable distribution. What we need is quality.

Solutions to the maladies afflicting the labour-law system are many. But the tragedy is that many of these, especially, in the form of recommendations of various Labour Commissions, have been put in the cold storage by successive Governments.

Firstly, we need a Government which is genuinely committed to the resolution of the legislative impasse we are facing today in the field of labour.

Secondly, the Government needs to consolidate all the existing labour laws and categorise under broad headings like Industrial Relations, Wages, Working Conditions, Social security et cetera. This may seem to be a utopian suggestion, but consolidation to the extent possible should be strived for.

Thirdly, we need to adopt a systems approach to the entire process of regulation of the employment relationship. Today, one body legislates, another enforces, and a third interprets. So far so good. But the problem is that these three functionaries have not been working in tandem with each other. The need of the hour is a concerted and a co-ordinated approach in which each of these bodies is viewed as a part of a system in which the actions of one affect the other. Let us also remember that new situations demand new solutions. Judiciary can still retain its jurisdiction, but in exceptional cases. Alternatively, Industrial Tribunals should take help from expertise of people from industry.

Fourthly, opinion-makers need to realise that today's workman is far more conscious of his rights than the worker of yore. He does not need over-protection. What he needs is parity of power between him/her and the employer.

Fifthly, legislators need to realise the proper function of law. Law is not to be seen merely as an abstract set of rules to be applied without any particular understanding of the relationships affected by those rules; it is, as Kahn-Freund puts it, a technique for the regulation of social power, and moreover one which could only be understood when one remembers that the main characteristic of all societies is an unequal distribution of power. Conventional wisdom suggests that industrial relations involves conflicts of interest between management and labour. At an individual level the employment relationship is a relationship between a bearer of power and one who is not a bearer of power. This imbalance needs to be redressed if the conflicts are to be fairly resolved. This attainment of the equilibrium of power should be the domain and function of law.

Sixthly, we also need to realise that the traditional models of industrial relations which begin with the presumption regarding the existence of conflict of interests between management and labour, need to be re-looked at. The traditional 'conflict' models often times are misleading.

Finally, realising the true function of law, legislators should leave the employment relationship to be governed, at least in part, by social forces, of which market forces are but one constituent. The emergence of Human Resource Management and Human Resource Development has been primarily in response to the market forces of competition, quality-consciousness and customer-focus, to name a few. No law has forced business to think on those lines. Market realities have brought more recognition and dignity to the individual worker than all laws put together have brought. In such a scenario, law should content itself with mere regulation. Nothing more, nothing less. Law should be used as part of a social policy strategy rather than relying on it as an exclusive source of protection.

After testing the hypotheses in the previous chapters, the following conclusions are drawn. Various settlement machinery under Industrial Disputes Act 1947 aimed at the settlement of disputes but due to lack of coordination among the stake holders the industrial disputes are not settled. The labour legislations are also not effectively enforced collective bargaining should be encouraged to settle the disputes amicably and promote industrial peace.

The industrial revolution has brought in its wake numerous problems and the worker today in any part of the world presents almost the same image. The industrial jurisprudence and the philosophy underlying Industrial Democracy are universal in theme though perspectives very, though the problems inherent in the system are global in nature and not regional or local. Many changes have taken place between the horse and buggy age and computer age. Managerial strategy has to be evolved to meet new challenges by keeping abreast of the rapidly changing trends in the realm of Industrial democracy in order to avert disharmony and industrial unrest and to promote productivity and efficiency.

Old theories are becoming obsolete under the tremendous pressure of modern social forces. New vistas need to be explored to subserve public good which is the aim of all welfare states in combating the pathological conditions in the legal system manifesting disregard of law and thus pave the way for achieving the goals of industrial democracy.

For effective and harmonious labour management relations in India, there is an urgent need to implement the Second National Labour Commission Report immediately, while taking the following suggestions into consideration:

1) The voluntary resolution of disputes should be encouraged over the settlement of disputes through adjudication

2) There should be a system of recognition of trade union as negotiating agent, so that the employer can negotiate with that recognized negotiating agent.

3) A tripartite National and State level councils of employment should be set up to monitor and plan problems relating to employment.

4) Training of workers and managerial personnel in the art of participative management is a prerequisite for the scheme of workers participation in management. Workers participation in management should be made compulsory without any distinction with the public, private and co-operative sectors.

5) As suggested by First National Labour Commission, Industrial Relation Commission should be constituted immediately at both Central and State level to adjudicate Industrial Disputes, conciliate and also certify trade unions as representative unions. At the same time, the existing machinery should be streamlined. Otherwise the desired result will not be achieved.

6) Collective bargaining cannot exist without the right to Strike or Lock-out. That's-why, the right to strike should be made at least as a legal right.

7) Code of conduct should be strictly applied to trade union organizations as well as employers.

8) As suggested by Second National Labour Commission, National Social Security Authority should be constituted.

9) As suggested by Second National Labour Commission, the existing Labour laws should be broadly grouped into five groups of Laws pertaining to (i) Industrial Relations (ii) Wages (iii) Social Security (iv) Safety v) Welfare and working conditions.

10) A Grievance Redressal Committee should be constituted to settle the Industrial disputes amicably.

SELECT BIBLIOGRAPHY

Books

Agrawal, S.I., '*Labour Relations Law in India*'. Macmilan Company of India Limited, New Delhi, 1978.

Arthur A. Sloane, Fred Witney., '*Labour relations*' Prentice Hall, Inc., Engletwood cliffs, N.J. 07362, USA, 1985

Arun Monappa., '*Industrial Relations*', Tata McGraw-Hill Publishing Co. Ltd, New Delhi, 1985.

Ashok Mathur, P.S. Raikhy., '*Economic Liberalization and its implications for employment*', Deep & Deep Publications, New Delhi, 2002.

Benjamin J. Taylor, Fred Witney., '*Labour relations Law*', Prenice-Hall, Inc, New Jersey, 1983.

Bhattacharya S. Joshi., '*Labour Law Digest (1966-69)*', law Publishing House, Allahabad, 1970.

Bhagoliwal, T.N., '*Economics of Labour and Industrial relations*', Sahitya Bhavan, Agra, 1987.

Chaturvedi, S.M., '*Labour and Industrial Law*', Central law Agency, Allahabad, 1995.

Chalapathi Rao, P.V., '*Labour Management Relations and Collection bargaining*', Anmol Publications Pvt. Ltd., New Delhi, 1995.

Don Bellante, Mark Jackson., '*Labour Economics Choice in Labor Markets*', McGraw-Hill Book Company, New York, 1983.

E.T. Mathew., '*Employment and Unemployment in Kerala, Some neglected aspects*', Sage Publications, London, 1997.

Gandhi M.K., '*Economic and Industrial life and Relations*' Navajivan Publishing House, Ahmedabad 1957.

Giri, V.V., *'Labour Problems in Indian Industry'*, Asia Publishing House, Bombay, 1965

Giriappa, S., *'Isues in Labour problems'* (A case study in fishing Plantations, and Crop cultivation), Ajanta Publications, Delhi, 1990.

Goswamy, V.G., *'Labour and Industrial Laws'*, Central law Agency, Allahabad, 1996.

Hugh Willamson., *'The Trade Unions'*, Heine mann Educational Books Ltd. London, 1970.

Immanuel Wallerstein., *'Labour in the world Social structure'*, Sage Publications, London, 1983.

Jagannadha Rao Vedula., *'The Labour code in Andhra Pradesh'*, Asia Law house, Hyderabad, 1991.

John A Fossum., *'Labour Relations (Development, structure, process)'*, Business Publications, Inc, USA 1982.

Justice Seth, D.D., *'Industrial Dispute Act, 1947'*, Law Publishing House, Allahabad, 1995.

Kangle, R.P., *'The Kautilya Artha Sastra'*, University of Bombay, Bombay 1972.

Kirpa Dayal Srivastava, Saran, G., *'Commentaries on Industrial Employment (Starding orders) Act, 1946 Together with (Central & State amendments Rules on notifications)'*, Eastern Book Company, Lucknow, 1991.

Kothari G.M., Kothari A.G. *'A Study of Industrial law'*, N.M. Tripathi Private Limited, Bombay, 1987.

Kumar, H.L., *'Labour Problems and remedies'*, Universal law publishing Co. Pvt. Ltd., New Delhi, 1996.

Lennart Levi, M.D, *'Preventing Work Stress'*, Addition – Wesley publishing company, London, 1983.

Malhotra, O.P., *'The Law of Industrial Disputes'*, N.M. Tripathi Pvt. Ltd. Bombay 1985

Malhotra, O.P., *'The Law of Industrial disputes'*, Universal Law publishing company, Delhi, 1998

Malik, P.L., '*K.D. Srvastava's Commentaries on Industrial Employment (Standing Orders), Act, 1946*', Eastern Book Compaany, Lucknow, 1998.

Malik, P.L., '*The Industrial Law*', Eastern Book Company, Lucknow, 1974.

Malik, S.K., '*Commentary on The Industrial Disputes Act, 1947*', Rajasthan Law House, Ahmedabad, 1998.

Mukhopadhyay, A., '*Laws on Industral relations*', Book corporation, culcutta, 1984.

'*N.G. Alexandrov's Soviet Labour Law in English*', translated by *Inder K. Nayer*, University Book House, Delhi, 1961.

Neil W. Chamberlain, *The Labour Sector*, McGraw - Hill Book Company, New York, 1965.

Peter Bowem., '*Social Control in Industrial organisations, Industrial Relations and Industrial Sociology: a strategic and occupational study of British steel making*', Routgledge Direct editions, London, 1976.

Prakash, S.S., *Bonded Labour and Social Justice*, Deep & Deep Publications, New Delhi 1990.

Prof. Madhavan Pillai, K., '*A text book on Labour & Industrial Laws*', Allahabad Law Agency, Allahabad, 1994.

Renana Jhabwala, R.K.A., Subrahmanya., *The Unorganized Sector (Work Security and Social Protection)*', Sage Publications, London, 2000.

Santosh sood., '*Trade Union Leadership in India (A Case Study)*', Deep & Deep Publications, New Delhi, 1989.

Sharma, A.M., '*Industrial Relations*', Himalaya Publishing House, Mumbai, 2004.

Sharma, G.K., '*Labour Movement in India*' *(Its Past and Present)*, University Publishers, New Delhi, 1963.

Sharma, R.N., '*Fundamental Rights Liberty and Social Order*', Deep & Deep Publications, New Delhi, 1992.

Srivastava, Kirpa Dayal, '*Law Relating to Trade Undons and Unfair*

Labour practices in India', Eastern Book Company, Lucknow, 1993.

Srivastava, K.D. *'Commentaries contract labour (Regulation & Abolition) Act, 1970'*. Eastern Book Company, Lucknow, 1992

Srivastava, S.C., *'Social Security and Labour Laws'*, Eastern Book Company, Lucknow, 1985.

Sukanti Priya Pattnaik., *'Strike* (A study of Conflict)', Gyan Publishing House, New Delhi, 1993.

Surya Narayana Mishra, Sudhir Kumar Mishra., *'An Introduction to Labour and Industrial Laws'*, Central Law Publications, Allahabad 1997.

Tripathi, P.C, Gupta, C.B., *'Industrial Relations and Labour Laws'*, Sultan Chand & Sons, New Delhi, 1996.

Yanai Tabb J. and Amira Goldfarb., *'Workers Participation in management, Expectations and experience'*, Pergaman press, New York, 1970.

Government Publications

Report of 1st National Commission on Labour.

Report of IInd National Commission on Labour.

Articles

Ahmedullah Khan., *'Settlement of Industrial Disputes'*, *JILI*, 1981.

Ajay Singh; *'Industrial Relations in Japan: Trends, challenges and Future Prospects'*, *IJIR*, January, 2000.

Bhatia, K.L., *'Labour laws research from a behavioural perspectives (Move from Doctrinal To Emperical generalization)'*, *JILI*, Oct-Dec, 1981.

Bhatia, K.L., *'Settlement of disputes – informal methods'* (An empirical study of the administration of workmen's compensation law in the states of Jammu & Kashmir and Panjab), *JILI*, July-December, 1981.

Chris Howell., *'Is there a third way for Industrial Relations'*, *BJIR*, March, 2004.

Christopher, L. Erikson, Sarosh Kunilla, Rene E. of renoe and Maria Asunuortiz., *'From core to Pheriphery ? Recent Development in Employment relations in the Philippines'*, *BJIR*, March, 2004.

Debi S. Saini., *'Leaders and Pleaders, Dynamics of brief case Trade unionism under existing legal frame work'*, *JILI*, 1995.

Deshpande D.S., *'A New concept of Industry'*, *JILI*, 1984.

Dond – One Kim and Seongses Kim, *'Globalization Financial crisis, and Industrial relations : The case of South Korea'*, *BJIR*, March, 2004.

Ernesto Noronta., *'Indian Trade Unions: Today and beyond Tomorrow'*, *IJIR*, July, 2003.

Harbhajan Sing & Niroop Mahanthy., *'The Role of Trade unions in bringing about performance oriental culture'*, *IJIR*, July, 2001.

Harish Chander., *'Contract of Employment and management prerogatives'*, *JILI*, 1994.

Indira Rothermund., *'Pattern of trade union leadership in Dhanbad coalfields'*, *JILI*, October-December, 1981.

Jain S.N., *'Child Labour'* *JILI*, July-December, 1981.

Kalpakam, P., *'Industry and Institutions other than "Industry"'* *JILI*, July-September, 1981.

Mallikarjuna Sharma., *'Right to Strike'*, *JILI*, October-December, 2004.

Mamta Panda., *'Industrial Relations environment and work culture in public and private sector organizations : A case study'* *IJIR*, April, 2004.

Mitra, N.L., 'Freedom of association for organised and unorganised workers : International Percept and Practice', *JILI*, July – Sept, 1993.

Nicola cunningharm Arma cost., 'Domestic workers in India – A case for legislative actions', *JILI*, 1994.

Pandey, M.S., 'Contract Labour and Social security Legislation', *JILI*, April- June, 1994.

Pandey, S.N., *Role of IR Manager in changing Industrial Scenario' IJIR*, April, 1989.

Parmar, O.P., *'ILO and India in pursuit of Human Right through Labour standards'*, *JILI*, October-December, 1981.

Pawan Sharma., *'Child Labour : A Socio Legal Study'*, *JILI*, April-June, 1994.

Phadtare, T.C., *'Government's power in relation to Industrial Disputes' JILI*, July-December, 1981.

Prasant Mishra and Upinder Dhar., *'Labour Management Partnershop : An Indian Perspective'*, *IJIR*, April, 2002.

Puri. M.L., *'Nature and scope of the jurisdiction of the tribunals U/s. 33 of the Industrial Disputes Act 1947'*, *JILI*, October-December, 1981.

Rajinder K. Pawar, *'Imapct of Agrarian legislation on Organised labourers of Panjab (A critical appraisal)' JILI*, 1994.

Santosh, Ram., ***'Note on Government's discretion to refer Industrial Dispatches for adjudication'***, *JILI*, 1980.

Sorab Sadni., ***'A model for Industrial Relations Audit From the specific to the General'***, *IJIR*, July, 2002.

Sudesh, V., ***'Vanishing rights of Workmen – A comment on Indian Drugs and Pharmaceuticals Ltd Vs. R.K. Shewarmani'***, *JILI*, Vol. 47, No.4, Oct-Dec, 2005.

Suresh C Srivastava., ***'Voluntary Labour Arbitration'***, *JILI*, July-December, 1981.

Suresh C. Srivastava., ***'Supreme Court and Labour relations'***, *JILI*, 1984.

Suresh Kumar Sharma., ***'Right to work'***, An assessment of constitutional policy and ethos, *KUJLS*, 1998.

Suresh, C. Srinivasa, ***'Labour Welfare and Law'***, *JILI*, 1975.

Syam Sundar, K.R., ***'Industrial Relations in China,'*** *IJIR*, July 2004.

Venkata Ramayya E.S., ***'A brief History of the liability of a participant in a strike in England'***, *JILI*, July-December, 1981.

Venkata Ratnam, C.S., '*Social and Labour Issues in Privitization – an overview*', IJIR, Oct, 1992.

Visweswaraiah, S.S., '*Discretionary Referrals Compulsory adjudication and the Industrial Disputes Act, 1947*', JILI, 1990.

Wadegaonkar, D.W., '*Concept of Industry*', JILI, July-December, 1981.

JOURNALS

Accidents Claims Journal (ACJ)

All India Reports (AIR)

Andhra Law Times (ALT)

British Journal of Industrial Relations(BJIR)

Cochin University Law Reviews (CULR)

Indian Factories and Law Reports (IFLR)

Indian Journal of Industrial Relations(IJIR)

Journal of Indian Law Institute (JILI)

Labour and Industrial Cases (LIC)

Labour Law Journal (ILJ)

Supreme Court Journal (SCJ)

INDEX

L

M

N

O

P

R

S

***